D1195484

DIALOGUE
on the way

Protestants Report from Rome on
the Vatican Council

38 4

edited by
George A. Lindbeck

AUGSBURG PUBLISHING HOUSE

Minneapolis   Minnesota

DIALOGUE ON THE WAY

Library of Congress Catalog Card No. 65-12140

A German edition is being published simultaneously by
Vandenhoeck & Ruprecht Verlag, Göttingen, under the title
Dialog unterwegs. A French edition is also in preparation.

Scripture quotations are from the Revised Standard Version
of the Bible, copyright 1946 and 1952 by the Division of
Christian Education of the National Council of Churches.

Manufactured in the United States of America

CONTENTS

iii

Translations from originals were prepared by Calvin Jacob Eich-horst, George A. Lindbeck, and Walter G. Tillmanns.

PREFACE

This book is the first extended evaluation of the Second Vatican Council by a group of Protestant observers officially delegated by their churches to attend its sessions. It is an international undertaking, bringing together authors of five nationalities and appearing in English, French, and German editions. This perhaps makes it even more important than usual to avoid possible misunderstanding by specifying clearly the nature, purpose, and limitations of this book.

It is in no sense an official Protestant reaction to the council. The authors speak only for themselves, and not for the churches which sent them as observers to Rome. Yet it seeks to give a balanced and distinctively Protestant summary and evaluation of what has so far happened at Vatican II.

There seems to be a pressing need for such an account. Catholics analyze with the greatest care even the most fugitive of the observers' comments. Protestants are often confused by the extremes of pessimism and optimism regarding the council which compete for their credence, and there is a grave danger that they will stumble bewildered and unprepared into a new ecumenical situation.

Thus this book is directed to both Protestants and Catholics, to both laymen and clergy. It seeks to be comprehensive and careful enough to be useful to all these groups while, at least in most of its chapters, avoiding theological technicalities as much as possible.

Enough has now happened to make possible a report which, while preliminary, can still remain useful after the council is over. Vatican II has virtually completed its specifically theological work in those areas which are directly relevant to Protestant-Catholic relations. We know what principles it will promulgate on Scripture and tradition (Chapter VI), and what it has already proclaimed on the liturgy (Chapter V), the church (Chapter VII), the Virgin Mary (Chapter VIII), and ecumenism (Chapter IX), even though doubt remains as to the extent and speed with which these principles will be put into practical effect in the documents still under consideration. (For a list of these, see the epilogue to Chapter IV.) The one major theological area in which the final shape of the council's action still remains obscure, viz., that of the church and the world, raises questions which go beyond our traditional disagreements. It is in some respects better suited to collaborative, rather than specifically Protestant, evaluation (see Chapter X).

Most of the authors of this book belong to that relatively small group of official observers and guests who were admitted to the closed sessions of the council and had the same access to its secret documents as did the council fathers. Two writers, Pastor Gerhard Pedersen and Dr. Wolfgang Dietzfelbinger, were assistants to officially delegated observers, but they also were present in Rome, read the council documents, and sometimes attended the closed sessions. The last chapter is written by Dr. Hermann Dietzfelbinger, Lutheran Bishop of Bavaria, who as chairman of the Board of the Lutheran Foundation for Ecumenical Research, and as the head of commissions dealing with Roman Catholicism of both the United Lutheran and the Evangelical Churches in Germany, is well qualified to comment on the significance of the council for the churches of the Reformation.

An effort was made to secure as authors those among the long-term observers (present for two or more sessions) who have special competence on the various subjects. Thus, for example, Professor Cullmann is the best known of the biblical scholars (including Catholics) who were present at the council. Professors Skydsgaard and Schlink, I think it would be generally agreed, are as well qualified as any Protestants in the world to write on current Catholic ecclesiology and ecumenism respectively. Dr. Vajta was the one Protestant liturgical specialist present for session after session. There are, of course, numerous observers of high qualifications who are not represented in this book.

It is in part accidental that all the writers can call themselves

"Lutheran" (though one can also call himself "Reformed," for he has double membership). Two of the originally invited non-Lutheran authors were unable to contribute. Further, while Lutheran authorship undoubtedly does give a special coloration to this book, the very nature of its subject matter means that there is little here with which many non-Lutheran observers would not also agree.

However, it should be noted that the original stimulus and continuing support for this book has come from the Lutheran Foundation for Ecumenical Research. This foundation, which maintains a research institute in Strasbourg, France, was established in 1963 by the Lutheran World Federation as an independent agency devoted to scholarly research. It is the successor of a Special Commission of the Lutheran World Federation which, in 1961, published a preparatory volume, edited by Prof. Skydsgaard, in English and German (*The Papal Council and the Gospel–Konzil und Evangelium,* Augsburg and Vandenhoeck & Ruprecht). The present volume, though its authorship is in large part different, may in a sense be considered a continuation of the Protestant evaluation of the council which was there begun.

As could be expected of a book in which each author speaks only for himself, there are certain differences of interpretation of the council in the following chapters. Compare, for example, the treatments in Chapters IV, VI, IX, and XI of the changes in the *Decree on Ecumenism* which were made as a result of papal intervention at the end of the third session. Nevertheless, my impression in reading the manuscripts is that we have here a basic consensus. The biggest contrast which I detect is between Americans (such as myself), who seem to have a greater inclination to emphasize the renewal now taking place in the Roman Catholic Church (perhaps because we have previously had little experience of it in the United States), and the Europeans, who often seem more inclined to speak of its limitations (for in trans-Alpine Europe they can presuppose greater familiarity with the new movements).

Not all readers will be equally interested in all chapters of this book. The first part is primarily for those who feel the need for information about the council. Thus the first chapter provides basic facts regarding organization, working procedures, and participants in the council, and the following three chapters outline the history of the first three sessions. Here a number of subjects are discussed which, though of great importance, are not dealt with fully in the remainder of the book. Examples of these are the statements on religious liberty and the Jews, and the problems of collegiality, decentralization, missions, the diaconate, and mixed marriages.

Those readers who are already well informed may wish to pass quickly to the second, specifically evaluative part. Here the chapters are arranged in a roughly chronological order paralleling the sequence in which the topics with which they deal were first discussed in the council. However, it makes little difference in what order they are read (although I would like to recommend the first section of Professor Schlink's treatment of ecumenism in Chapter IX as an excellent summary of the complex problems involved in evaluating a council document).

In conclusion, it might be well to note some of the things which the reader will not find in this book. Some of these result from the haste in which it was produced so that it would be useful, not only after the council, but also before and during the fourth session scheduled for next fall. An example is the lack of a complete guide to the immense literature on Vatican II which has already appeared (although there is a brief bibliographical note appended to the volume).

However, there are also more substantial omissions which are perhaps inevitable in a work of this kind. With the exception of some passages in the historical chapters, there is little here which attempts to convey the high drama and emotional impact of the council, although every observer was, on occasion, deeply moved by them. Nor is there much about the reactions of the observers and of Protestants in general. This volume, after all, is itself a Protestant reaction, rather than description of such reactions.

Further, the fact that this is a study of Vatican II from the viewpoint of the Reformation Churches means that there is little here regarding the roles of other Christian bodies, such as the Orthodox and the Anglican, in the present ecumenical situation. Needless to say, the authors are intensely aware of the importance of these roles and, despite their relative silence on this point, they think of the Protestant-Catholic encounter as inseparable from dialogue between all parts of Christendom.

Most serious of all, however, is the absence of extensive Protestant self-criticism. It could not be otherwise in a book written about a Catholic council, and yet it is unfortunate that this is so. If the authors had written on the need for renewal in Protestantism, they would, I suspect, have been at least as critical of aspects of their own churches as they are of certain features of Catholicism. Indeed, this will often be evident to the reader from the way in which they phrase their reservations about the council.

Nevertheless, it seems to me that we must in all fairness admit that there is, at present, more Catholic self-criticism in the light of what Hans Küng calls "justified Protestant desiderata" than there is Protestant self-criticism in the light of Catholic desiderata. This probably makes it easier for ecumenically-minded Protestants to speak frankly, as they do in this book, regarding the limitations of the current Catholic renewal than it is for Roman Catholics to express themselves on the need for Protestant renewal. It is hoped that the present book will stimulate equally frank Catholic responses.

In short, our hope is that this book will be a genuine contribution to the conversation between separated Christian brothers. We believe that the dialogue has now reached the point where it is no longer necessary to be either defensive or carefully polite, where one can both praise and criticize the other side, without being automatically stereotyped as "pro" or "anti" Catholic (or Protestant). The bonds of Christian love hold us together in discussions which are both rewarding and difficult. We cannot escape, for God's Word of redemption and judgment grasps us all and impels us to grapple together with the truth, unity, and wonder of the Gospel.

Finally, as editor I would like to express my great appreciation to the authors for their work. They, in turn, I am sure, join with me in thanking all the Roman Catholics, especially Cardinal Bea, Bishop Willibrands, and the other members, consultants, and staff of the Secretariat for the Promotion of Christian Unity, who by their unfailing hospitality, help, and Christian fellowship made our task as observers in Rome both enjoyable and rewarding.

GEORGE A. LINDBECK

Part I
Descriptions

Chapter I

Structures and Procedures
of the Council

The composition and procedures of the Second Vatican Council have changed considerably from session to session. The difference between the first and second sessions was especially great, and consequently it is mostly to the second session that we shall refer in the following descriptions.

As the second session commenced on Sept. 29, 1963, it was no longer John XXIII who sat on the throne in front of the high altar in St. Peter's basilica. Instead of his imposing bulk, which awakened trust and joy wherever it appeared, one saw the ascetic figure of the new pope, Paul IV. The bishops had been moved up to fill the 72 seats which had been emptied by death during the course of the year, and at the far end of the rows occupied by the council fathers were gathered 98 prelates who had been consecrated in the nine months since the end of the first session. Approximately 2,250 bishops, abbots, archbishops, cardinals, and patriarchs were gathered in the basilica for the opening service. Further, the thousands of clerics and laity who had gained admission on this occasion, filled the church almost to bursting.

The next day the work which had been interrupted in December, 1962, once again started. Two kinds of meetings were held, the daily

3

general congregations and the so-called *public sessions* in which conciliar documents received final approval.

General congregations always started with mass celebrated by one of the council fathers. Immediately afterwards a medieval manuscript copy of the Gospel was enthroned upon the altar as a symbol that the Gospel should be at the center of the conciliar proceedings. Then the oldest member of the board of presidents, Cardinal Tisserant, began the ancient council prayer, *Adsumus*,[1] which was repeated in chorus by all the council fathers. Afterwards everyone sat down, and the voice of the General Secretary intoned through the loud-speaker, "Exeant omnes." This phrase was the signal for all those not authorized to remain to leave the council hall. There was a general exodus of liturgical assistants, such as choir members and acolytes, and of journalists, theologians, and visitors who had received special permission to attend the mass but not the other parts of the council proceedings.

As soon as the last unauthorized person had left the church, the General Secretary proceeded to the lectern where he read the announcements of the day as well as the list of those who had asked to speak. Discussion now began, with the moderator announcing the name of each speaker beforehand and asking the following speaker to proceed to a microphone so that he could commence immediately as soon as his turn came. According to the council regulations, a speech could not last longer than eight minutes (in the first session ten minutes). This time limit was enforced by the presiding moderator who, when necessary, interrupted the speakers.

Exactly who were the participants in the council? We can best visualize the answer to this question if we make a circuit of St. Peter's during a general congregation. In front, just before the high altar, stands the papal throne. It is empty, because the pope does not take part in the daily proceedings of the council. Below the papal throne is the great circular entrance to the crypt, and to the left (south) side of this are rows of tables at which sit priests who are doing the secretarial work of keeping records, as well as some theologians whose job it is to report at the press conferences which are held each day immediately after the conclusion of the general congregation.

In front of the entrance to the crypt are two low platforms. On the one closest to the crypt and farthest from the bishops, sit the twelve cardinals who make up the board of presidents. In front of them on the second platform sit the four moderators, the cardinals who act as legates of the pope and lead the daily proceedings in his name. (Moderators were not present at the first session, but were added by Paul VI.)

To the left (south) of the presidents' platform stands the table of the five archbishops and bishops who serve as general secretary and assistant secretaries to the council. There is more movement here than anywhere else. Bishops and others make a constant stream as they approach the table with requests to speak, manuscripts of speeches, or other business.

Next, just before the beginning of the great central nave of St. Peter's, we come to two tribunes, one on each side, facing the high altar, and overlooking all the officials of the council whom we have so far mentioned. In the tribune on the north, to the right of the presidents and moderators, sit the *auditores* and *auditrices,* prominent Catholic lay men and women who were invited to observe the council proceedings. (In the first session, there was only one of these, the noted French author Jean Guitton, who attended, rather unofficially, on John XXIII's personal invitation, and sat, of all things, among the non-Catholic observers. And until the third session no woman attended the council proceedings.) On the same tribune are gathered a large number of the 400-odd *periti* (theological experts) of the council. The tribune on the opposite side is far from full, for here are authorized to sit only the approximately 70 non-Roman Catholic observers (most of whom are in Rome only part of the time during the council sessions), together with the few priests from the Secretariat for Christian Unity who translate for them or in other ways help them.

Now we come to the great assembly of the council fathers themselves, who are seated on two facing tiers of seats which have been erected along the entire length of both sides of the central nave. The first part of the north side is reserved for cardinals. Opposite them, and facing them, directly under the famous bronze statue of the Apostle Peter, are the six Oriental patriarchs. Then on both sides, all the way to the distant door, are seated in order of seniority the archbishops, bishops, and heads of the ancient monastic orders.[2]

At the beginning of the council, there were 2,427 persons eligible to take part as council fathers. Of these, 75 were cardinals, 2,228 were bishops and archbishops, 59 were apostolic prefects[3] and 65 were heads of religious orders. Since the opening, the number of council fathers has increased somewhat.

In addition to those already mentioned, a large number of assistants of one sort or another are present. Some help with ceremonies, others with the clerical work, while still others are available to aid the council fathers in the preparation of their contributions to the discussions (e.g. translators and Latinists).

Thus on an ordinary working day one could count on an attendance of over 2,500 persons during the proceedings in St. Peter's.

I. Tendencies at the Council

Many different positions are represented in this great assembly. This became manifest in the first session, and continued to be evident also during the later proceedings. It has become customary to group the various points of view into two chief tendencies, the "conservative" and the "progressive." We shall now try to indicate what is meant by these terms.

The conservative tendency was represented chiefly by the Roman curia, the central agency in the Vatican of the Catholic Church. Basically its structures and functions go back to the end of the 16th century, but their ultimate source can be found in the medieval papal court. Originally the curia was supposed to be the purely administrative organ of the papacy, but its influence so increased in the course of the 19th and 20th centuries that in some respects it is now the body which rules the Roman Catholic Church.

The officials of the curia are mostly Italians whose special "Roman" training in theology, church law, and the Latin language make them particularly adept at adapting themselves to the traditional system which governs the daily work of Vatican administration. The few foreigners who become part of the curia are generally quickly influenced by the system and become accustomed to thinking along the standard, rigidly predetermined lines. The curial mentality represents a kind of higher synthesis of Roman legalism, Latin culture and language, medieval feudalistic thinking, political and ethical conservatism, and modern anticommunism.

With its minutely elaborated regulations and protocol, the curia invades the daily life of the pope himself. Further, to name a few examples of its activities, it gives directives in the name of the pope to the bishops of the entire world, condemns "heretical" books, prepares for the canonization of saints and decides—after not inconsiderable payment and years of deliberation—on difficult matrimonial cases.

It was therefore to be anticipated that the curia would be the watershed of the council. On the one side stand the conservatives who are in agreement with the status quo of ecclesiastical administration. They believe that a completely authoritarian regime constitutes the only means by which church unity can be maintained. Naturally there are some bishops of this kind everywhere, but they are most numerous in Italy, Spain, Portugal, parts of Latin America, and, interestingly enough, the English-speaking countries. On the other side stand the "progressive" bishops, especially from trans-Alpine Europe, but also, to a remarkable degree, from South American countries,[4] and from mission lands. It is they who, from the beginning of the council, have entered the lists against the curial system.

In recent decades even the popes have felt themselves under pressure from the increasing power of the curia. Paul VI is the first, however, who has spoken openly and directly of the need of change. He called the members of the curia together shortly before the opening of the second session, and informed them that he intended to carry through a reform of the curia. He took the opportunity to emphasize that the curia is a purely administrative and executive agency, and that it owes absolute obedience to the pope even when he decides to reform it![5]

The second and third sessions showed clearly that the opposition between council and curia is the major one in the conciliar proceedings. This became apparent in the discussion on the collegiality of the bishops and on the increase of episcopal power which this implies. One of the high points of the session was the sharp attack of Cardinal Frings (Cologne) on the Holy Office (which is the highest body within the curia) and Cardinal Ottaviani's reply to this.[6]

However, this basic division is related to other disagreements especially of a theological nature. These are a consequence of the movement which has developed in the last fifty years, particularly in the field of biblical research. From this has arisen criticism of traditional scholastic theology. The new tendency was represented at the council by, for example, Cardinal Augustin Bea and other exegetes. On occasion they called attention to the highly questionable use of the Bible in many of the schemas which were submitted to the council. In many cases the drafts did not sufficiently express the meaning of the biblical texts which were cited or presupposed. In their answers the conservatives frequently showed a disconcertingly small knowledge, and even less understanding, of recent biblical research.

Differences of opinion also arose over the church's relation to wealth and poverty. A good number of bishops pleaded for the abolition of the pretentiousness, the high-sounding titles, and the pomp and splendor which surround the Roman clergy. The church should bear the marks of poverty and service. Such proposals came especially from bishops who, it should be noted, have sometimes already begun to live in the way they preach. They have sold their palaces, their large automobiles, and their precious insignia. They have used the money for social work and for teaching in their dioceses. Nothing was said in reply to them by the conservatives, but the ceremonial of the council showed that the Romans were not willing simply to abandon their beloved spectacles.

A third area of conflict became apparent through speakers from the so-called uniate churches, i.e., those Oriental churches which in past centuries have separated from the ancient Orthodox communions and adhered to the Roman See by recognizing the primacy of the pope. While they have succeeded in retaining their own liturgy and church law, they still have reason to complain of the efforts made by the Roman curia to Latinize them. Their concern was to emphasize that unity of the church is not synonymous with uniformity based on the Roman pattern. As a practical example of this, Patriarch Maximos IV Saigh of Antioch insisted, against all rules and regulations and despite repeated admonitions, on delivering his speeches in French. Further, the patriarch and his colleagues were not interested simply in the problems of their own church, but tried to speak on behalf of all the Orthodox churches of the East. They stressed that there could be no hope of reaching an understanding with the separated Orthodox without willingness to surrender Roman uniformity.

This position was sharply attacked, not only by bishops of the Latin rite, but by some uniates. This was especially true of the Armenian Patriarch Ignatius Peter Batanian XVI who made common cause with the curia and showed the total dependence of his particular church on the firmly established Roman central authority. On the other side, however, many bishops maintained that Latinization is just as much an error in the West as in the East, and that it is necessary that the Catholic Church adapt itself, also in the Western world, to the particular peoples among which it preaches the Gospel.

It is evident from this that the expressions "conservative" and "progressive" do not refer to two homogeneous blocs, but to a multitude of overlapping oppositions. It was therefore possible for the bishops who were clearly progressive in social matters to express conservative theological opinions. Similarly, many of those who were theologically progressive in some areas found it difficult to accept the ecumenical openness of other bishops toward non-Roman Catholic Christian communities. Further, there is no doubt that many bishops changed their positions on various points during the course of the council as they encountered the well-founded arguments of colleagues or of theologians who had more experience or insight than they had.

Whatever the character of the conciliar decrees which finally emerge from this melting pot of opinions, there is no doubt that the episcopacy as a whole has been forced into a movement away from traditional scholastic thinking toward a more biblical way of understanding the church and its teachings. It is said that the conservatives in Rome comfort themselves with the thought that popes and councils come and go, but the curia continues as before. Nevertheless, the curia has received some hard blows in the course of this council from which it is not likely to recover completely.

II. The Working Methods of the Council

In order to provide some insight into the work of the council, we shall now follow the path of a council document from the initial stage of theological raw material to the final form of an official conciliar decree.

The documents which were prepared before the council had their origin in an enormous collection of material which was assembled during the preconciliar preparatory stage. The *commissio ante-preparatoria* which worked from May, 1959, to June, 1961, gathered a mutitude of proposals by means of a questionnaire sent to all the bishops and Catholic universities of the world. This material was processed by the ten preparatory commissions and printed in fifteen volumes totalling 9,520 pages.[7]

The task of the ten commissions was to select a manageable amount of material out of this overwhelming mass, and present this to the council. This was done by preparing *schemata* (i.e. "schemas") which were supposed to reflect the suggestions of the bishops and were to be distributed to the bishops for their consideration before the council opened, or at least to be completed by that time. It will surprise no one to hear that this project was not completely carried out. At the outset of the first session in the fall of 1962, 70 schemata had been worked on by the commissions, but only nine of these were ever distributed to the bishops, only five were discussed, and none was completely processed in the first session. In view of the slowness of the proceedings, the number of the schemas has been gradually reduced to a total of thirteen.

It is impossible for us to go into detail on the origins of a schema. It is obviously an extraordinarily complicated process which requires long negotiations among the members of the commissions and the experts. It is not enough simply to agree on the themes which are to be dealt with by a given commission, but a theological consensus must be reached on how to handle the theme. Then the question arises of how to put this into words. This often creates great difficulties, especially because Latin is so closely tied to scholastic theology that it lacks expressions for many modern theological categories. There is no reason to be astonished, then, when one hears that the second version of the schema on the church was rewritten sixteen times before it was presented to the council.

To return now to the period before the council. After a preparatory commission had completed a schema, it was submitted to the central commission. This reviewed all 70 of the preparatory schemas, and sent out a volume containing seven of these before the beginning of the council. Many bishops had already submitted their remarks on these seven schemas before the opening.

At the very beginning of the first session ten conciliar commissions were selected, each composed of 25 members, 16 selected by the council and nine appointed by the pope. These took over the continuation of the work of the preparatory commissions. Between the first two sessions, a commission of coordination was chosen which replaced both the preparatory central commission and a special commission which had responsibility for new or unusual questions.

Turning now to the conciliar debates on the various schemas, these were introduced by a *relatio* explaining the schema presented by the commission responsible for it. Each *relatio* was printed and distributed to the council participants, but it was also given in oral form by a spokesman of the commission. After this came the discussion of the schema as a whole, which provided opportunity for opinions to be expressed on such matters as the basic principles of the schema, their mode of expression, and the relation of this schema to others. Also, complaints were sometimes made regarding the way the schema had been prepared. For example, during the general debate on "Bishops and Government of Dioceses" in the second session, one bishop from Colombia asserted that the conciliar commission which was supposed to deal with this subject had never been called together, that the *relator* who presented the schema to the council had not been chosen by the commission, and that his *relatio* had not been submitted to the commission for its approval. This, admittedly, was an extreme case, not typical of other schemas.

This debate on the schema as a whole closed with a vote on whether to accept the schema as a basis for further discussion. If this was affirmative, then each chapter was treated in turn.

However, the treatment of individual chapters did not take place only through speeches made in the council hall, but to an even greater degree in writing. The regulations prescribed that the changes which the council fathers intended to propose in their speeches should be handed in to the Secretary General three days beforehand. Further, the bishops could submit their observations without delivering them orally. The moderators repeatedly stressed that these written contributions would be given just as much attention by the commissions as those which were presented in the form of speeches. This made it possible for bishops to deal with themes which they did not wish to discuss publicly.

The debates were often wearisomely long, but it is understandable that the moderators considered it important that no one should feel that he had been deprived of an opportunity to present his point of view. However, when a given subject had clearly been exhausted, a vote on closure of debate was taken. In all the cases where this was done the votes were overwhelmingly affirmative. Even after closure, however, those speakers who were already inscribed, and did not wish to withdraw, were generally allowed to present their contributions.

After the discussion the competent commission reviewed the schema in the light of all the observations which had been made, and prepared and distributed booklets containing the *emendationes* (proposed amendments) as well as the comments of the commission. The amendments approved by the commission were then voted on by the council one after another.

Those amendments which were adopted were inserted into the text of the schema by the commission, and the revised schema was presented to the council by still another *relatio*. Then followed additional votes, first on the individual chapters, and then on the text in its entirety. If this was not affirmative, the whole complicated process started over again.[8] The text finally approved was submitted to the pope for approval and promulgation as a conciliar decree.

Normally, except for the question of closure of debate, votes were taken by ballot. The authorized ballots made it possible to vote in one of three ways: *placet* ("yes" or, literally translated, "it pleases"), *non placet*, and *placet iuxta modum* ("yes, with reservations"). This last type of vote was allowed only when a schema, or part thereof, was still in a position to be amended. Those council fathers who voted *placet iuxta modum* were required to submit their reservations *(modi)* in writing to the secretary general. When numerous

enough, these led to additional *emendationes.* A two-thirds majority
was needed for the final adoption of a text.[9]

The texts adopted by the council and approved by the pope were
then promulgated. This occurred at public sessions. These started
in the same way as a general congregation, except that the pope
was present in person and himself read the *Adsumus* prayer and
struck up the hymn *Veni Creator Spiritus.* After the conclusion of
the worship part of the session the general secretary received the
decrees to be promulgated from the hand of the pope, proceeded
to the lectern, and read summary portions from them.

After this reading came the formality of final solemn votes. Once
the result of a given vote had been announced to the assembly, the
pope proceeded to promulgate the document.

This, then, is the process by which conciliar decisions are endowed with canonical authority in the Roman Catholic Church. It
should not be thought, however, that they are considered unconditionally infallible, unless this is made explicit in the text. Indeed,
because this council has viewed its task as pastoral, not dogmatic,
it has tried to avoid making "irreformable," i.e. explicitly infallible,
pronouncements. Nor should it be supposed that a decree, once
promulgated, takes effect immediately. Normally it provides general
directives, and it is up to the administrative authority to determine
how those should be put into effect in the life of the church. Thus,
for instance, in reference to the constitution *De Sacra Liturgia,* the
pope warned in his concluding speech to the second session that
no one should begin to change the liturgy or introduce private reforms and special rites before the publication of the particular liturgical changes which would be worked out by the appropriate Vatican authorities or by post-conciliar agencies.[10] From this point of
view, the work which follows the council will be at least as extensive and important as that which was done by the council itself.

III. What Is a Council?

On the basis of the preceding description of the organization and
procedures of the council, one might get the impression that this
was simply a kind of ecclesiastical parliament, conducted in good

democratic fashion, where—despite the use of the venerable Latin language and of elaborate ceremonials—there was no inclination to deny the basically human character of the whole assembly. It is true that after what happened in the various sessions, no one can pretend that the purely human, the historical, and the accidental did not play a great role in the work of the council. There were disputes about prestige, titles, and the proper dress to wear, as well as much maneuvering behind the scenes. It was not only the observers who disliked the human pettiness which was often visible behind the pompous titles and documents. There were Roman Catholic critics who were even more severe. The bishops themselves were sharply self-critical, as was indicated by the many bitingly ironical jokes and anecdotes which circulated in the corridors of St. Peter's.

Yet, despite this recognition of the human element, the council thinks of itself as much more than a kind of parliament. On this point progressives and conservatives are at one. To be sure, this agreement ceases when they try to describe precisely what a council really is. This is true, in part because the theological nature of a council has never been fully defined, in part because of a fundamental difference in the conception of the relation between Pope and council.

According to the most recent (1917) revision of the *Codex iuris canonici,* which is the authoritative collection of the laws of the Roman Catholic Church, "An ecumenical council exercises supreme authority in the universal church" (can. 228, §1). However, it is also said: "There can be no appeal from the decision of the Roman Pontiff to an ecumenical council" (*ibid.,* §2). One way of expressing the division of opinion on this matter is to say that the conservatives place the greatest weight on §2, while the progressives emphasize especially §1.

For the conservatives, the council is completely dependent on the pope. The decisions of the council have no worth in themselves, but acquire all their authority from the fact that they are approved and promulgated by the pope. Further, many of the conservatives give the impression of identifying the Petrine office with what canon law (can. 7) calls the "Apostolic See," i.e. pope *and* curia. It would seem that this is why Cardinal Ottaviani asserted in the council that the criticism which various bishops had directed against the Holy Office were actually attacks on the pope himself who has the title of prefect of this body. Also the cardinal, who as secretary of the Holy Office is also president of the council's Theological Commission, argued that the five questions which were voted on Oct. 30, 1963, should first have been submitted to his commission. In other words, the conservatives tend to regard the council as an instrument in the hands of the pope. A council is basically an advisory body called together on extraordinary occasions in order to assist the pope in matters which he, as chief bishop of the church, could in principle decide by himself.

The progressive case against this curial view is theologically rooted in the conviction that the church is not in the first place a juridical institution culminating in an infallible teaching office, but rather a communion analogous to a living organism. Consequently, the council is not simply an instrument of the pope, as the curia is, for example, but rather a particular expression of the community of all the bishops, which includes the pope. Thus the pope, even when apparently ruling the universal church by himself, actually does so in his capacity as head of the "college" of bishops, and the college of bishops, in turn, always acts *together with* the pope.[11] An ecumenical council is, therefore, genuinely a representation of the entire church, even though not in a democratic sense (e.g. the individual bishops are not elected by the people). Each bishop, so to speak, brings a local church, with its needs and joys, to the council. Various opinions struggle with each other, and human differences unfold into rich diversity. Yet behind this diversity lies a brotherly unity in faith and in doctrinal consensus. The purpose of the council is to advance this unity and bring it to expression. What the council decides should represent a basic consensus in which all are agreed. Those questions on which quasi-unanimity cannot be obtained should be laid aside because they are not yet ripe for decision. A guarantee of this unity lies in the fact that the pope, while he cannot contradict the council, still has the right to postpone its proposals for possible consideration at some indeterminate future time.

It is significant in this connection to observe that the formula for promulgation was changed in the course of the second session. This according to the "Regulations" was supposed to read, "The decrees and canons previously read have pleased the fathers. . . . And we, with the approval of the Holy Council, decide, appoint, and confirm that which has been read." However, the wording was suddenly replaced in the public session of Dec. 4, 1963, by this: "In the name of the Undivided Trinity of the Father, the Son, and the Holy Spirit. The decrees read in this most reverend Second Vatican Ecumenical Council, here validly assembled, have pleased the fathers, and we, with the apostolic power bestowed on us from Christ, approve, decide, and appoint these decrees in the Holy Spirit and together with the reverend fathers. And that which has been synodically decided, we command to be promulgated to the honor of God."[12]

The idea expressed here, it would seem, is not that the decrees are fundamentally the decision of the pope in agreement with the council but that they are the decision of the council *(synodaliter statuta)* which the pope in his capacity as the leading bishop, *together with the bishops of all the world,* proclaims as the law and norm of the entire Roman Catholic Church.

This supports the progressive point of view and suggests that the balancing of the papacy by the episcopacy which was hoped for from the council is taking place. If this occurs, it will open the way for new theological reflection on the question of councils, not only within the limits of Roman Catholic theology, but also within the wider perspectives of ecumenical research.

Notes

1. We are gathered together, O Holy Spirit, we are gathered here, conscious of our exceeding sinfulness, yet assembled together especially in thy name. Come to us and be with us. Deign to enter our hearts. Teach us what to do and how to walk, and show us what we shall accomplish so that, with thy help, we may in all things be pleasing unto thee. Be thou the sole prompter and director of our decisions, O thou, whose name is glorious, together with God the Father and his Son. Suffer us not to undermine justice, O thou who dost love equity above all things. Nor let ignorance draw us astray, nor partiality mislead us, nor bribes nor favoritism corrupt us. Rather may we be steadfastly joined to thee by the gift of thy grace alone, so that we may be one in thee, and in nothing depart from the truth. As we are assembled in thy name, so may we in all things be guided by true piety to the maintenance of righteousness, in order that our thoughts may here in

no way depart from thee and the eternal reward for deeds well done may follow us in time to come.

2. Cf. *Ordo Concilii Oecumenici Vaticani II Celebrandi,* Editio altera recognita, Typis Polyglottis Vaticanis, 1963 (cited as das *Ordo*), Art. 4.

3. An apostolic prefect is the head of a mission area which has not yet been organized into a diocese. He is not a bishop, but is a prelate who, under certain circumstances, has the right to wear episcopal garb within his own territory. These prefects were not present at the first session, but John XXIII decided that they should be invited to later ones.

4. It will no doubt be surprising to many that Latin America, where the Roman Church is in such a sorry state, should be mentioned in this connection. However, the very gravity of the situation in this area has led many of its bishops to insist on the necessity of major reforms. See the article, "Des évêques et des hommes," *Informations catholiques internationales,* no. 177 1962, pp. 21-39.

5. This speech is printed in *Osservatore Romano,* Sept. 22, 1963.

6. For additional information supplementing that given in this article, regarding the history of the council, see Chapters II-IV in this volume.

7. Cf. *The Papal Council and the Gospel* (ed. K. E. Skydsgaard), Minneapolis: Augsburg, 1961, pp. 98 ff.

8. *Ordo,* Art. 31 e.

9. *Ordo,* Art. 34, §1.

10. *Acta Apostolicae Sedis,* Vol. 56, 1964, p. 35. Cf. the pope's *motu proprio* of January, 1964, in which he gives permission to make some changes beginning with the First Sunday in Lent, Feb. 16, 1964. (*ibid.,* pp. 139-144.)

11. The theological basis for this view is developed in two composite works written by certain theological experts of the council: *L'Episcopat et l'Eglise universelle,* ed. Y. Congar & B.-D. Dupuy (Unam Sanctam 39), Paris: Cerf, 1962, and K. Rahner & J. Ratzinger, *Episkopat und Primat,* (Quaestiones disputatae 11), Freiburg-Wien-Basel: Herder, 1961.

12. Cf. A.A.S., Vol. 56, 1964, p. 134.

Chapter II

Pope John's Council:
First Session

The preceding chapter has described the structure of the Second Vatican Council. Later essays will present theological analyses of its treatment of certain major themes. The purpose of the present and two following chapters is to supply primarily historical information and interpretation.

The view supported by these pages is that the current Roman Catholic renewal is both profound and, in a real sense, "evangelical." It is, however, also thoroughly "Roman." Its representatives are deeply loyal to their church and are not in the least inclined to repudiate any of the dogmas of the past, even though they often reinterpret them. In short, neither the conviction that "Rome never changes," nor the belief that Christian reunion is rapidly approaching is justified. Difficult as this is for us to understand, it seems that the Roman Church may become much more faithful to the Christian Gospel than in the past while it still continues to maintain false doctrine regarding, for example, the Virgin and the pope.

This possibility of a radical renewal of Roman Catholicism does not necessarily become apparent when one looks at the council by itself, as if it were an isolated event. On most points it has lagged, and probably will continue to lag, far behind the best of contem-

18

porary Roman Catholic theology. It often seems to have ignored
the most moving and prophetic voices among its own participants.
Its pronouncements will strike many as tragically lacking in the
courage to innovate, to take risks, which is demanded by the present
crises situation of Catholicism and of all Christianity. Even when
looked at in terms of the practical possibilities of what the majority
of bishops would have been willing to vote for, it seems likely that
the council failed to do much that it could have done. In brief,
measured by the hopes of many Roman Catholics and non-Catholics
alike, the Second Vatican Council could be considered a failure.

However, entirely different conclusions are warranted when one
views it in historical perspective. Then the council appears as one
phase in a movement of renewal which started long before it opened
and may, in a few decades, advance far beyond it. It represents a
critical turning point in that movement. The reactionaries were
mobilizing to crush the new developments, but they were themselves defeated. More than that, the Roman Church as a whole,
acting through its highest authorities, is for the first time placing
itself on the side of reform. The council could, no doubt, go farther
than it has done, but this simply means that, instead of advancing
as fast as possible, it has merely moved rapidly. Before the council,
the forces of renewal were able to progress without, and often
against, official support. Now they have been immensely encouraged and strengthened. Possibilities which were unimaginable six
years ago have been opened. We, of course, cannot be sure to what
extent, and how rapidly, these possibilities will be actualized, but
there can be no doubt that they are genuine and must be taken into
account.

In this connection it should also be remembered that no church
is ever transformed by legislative fiat, whether that of a council, a
pope, or a synod. The role of a council is strictly limited, even
though it can be of decisive importance. It can, so to speak, open
and shut doors, but that is all. It can ban a given movement or
position, and encourage another, but it does not create them. Even
the first council at Jerusalem did not do more. It approved the mission of Paul to the Gentiles, but it did not initiate it. Councils, like
other legislative assemblies which try to maintain continuity and
avoid schism, are not themselves adventurous or prophetic. Their

job is to enact reforms or issue condemnations when a church as a whole is persuaded that these are needed. More than this we cannot rightfully expect. Measured by these standards, Vatican II is already most emphatically a success even from the Protestant point of view.

I. The Background[1]

Before embarking on the story of Vatican II, we must say a word more about the major factors which have shaped it. In addition to the forces of renewal, we must mention the conservative opposition, especially as this centers in the Vatican curia, and also the role of the papacy.

The forces promoting renewal, it should be remembered, are of two very different kinds. First, there are the external pressures represented by the social, political, and intellectual developments of the modern world. These are depriving the Roman Church of its previous sources of strength even in traditionally Catholic countries. Already at the time of the French Revolution it had lost most of the intellectuals, and much of the financial and political leadership, even in traditionally Catholic societies. During the 19th century the growing urban masses became more and more hostile and indifferent. Finally, in our day, with the disappearance of the traditional peasant society, it is even losing its grip on the countryside. While traditionalists try to ignore the significance of these facts, there are multitudes of Roman Catholics who are convinced that modern social, political, and intellectual developments demand profound changes in their church if it is to work effectively in the new situation. As is often said, the "Constantinian era" is at an end.[2]

However, in addition to these external pressures, there is a widespread movement of renewal within the Roman Church. Two aspects of this can be conveniently distinguished, although they are in practice generally joined together. First, there is a kind of practical reformism which is a more or less direct response to the external pressures we have mentioned.

It is this, probably, which explains the strong stand of otherwise conservative North American bishops at the Council in favor of religious liberty and against the kind of church-state relations which prevail in countries such as Spain and Colombia. It also accounts for much of the passion for social justice and genuine concern for the poverty-stricken masses which prevails in some Latin American hierarchies (as well as elsewhere). This interest in practical reforms should not be minimized. Not only is its motivation often authentically Christian, but it leads, in many cases, to a desire to return to the simplicity of the early church and opens hearts and minds to the need for a renovation of theology and piety.

Taken by itself, however, the desire to meet modern conditions simply creates the willingness to change but does not indicate what form the changes should take. Therefore the decisive factor in the current renewal is not the increased openness and sensitivity to the modern world but rather the return to the sources of the Christian faith in the Bible and in early centuries of the church. It is this which provides theological direction and evangelical impetus to the whole development. To be sure, the return to the sources is not unrelated to external pressures. As its traditional bases of power disappear, the Roman Church is learning—or being driven—to rely more upon the Gospel. Furthermore, the pressure of modern historical scholarship is also forcing the return to the sources. It is this scholarship which is stripping away the incrustations of later centuries and thus making possible the rediscovery of the original character of Christian proclamation and worship. It is this which has provided the main stimulus for the two greatest forces in the current renewal, the liturgical and biblical movements. It has also played an essential part in creating a new ecumenical atmosphere. Through it the different confessions are learning to read the Bible in ways more similar than before, and they are beginning to see that the history of Christian schisms is one of tragic complexity rather than of simple black and white. Thus critical, objective, and apparently relativistic studies of the kind which have often been thought of as opposed to piety have done much to promote what is a profoundly spiritual awakening.

Needless to say, the opposition to these developments is powerful and widespread. However, the council has taught us that it should not be exaggerated. Part of it comes simply from ignorance. In most parts of the Roman Catholic world the movements of renewal are astonishingly recent. Outside of Europe north of the Alps, even students and professors have become aware of them only since the last war. The bishops, in most cases, were ill informed, or misinformed. As a consequence, the council has served as a kind of episcopal university in which many of the participants admit they have had their theological horizons immensely enlarged. They have found themselves agreeing with ideas which were before unknown, or thought to be subversive. This fact helps explain the unexpected strength of renewal at the council. It accounts, to take a specific case, for the way in which the North Americans surprised themselves and the world by voting fairly consistently in favor of reform. Their reputed conservatism proved to be, in large part, not a matter of theological conviction, but of habits—the habits of ecclesiastical bureaucrats who had been exposed to no new ideas since they left seminary.

However, the traditionalists do have a hard core, and a very powerful one. Numerically this group is a minority among the bishops in most countries, but especially in the early phases of the council it dominated the central administrative body of the church, the Vatican curia (although some members of that body—e.g. Cardinal Bea—are of a very different type). It was for this reason that the curia was able, before the council, to persuade both itself and others that its position was quite simply that of the Roman Church, and that movements of reform were peripheral and could easily be suppressed if need arose.

It is not quite accurate to call this group simply "traditionalist" or "conservative." In its efforts to preserve the post-Tridentine form of Catholicism, it pays far less attention to early Christian, and even some medieval, traditions than do the supporters of renewal. It seeks to conserve a particular type of Romanism, rather than the total Catholic tradition. Many of its members become what might be called "radical rightists" and favor what are, in fact, novelties which further isolate the Roman Church from other Christian communions and from the contemporary world. They wish to place an even greater emphasis on the role of the Virgin Mary and to increase the centralization of authority or, as they put it, the power of the pope.

This, then, brings us to the role of the papacy. One of the revelations of this council to almost all Protestants and to many Catholics is that there can be in practice, even though not in Roman theory, a sharp opposition between the pope and the curia. Theoretically the curia is simply the instrument of the pope. It is the administrative tool which he uses to carry out his wishes. The men of the curia like this identification. It enables them both to think and to claim that their actions are the actions of the pope.

However, the absolute monarch of a centralized regime is always in danger of becoming the prisoner of his courtiers, of his bureaucrats. There are no centers of power outside of his own administrative apparatus to which he can appeal for help when this apparatus fails or becomes recalcitrant. Many Oriental despots, for instance the Japanese Mikados, became mere figureheads, even while they remained theoretically supreme. The beginnings of a similar development are to be seen in Rome. In the course of centuries the pope has been surrounded by an elaborate ceremonial which is supposed to exalt him, but which actually isolates him and deprives him of independence. The curial officials remain, while popes come and go. These officials are the only ones who know how to operate the complicated administrative machinery of the church. The pope must always be careful not to antagonize them completely, for without their willing cooperation the administration of the church would become chaotic. Further, it has been assumed, perhaps too unquestioningly, that the prestige of the papacy would suffer severely if it became publicly known that there were disagreements between the pope and those most closely associated with him in governing the church. For these reasons the facade of unity has been well preserved, and it is only now, through the council, that we have become aware that it is sometimes only a facade. We can no longer assume that the phrase "Rome speaks," or "the Vatican thinks," always refers to the pope. Very often it refers to subordinates who, perhaps in all sincerity, believe that they know what the pope wants, or should want, better than he does.

However, the papacy is not only an institution, it is also men. To understand its recent role, we must say something, first of all, about the remarkable Pope John XXIII who convoked the council.[3]

As all the world now knows, he was a man of warm and generous heart who not only loved but liked human beings of all kinds and had a tremendous capacity for eliciting their affection. Further, he lived abroad much of his life, and this gave him greater opportunity

than have most Italian prelates to know and appreciate different
kinds of Roman Catholics, non-Roman Christians, and even secu-
larists and atheists. These factors help explain his passionate interest
in ecumenism and his concern for social justice and world peace as
expressed in his encyclicals *Mater et magistra* (1961) and *Pacem
in terris* (1963). They also explain his willingness and desire to develop more friendly relations with Communist governments and
parties. Even while repudiating their tyranny and their opposition
to religion, he recognized that they were capable of some good, and
wished to encourage this.

However, Pope John was not a theologian. He once remarked,
in his humorous way, to an American Protestant visitor that even
though he was infallible, he still had to consult his theologians on
complicated theological issues.[4] He had little knowledge and some
doubts regarding the newer biblical scholarships, although, once
he became pope, Cardinal Bea and others appear to have reassured
him. He had not worked out a program of reform, despite his awareness that one was needed. He had simply been, during most of his
life, a faithful member of the Vatican diplomatic corps, who had
never caused any particular difficulties to his superiors. In many
ways his piety remained that of his devout Italian peasant forebears.
Thus he accepted the traditional Marian cult as completely natural,
and apparently did not see it as opposed to the greater devotion to
Christ and the reading of the Bible which he frequently urged upon
the people. He made a sensational pilgrimage to Loretto to pray for
the success of the council just before it opened, and thereby gave
implicit support to one of the grosser forms of Marian superstition.
Sometimes, even when he was trying to be ecumenical, he uninten-
tionally offended non-Roman Christians, because he did not know
the right way to address them.[5] It is this traditionalist side of his
character, no doubt, which explains why he was considered a safe
interim pope when he was elected in 1958.

What accounts for the startling change in the behavior of this
77-year-old man once he became pope? One way of explaining it
is to say that for the first time he could follow the intuitions of his
heart regarding the needs of the Roman Church, rather than follow
the policies of others. However, what was really decisive was his
deep and serene trust in God's guidance. He himself expressed this

most movingly in his speech to non-Roman Catholic observers just after the Council opened: "Blessed be God every day; he carries our burdens, the God of our salvation" (from the Vulgate: Ps. 67:20). He had learned, the pope explained, to accept in "obedience and peace" everything as coming from God. This is the way he had done the tasks given him by others before he became pope, and this is the way in which he accepted and put into effect the idea of calling the council.[6] In short, it was not Angelo Guiseppe Roncalli who changed when he became John XXIII; it was only his responsibilities. He proceeded to lead the Roman Church into new paths with the same quiet confidence in God's guidance with which he had previously carried out the orders of his superiors.

II. The Calling and Preparation of the Council[7]

It is against this background that we must place John XXIII's announcement on Jan. 25, 1959, that he would convoke a council. By his own testimony, the idea had come as a surprise even to him. He knew that the church needed major changes, but not what specific measures to take. Further, he was well aware that he could not do much by himself. He felt trapped by the curia. In his own words, reported to have been said to Cardinal Cushing of Boston, "I am in a bag here."[8] It was under these circumstances that the plan of calling the council occurred to him. The assembled bishops would help him, not only by counterbalancing the curia, but by deciding better than he could alone what was necessary to rejuvenate the church.

John XXIII did, of course, have an intuition of what was needed: renewal, ecumenism, and mission. The Roman Catholic Church should first renew itself. This would help meet the objections of non-Roman Christians and prepare the way for the union of the churches. The mission of the church to the world would thereby be furthered, as is indicated by Christ's prayer that his disciples "may all be one, . . . so that the world may believe that thou hast sent me" (John 17:21 RSV). These, to be sure, are not three chronologically distinct steps. Internal renewal of the church should immediately lead to an increase in ecumenical openness and missionary concern. The council must concern itself with all three, but its first order of business should be the internal reform of the church. It was in some such fashion as this that Pope John envisioned the purpose of the council, even though we have stated this purpose more systematically than he ever did.[9]

The Roman curia, as could be expected, tried hard to delay, and if possible, defeat, these plans. From the point of view of prudent and cautious administrators, a council is a risky venture. The bishops necessarily would have freedom to express themselves about all sorts of questions on which they were ill-informed. What if serious conflicts arose among them, or between them and the curia, or them and the pope?

It proved impossible to stop the council from taking place, but the curia was able to control the preparations. Many of those who helped with the preparations were in favor of renewal. However, with the exception of the Secretariat for Christian Unity, everything was managed through the regular Vatican bureaucracy and, consequently, most of the final drafts were highly biased in favor of the curial point of view.

The course of events during the three years of preparatory work was baffling to outside observers because they were unaware of the depth of the disagreement between pope and curia. Indeed, some of the curial officials themselves perhaps did not realize the extent of the conflict. John XXIII liked people, and disliked disputing with them, so his opponents may sometimes have wrongly assumed agreement where none existed. In any case, whether or not this is true, there is reason to believe that he disapproved of a good many of the things done in his name during this period. Karl Rahner, probably the most influential contemporary Roman Catholic theologian and a leader of renewal, was put under Roman censorship and ceased writing. The investigations of biblical scholars were attacked, and Fathers Zerwick and Lyonnet, the two senior New Testament exegetes at the Pontifical Institute in Rome, were suspended from teaching.

Veterum sapientia, an Apostolic Constitution actually signed by the pope, reinforced the use of Latin in seminaries and condemned those "who out of a desire for novelty" talk or write against its use in the liturgy.

Nevertheless, immense hopes and expectations were raised in both Catholic and non-Catholic circles by the reformatory and ecumenical purposes assigned to the council, by many of the pope's acts and speeches, by the unprecedented sending of official Roman Catholic observers to the World Council Assembly in New Delhi and, above all, by the establishment of the Secretariat for the Promotion of Christian unity with Cardinal Bea at its head, together with the invitation to non-Roman Catholic confessional groupings to send observers to the council.

By and large, the observers were not among the most enthusiastic, but they were moderately optimistic.[10] They expected that the schemas prepared for the council would reflect at least some of John XXIII's spirit, that they would represent an objective effort to strike a balance between the various viewpoints in the Roman Church, and that they would therefore avoid condemnations and would make at least some advances toward reform and ecumenism.

If this had been the character of the preparations, perhaps the council would have moved swiftly and smoothly to its conclusion after a single session. This was the expectation of many bishops. They believed that matters had been so skillfully arranged that there would be little for them to do except approve the 70 schemas drafted by the preconciliar commissions.

III. The First Session

Instead of a harmonious display of Roman Catholic unity, the first session revealed a depth of conflict which surprised both many inside and those outside the council. The curial leaders and their allies were unwilling to make even the relatively small advances which might have satisfied the majority. Instead they tried to turn back the clock and close doors which were already open. Many of them were genuinely fearful of what they considered the heretical tendency of new developments. This attitude forced their opponents to react much more vigorously than they probably otherwise would have done. In doing this, the forces of renewal discovered that they are far stronger than either most Roman Catholics or non-Roman Catholics had thought.

1. The Opening of the Council

The first days of the council were a mixture of hope and anxiety for the observers and many others. Most hopeful was the way in which they were welcomed, not only by the pope in his audience on October 13 and by Cardinal Bea on October 15 (at which Prof. Schlink spoke for the observers),[11] but by many of the bishops and theologians. In these encounters there was not only friendliness but sometimes astonishing frankness and a strong sense of unity in Christ. The observers often felt more like collaborators for the renewal of the entire church, Roman and non-Roman, than like outsiders, even though they also generally remembered the necessity of staying within their official functions of collecting information and reporting to their church authorities.

More mixed was the impression left by the opening session of the council on October 11. The observers were honored by being given seats closer to the papal throne than anyone else, but the baroque splendors of the ceremonies were distasteful, not only to them, but to many bishops who would have preferred a celebration influenced by liturgical reform. Pope John's address[12] contained encouraging passages condemning the "prophets of gloom" who see nothing but evil in the modern world. The new, he said, is often good, and the church has the responsibility of *aggiornamento,* of bringing itself up to date, both in its theological formulations of the unchanging substance of truth, and in its structures, life, and relations to non-Catholics. It should use love, rather than the condemnations so often employed in the past. These words were generally interpreted as a strong attack on the conservatives, but this was by no means clear to all. The pope did not explain concretely what he had in mind, and most of the speech was highly traditional in its phraseology. Later, in the conciliar debates, both the opponents and the proponents of renewal cited this speech in favor of their positions.

It was typical of John XXIII to speak in this rather vague way. He stayed in the background of the council proceedings, and generally limited his own actions to the support of whatever seemed to be majority opinion. If he had done otherwise, the freedom of the council would have been destroyed. So exalted is the pope in contemporary Roman Catholicism that it is unwise publicly to disagree with him even on matters where this is canonically permissible.

A similar ambiguity clouded other opening events. To be sure, the bishops dramatically asserted their independence of the curia-dominated General Secretariat of the council by choosing their own candidates for 160 places on the council's ten commissions rather than simply approving the lists of preconciliar commission members which were presented to them. Through this action they learned to consult together outside the formal structure of the council through national and regional episcopal conferences. However, the conservative strength on the commissions remained great, for their presidents were members of the curia, and the 90 members appointed by the pope were generally curial allies. Further, a "Statement to All Humanity," which was noncurial in its origins and in many ways excellent,[13] was discussed so briefly by the bishops that it had to be considered a public gesture rather than a document expressing their views. All this contributed to a mood of uncertainty, despite the streams of laudatory prose which issued from the council press office. The newspapers began to speak more and more frequently of the conflict between what they labeled the "conservatives" and "progressives," and many were of the opinion that the conservatives were the stronger.

For the observers and the bishops uncertainty grew into anxiety as they studied the nine schemas totalling 390 pages (including notes) which were distributed during the first session. While the one on the liturgy was encouraging, and that on "The Means of Social Communication" was theologically unimportant, the other seven were poor, and the six prepared by the Theological Commission were deeply disturbing. Three of these theological schemas[14] were withdrawn before they were discussed. We shall say no more about them, because the texts are still secret. Another, "On the Blessed Virgin Mary," is best treated in connection with later sessions. The remaining five will be dealt with in the order in which they appeared before the council. Because of the rule of secrecy, our comments will generally be based on published reports of what the bishops said about them with supplementation from our own notes.

2. The Schema on the Sacred Liturgy

The only document from the first session which is no longer *sub secreto* is the 45-page one on the liturgy. It was officially approved in slightly modified form and promulgated as a "constitution" at the end of the second session. As its contents are discussed at length later in this volume, we are here mainly concerned with the course of debate on the schema from October 22 to November 13.

This schema is so much better than the other preparatory drafts (with the exception of those prepared by the Secretariat for Christian Unity) that a word of explanation is needed. Its excellence reflects the progress of liturgical studies in the Roman Catholic Church. Any group of outstanding experts in the field would have been basically in favor of renewal. When, shortly before the council, the curial conservatives discovered what the liturgical commission had done, they were apparently most unhappy. The secretary of the commission, Bugnini, was relieved of both his secretaryship and his professorship at the Lateran University, and was banished from Rome. Just before he left, Bugnini succeeded in having a note added to the schema saying that the implementation of its provisions would be completely dependent on the Holy See. This note was later removed as a result of the conciliar debates, but it has been suggested that without it the conservatives would have tried to prevent the schema from coming before the council.[15]

For the conservatives, the pastoral issues raised by the reform of worship were not as important as the more theological questions dealt with by later schemas. One Italian commentator explained the traditionalist position by saying that they thought of "liturgy as decorative ceremonial . . . . The liturgy was considered useful for uncultivated people who need exterior elements to raise themselves to the thought and especially the 'feeling' of spiritual things. To such an extent it was always viewed as in some way peripheral to the spiritual life, that practices of individual piety were considered superior to the mass itself."[16]

In contrast to this, those in favor of the schema regard communal worship as the central act of the church, as fundamental to the whole Christian life. The way in which men learn to worship God forms their piety and their characters, and ultimately influences even theology and the structures of the church. The success of the council depends more than anything else on the degree to which it furthers liturgical reform. And liturgical reform, in turn, is a matter of renewing, in forms appropriate to the present day, the fundamental structure and experience of the encharistic worship, centered on the crucified and risen Christ, from which the church lived in the early centuries.

Consequently the mass must cease to be a spectacle which the congregation passively watches, or uses as an occasion for private meditations, or for discharging a religious duty, or for gaining merit. All must be helped to participate actively with mind and heart. They must understand, and this means that the liturgy must be in their mother tongues, not in Latin, and that the prayers and responses must be said aloud by priest and congregation, not silently nor by only one assistant. Liturgical forms must be changed and adapted to different times and cultures so that their basic meaning becomes accessible to all. As one Japanese bishop pointed out, kneeling makes no sense in the Far East and should be replaced by some other sign of reverence. African bishops suggested that native music, including drums, be adapted for use in church. As a matter of fact, African drums beat during the council in St. Peter's on days when mass was celebrated according to the Ethiopian rite.

Most important, however, is the recognition in the schema that biblical preaching, reading, and instruction ought to be greatly increased in order to foster full participation in the liturgy. The purpose of the liturgy is to celebrate God's mighty acts in history, to make them present so that men in worship may come to share in these saving mysteries. It is through the Scripture, however, that we come to know about these acts, these mysteries. The better men know what Scripture says, the greater the possibility of their sharing in the full meaning, the fundamental content, of the liturgy.

In order to carry out reforms along these lines, the government of the church needs to be decentralized. Only the local authorities have the intimate knowledge of local conditions which is required for intelligent and effective adaptation and change. Therefore the initiative, and part of the control, in liturgical matters should be taken from Rome and placed in the hands of national and regional bishops' conferences.

When summarized in this brief way, the liturgical schema sounds revolutionary, at least to Protestant ears. We should remember, however, that many of its main ideas have already become familiar even at Rome, first, sixty years ago, through Pius X, and most notably, through Pius XII's encyclical *Mediator Dei* (1947). This schema goes considerably farther, but it is couched throughout in moderate language which disguises the radicalness of the denunciation it implicitly contains of many past and present practices.

There was surprisingly little attack on the theological framework of the schema. Cardinal Ottavianti and Archbishop Parente of the Holy Office criticized its "unclear," i.e. nonscholastic, character. In other words, they and some others objected to the basically scriptural and patristic language which the schema uses. However, the basic ideas were left untouched and only a few additional scholastic terms were introduced.

It would seem, in other words, that the conservatives were not much interested in the theology of worship which the schema presents. For them the church is not fundamentally a worshiping community, but rather, as Cardinal Ruffini of Palermo put it in a press conference, it is like a highly disciplined army.[17] From this point of view it is the practical recommendations of the schema which are dangerous. It encourages change, but this upsets the simple soldiers who are the laity. In two different ways it threatens the unity of the church. First, by favoring a diversity of liturgical languages and forms, and, second, by decreasing central control of the church.

The most passionate opposition was aroused by the suggestion that the vernacular languages be used more, and Latin less. One Italian bishop argued that "a single step away from Latin is a step toward schism," and cited the Lutheran Reformation as an example. Some of the more extreme defenders of Latin were incredibly insensitive to the conciliar situation. Not only were there observers present, but also large numbers of uniate bishops from nonwestern rites whose liturgical languages are not Latin. The most notable of them, eighty-four-year-old Maximos IV Saigh, Melchite Patriarch of Antioch, was unique in refusing to speak Latin in the Council (instead he spoke French). In reference to the sacred character which Latin has acquired in the West, he bitingly pointed out that Christ spoke Aramaic and the New Testament was written in

Greek. Further, "The Latin language is dead: but the Church remains alive: and language, the vehicle of grace and of the Holy Ghost, should be clear and alive . . . no language should be untouchable." Yet even after this, Cardinal McIntyre of Los Angeles and a number of others spoke as if it were a sin to question Latin. One Italian, Battaglia, asserted that to say Latin was a dead language was a crime against Holy Mother the Church, whose language it is.

There was a note almost of anguish in some of the replies. Spülbeck of Meissen, speaking in the name of all East German bishops, said that for them the vernacular was a matter of life and death. In Communist countries the church has no schools, no radio stations, no printing presses, and little opportunity even for catechetical instruction. Its contact with the people is almost exclusively through the liturgy, so it is imperative that this be intelligible. Kobayashi of Japan went so far as to say that to insist on Latin was equivalent to denying Christ to his nation. The salvation of souls should not be sacrificed to an external uniformity. This uniformity is not necessary for the true unity of the church in faith and love, and it should not be supposed that loyalty to the Holy See is so weak that it would disappear if Latin were eliminated. Jenny of France asked, "How can the people understand what Jesus says if the Gospel is read in an incomprehensible language? How can they really pray if they do not understand what they are saying? Let us not deprive the world of the Word it is thirsting for." On a somewhat different theme, Garcia Martinez of Spain complained that the church is embarrassed by such relics as Mary's supposed milk and veil, or Joseph's sandals. "Let such things be reverently buried and heard of no more." It took courage to say this. Immediately before, Dante, papal Master of Ceremonies and Secretary of the Congregation of Rites, which is the supreme authority on liturgical matters in the Catholic Church, had criticized the schema for making no mention of the veneration of relics.

While the vernacular was the main issue, three other subsidiary centers of controversy should be mentioned. The first was the proposal of the schema to give communion to the laity under both kinds, in the form of wine as well as bread, at least on special occasions such as nuptial masses. The present practice of reserving the cup for clerics became general only between the 12th and 14th centuries. Further, it has never spread even to those churches of Eastern rites which are in communion with Rome. There is, therefore, no dogmatic objection to reintroducing the original practice. Yet traditionalists resisted strongly. Cardinal Godfrey of London, for example, claimed that giving the cup was unhygienic, offensive to teetotalers, dangerous for former alcoholics and likely to be misunderstood as the beginning of surrender to Protestants. The source of such objections lay deeper and was expressed by Cardinal Ottaviani: "Are the Fathers planning a revolution? Would not the faithful be scandalized by all these changes?" Cardinal Alfrink of Holland, one of the leaders of the progressives, presented the center of the opposing position. While no Catholic, he said, doubted that communion under one kind is full and complete, nevertheless Christ has commanded both kinds, and this more effectively symbolizes the fullness with which he gives himself to us in the Lord's Supper.

A second subsidiary point of controversy was "concelebration." This refers to the practice of the joint celebration of one mass by a number of priests using the same altar and chalice. It has been retained in the Latin rites only in the consecration of bishops and at ordinations. The schema proposes that it once again become normal whenever a group of priests are together, as at conferences or retreats, or in religious communities. As usual, the basic objection to this was that it involved change. Only occasionally, as from Cardinal Spellman, was the old theological view presented that grace is multiplied for the church in proportion to the number of separate masses. It is this view, which implies that the eucharistic sacrifice is something which man does in order to gain God's favor, which was the basic reason why the Reformers so vigorously denounced "the abomination of the mass." Now, however, even most conservatives avoided this theological reasoning and based their opposition to concelebration on "practical" grounds.

Conservatives also objected to the schema's recommendation that control over liturgical matters be decentralized and partially given to bishops' conferences. They argued that this represented an attack on papal authority (to which one bishop replied, "It is not Peter, but Peter's secretaries, whom we fear"). From the conservatives' point of view, the liturgical schema was relatively harmless as long as its implementation remained centered in Rome. It would then be possible to delay, or even prevent, reform. For them, therefore, the provision for decentralization was the most objectionable feature of the schema. However, a full-scale debate on this question was postponed until later sessions.

After 328 speeches, 253 speakers, and 625 written communications which lack of time prevented from being orally presented in council, the discussion of the liturgy was brought to a close. Everyone was weary. Nearly five weeks had passed. More than half the first session was over, and only one of the 70 schemas had been considered. Further, the conservatives had attacked this schema so vigorously that there was some doubt whether it would be approved. The final outcome, therefore, was a welcome relief. Only 46 out of 2,215 bishops voted against it.

Yet it was hard to know what this signified. Many conservatives had apparently voted affirmatively because they feared that rejection of the schema would cause a public scandal. Also, it was not for them of crucial importance, and they believed that they could prevent its provisions from being quickly or fully put into effect.

On November 13, the last day of discussion on the liturgy, Pope John announced that the canon of the mass would be changed for the first time in 1200 years by the insertion of the name of Saint Joseph into one of its prayers. This change was in itself trivial, but it was also bewildering. Was the pope demonstrating to the conservatives that change is possible? Or was he in fact yielding to the requests of the small, and in general highly conservative, group of "Josephologists" who had spoken vociferously in favor of their cult in the council? Actually, it seems that John XXIII acted out of personal sympathy for a Jugoslav member of this group who had suffered greatly from the Communists.[18] Whatever its explanation, the pope's act contributed to the general uncertainty. No one was confident of the results of the next debate on "the Sources of Revelation."

3. The Schema on "The Sources of Revelation"

This schema represented the heart of the traditionalists' attack on the center of the contemporary Roman Catholic renewal, viz. the biblical movement. It not only tried to prevent this movement from advancing farther, but also to close some doors which had been opened by Pius XII's encyclical *De Divino afflante Spiritu* (1943). This latter document, which was inspired and largely prepared by Cardinal Bea, at that time Rector of the Biblical Institute in Rome, has served for two decades as the charter of freedom for contemporary Roman Catholic scriptural studies. If that freedom were limited in the way proposed by the conservatives, it would greatly hinder renewal in all areas of thought and life.

At first it seemed that there was a real chance that the conservatives would be successful. Their schema was in possession of the field. They often emphasized that the pope had authorized its presentation to the council for discussion. Admittedly it could be amended, but to reject it entirely, so they claimed, would be an insult to the Holy Father. When it was pointed out that the "Regulations" of the council specifically mention that a schema can be rejected, they argued that rejection would waste time. A new schema would have to be prepared because the substitute drafts which progressives were circulating among the bishops were unauthorized and subversive efforts to upset proper conciliar procedure.

Further, this schema had all the prestige of the Holy Office, the most powerful congregation of the curia, behind it. The Theological Commission, which had prepared the schema, was controlled by Cardinal Ottaviani and his associates. They tried to maintain their role within the council as the supreme guardians of orthodoxy. It was not easy for bishops, who all their lives had trembled before them, to realize that they now had the right and responsibility to make their own theological decisions.

Lastly, many—perhaps most—of the bishops were genuinely troubled by the newer biblical studies. To be sure, only a few were what, in Protestantism, would be called fundamentalists. Most bishops, for instance, had become accustomed to the view that theories of evolution do not contradict the doctrine of creation. They were not overly shocked when told that, historically speaking, it is absurd to impute the intention of writing modern science, rather than theology, to the author of Genesis. They were willing to accept the suggestion that his purpose was to explain in a way intelligible to his contemporaries, using their thought forms and stories, the affirmation that God had created a good heaven and earth and that it was through man's fall that sin entered into the world. However, when this same critical historical approach was applied to the New Testament many became uncomfortable. They heard reports that Catholic exegetes even at the Biblical Institute in Rome were saying that "you are Peter, and on this rock I will build my church" (Matt. 16:18 RSV) should be assigned to the post-resurrection period, and that the story of the three wise men was not intended by its author as what we call history, but as "haggadah" (i.e. a story of a type often told by the rabbis which illustrate the meaning of events, rather than reports them).

Pamphlets were distributed to all the bishops claiming that an effort was being made through the Biblical Institute "to introduce rationalist criticism into the church" to make young men "lose all that they have learned during their theological studies." The great culprits cited were Wellhausen, Gunkel, and form criticism.[19] Similar fears were expressed by a number of speakers in the council, most dramatically, perhaps, by an Italian who concluded by quoting from 2 Tim. 4: "For the time is coming when people will not endure sound teaching . . . and they will turn away from listening to the truth and wander into myths" (RSV).

The schema itself, of course, did not go to such extremes. After all, biblical scholarship had been encouraged by popes. However, with one small exception, the schema's references to scriptural studies took the form of warnings. It spoke of the inspiration, inerrancy, and historicity of the Bible in ways which were stifling. It ignored newer understandings of the divine origin of Scripture which not only allow, but encourage, objective scientific historical research. This prompted Bishop Charue of Belgium to say, "the Council must not set the stage for another Galileo incident."

Biblical studies were not, however, the chief theme of debate. This centered, rather, on the schema's assertion that Scripture and tradition represent *two* sources of revelation. Until recently this has been the almost universal interpretation of the Tridentine formula which says that knowledge of revelation is transmitted through Scripture *and* tradition. It has been assumed that this means that some truths are contained in Scriptures, but others (e.g. the Assumption of Mary) are known exclusively through tradition. This tends to emancipate parts of dogma and theology from any kind of reference to the Bible. Roman Catholics, of course, assert that no article of faith can be in conflict with the Bible, but on the two-source theory, room is left for independent developments of tradition (as interpreted by the magisterium) which need not even pretend to have a scriptural source.

In recent decades another view has become widespread.[20] It asserts that the Council of Trent can be understood as affirming that all revealed truth is contained both in Scripture and in tradition (not partly in one and partly in the other). Some biblically-minded theologians go farther and contend that the authoritative tradition of the church is simply its tradition of interpreting Scripture. They are willing to use the phrase *sola scriptura in ora ecclesiae* ("Scripture alone in the mouth of the church"). Those who say this, to be sure, find it difficult to find any kind of scriptural evidence for some dogmas (notably the Assumption, as we have already mentioned). However, they insist that it is necessary to seek for such evidence. One must learn to read Scripture in such a way that, for instance, the Assumption appears as a natural consequence. Otherwise the dangers of extrabiblical theological developments are increased, and the Bible loses that primacy which it had in the early centuries.

A Protestant naturally finds himself sympathetic to the intentions of this second view, even though he is also likely to think that it is inconsistent for a Roman Catholic to hold it. Further, he suspects that the effort to find biblical support for nonbiblical Roman dogmas tempts precisely those Roman Catholics who value the Bible most highly to distort the meaning of some biblical texts more than do the traditionalists. Yet this process of distortion affects the dogmas also. That is, the effort to provide them with a biblical basis can also result in their being interpreted in ways which are closer to the Gospel.

However, what has so far been said only touches the surface of the disagreement between these two views. Their difference is rooted in divergent ways of conceiving revelation. The two-source theory is generally associated with an intellectualistic and scholastic view of revelation as consisting of truths which can be adequately expressed in words and propositions. Such truths are, so to speak, atomistic and can be parceled out between the two sources. The newer position, in partial dependence on recent Protestant work, thinks of revelation, not primarily as the words in which revelation is expressed, but as God's mighty acts in the history of salvation as this is recorded in the Bible. These revelatory events are summed up in the person, life, death, and resurrection of Jesus Christ. Revelation is not so much the statements of or about Christ, as it is the indivisible reality of the Incarnate Word himself. It cannot, therefore, be partly assigned to Scripture and partly to tradition. Christ comes to us through both. Tradition itself, in this view, is not primarily orally transmitted truth, but is rather the life of the church in all its fullness, especially as this centers on the Sacraments. Tradition is the vital milieu in which alone Scripture can be properly interpreted. A final consequence is that it denies that words succeed in grasping revealed truth, as the traditionalist position assumes. Rather, dogmatic formulations (although without positive error, and in that sense "irreformable") are faltering and inevitably inadequate (although true and indispensable) pointers and guides to the inexpressible mysteries through which God grasps us in faith and love. Those formulations can be indefinitely improved, and must often be re-interpreted in order to be intelligible in new historical situations.[21]

These fundamental issues were discussed more outside St. Peter's than within the council hall. Bishops from nearly all lands (including Spain and Latin America, but only rarely from Italy) crowded the lectures by such leading theologians as Conger, Danielou, Tavard, Rahner, and Küng, not to mention many others. One of these others, an American exegete, commented that in the United States he practically never spoke to bishops, while in Rome he had been doing nothing else for weeks. The observers and guests also contributed to this educational process. A remark of Professor Cullmann's to the effect that the schema completely ignored the great exegetical accomplishments of Roman Catholics in the last decades was widely quoted. This prompted one bishop to quip that only cardinals and observers were really listened to in the council. There is no doubt that these discussions did much to remove the anxieties of many bishops regarding the newer Roman Catholic biblical and theological scholarship. It is, they discovered, respected outside the Roman Church and yet unquestionably loyal to Rome. It is also

better grounded in the total Catholic tradition (which includes the
Bible and the early centuries) than is the narrow Post-Tridentine
scholasticism in which most bishops have been reared.

The curia recognized the danger. Ottaviani is reported to have
asked the pope to banish Karl Rahner from Rome, but John XXIII
replied that he had a written statement from three cardinals praising him, and that if Ottaviani had doubts about him, he should speak
to these men.[22]

The council debates themselves did not deal with the substantive
theological issues so much as with the "style" and "opportuneness"
of the schema. The progressives were led by Cardinals Lienart
(France), Frings (Germany), Léger (Canada), König (Austria),
Ritter (U.S.), Alfrink (Holland), Suenens (Belgium) and Bea
(curia), with support from Silva Henriquez (Chile), Rugambwa
(Africa), and Gracias (India). They argued that the schema did
not fit the pastoral and ecumenical aims which had been assigned
to the council by the pope himself. It was condemnatory, trying to
impose the views of one particular theological school on the whole
church. This council, like Trent, should not try to decide issues which
were still being debated among Catholic theologians. Further, the
schema was too technical and scholastic. It did not speak a language which modern man could understand. Lastly (though perhaps most frequently mentioned), it spoke of Scripture and tradition
in a way which would widen the gap between Catholics and other
Christians.

The conservatives were led by Cardinals Ottaviani and Browne
of the Curia, and Ruffini and Siri of Italy (though with support from
Latin America, Spain, the Philippines, and Cardinal McIntyre of
Los Angeles). They replied that the schema was actually both
pastoral and ecumenical because it simply tried to remove confusion by stating fully and clearly the Catholic position. By a "clear
statement," they meant a scholastic one. Scholastic theology, they
argued, has been developed by the church over long centuries precisely in order to give unambiguous expression to the changing
faith of the church. Only confusion can result from following current fashions and adopting a new language which would in a few
decades become incomprehensible. This might be appropriate for
popular preaching, but surely not for conciliar pronouncements

which become part of the enduring heritage of the church. Finally, the theology of this schema is not that of a particular school. It has been generally accepted in the church for centuries (here they were, of course, right), and theologians of all tendencies were consultants for the commission that prepared it. (However, Ottaviani, who made this point, should have added that the progressives were granted little opportunity to speak.)

The conservative argument that "ecumenism requires clarity" created so much confusion that Bishop de Smedt of Belgium replied on behalf of the Secretariat for Christian Unity in a speech which many bishops acclaimed as one of the great events of the council. De Smedt pointed out that it is not enough in the ecumenical dialogue to explain the truth in the way which seems clearest and best to oneself. The other party is likely to misunderstand. It is necessary, rather, to enter so completely into the other's world of thought and feeling that this becomes as familiar as one's own. It then becomes possible to present the Catholic position in the language of others, in terms which they will understand. Only then will clarity be achieved. Only then will it be possible to determine how much Christian divisions are based on misunderstanding, and how much on genuine disagreement.[23]

As these summaries indicate, the fundamental issue which the bishops were asked to decide was not that of Scripture and tradition per se, but rather that of theological diversity. Can and should the church express the one unchanging substance of the truth in different ways to fit different times and mentalities? Or should traditional scholasticism be considered permanently normative? Stated in more general terms, the decision was between two mentalities: a rigid and defensive "Counter-Reformation" mentality and one which is more open to rethinking old problems in the light of the Bible, the early church, modern developments, and the beliefs of other Christians.

When the vote came on Nov. 20 after five days of debate, 822 bishops were in favor of keeping the schema as a basis of discussion and 1,368 were opposed. However, the question was phrased awkwardly (whether because of conservative machinations or for other reasons is not certain). It was necessary to vote *placet* (affirmatively) in order to close discussion, and *non placet* to continue it.

As the "Regulations" of the council require a two-thirds affirmative majority in order to pass any major motion, this meant that the schema, although opposed by a large majority, was still officially on the floor. John XXIII, seeing that this was an impossible situation, intervened to send the schema for complete reworking to a mixed commission composed of members of the theological commission, under Cardinal Ottaviani, and of the Secretariat for Christian Unity, under Cardinal Bea.

Later, during the intervals between the sessions, this mixed commission completed its work, producing a compromise document, now entitled simply *De Revelatione*, which was discussed in the third session and will probably be promulgated in the fourth.

Despite this lack of positive results, the debate on the sources of revelation was probably the most decisive event of the initial session. Men who had been victimized by the curia became the heroes of the Council. This does not mean that the majority of the bishops suddenly became "progressive" over night. It takes a long time to learn a new pattern of theological thinking. Yet many who admitted that they would remain "scholastic" to their dying day voted with the progressives in the full knowledge that this opened the door to a very different style of theological thought in the future. As in the case of the liturgy, they decided for diversity and change in preference to immobile uniformity.

4. The Schemas on "Communications," "Unity," and the "Church"

The last three weeks of the first session may be viewed either as an anticlimax or a prelude. First, two-and-a-half days were spent discussing "The Means of Social Communication" (press, radio, cinema, television). This schema echoed familiar traditional themes to the effect that the church should, when possible, use modern mass media to spread the truth, and that it should try to insure that they respect the laws of morality. The language, however, was less repressive and authoritarian than in many past statements. It seemed relatively unobjectionable to both progressive Roman Catholics and to most observers (who, to be sure, paid little attention to it). Criticism centered on its excessive length and its lack of any fresh, positive, and helpful approach to the problems created by modern communications. Serious doubts, prompted largely by the outraged comments of lay Catholic specialists, became widespread only in the second session. Many bishops became convinced that, despite its nontheological character, the subject was far too important to be dealt with in the manner of the schema. Further, they came to fear that the schema did not sufficiently safeguard freedom, and that it could, at certain points, be misused in order to justify repressive censorship.[24] However, there was no further discussion in the second session, and a shortened version of the original schema was approved on November 25, 1963, by a vote of 1,788 to 503, and later promulgated by Pope Paul VI. Almost certainly the results would have been different if opportunity for additional debate had been granted.

The last two weeks of the first session were spent on two schemas which, it was now evident, were so traditionalist that they had no chance of acceptance, but which were too important simply to drop from the agenda (as was done with three other clearly unacceptable drafts).

The schema on "The Unity of the Church" was a curious document. It had been prepared by the preparatory Oriental Commission—a highly conservative group—but this was not mentioned. It could easily have been thought, therefore, that it came from the Secretariat for Christian Unity which was officially charged with ecumenical matters. If this schema had been made public, it might well have raised an uproar. Because it dealt with the Orthodox in complete isolation from other non-Roman Catholics, it could have been interpreted, for example, as an effort to break up the World Council of Churches.

To be sure, there was no possibility that this schema would attract the Orthodox. Many of the bishops saw this point clearly and expressed it vigorously. What the draft called for, in effect, was complete surrender to the most rigid interpretation of Roman papal claims. As Vuccino (retired Latin Archbishop of Corfu) said: "The description of the unity of the Church contained in the present decree not only would not arouse the least sympathy among our Orthodox brothers, but on the contrary would cause instinctive repulsion among them. Let me be properly understood, however, it is not a question of modifying doctrine, but the manner of presenting it to

Christian brothers. We Latins have the habit, as the heirs of the Council of Trent, to affirm with special insistence, sometimes in strident terms, the authority and power of the Catholic Church, and especially of its supreme head. If we intend to encourage union among Christians, let us keep from using such language. . . ."[25]

After a week, discussion moved on to "The Church" (De Ecclesia), but not before Ottaviani had made an unsuccessful attempt to take up the Statement of the Virgin Mary as the next item. He argued that all the bishops could easily agree on the Marian statement. They would, therefore, be able to go home with at least one positive accomplishment and, furthermore, the Orthodox would be pleased because they also venerate the Virgin. Both arguments were more than questionable.

De Ecclesia was a highly traditionalist document, even though in some respects better than the other drafts from the preparatory theological commission. In a phrase that has become famous, Bishop de Smedt of Belgium attacked it for its "triumphalism, clericalism, and juridicism." The church, he said, is a "little flock," not a conquering army applauded by the world. It is not, contrary to what the schema suggests, a pyramid with the laity at its base representing nothing, and the pope at its summit representing everything. Bishop Huyge (France) criticized the medieval way in which the schema spoke of the church as a power which wishes to bring all nations into subjection, instead of making clear that in the church founded by Christ, authority should be exclusively a matter of service. In a similar vein, Lercaro of Bologna, the most socially progressive of the Italian cardinals, gave a speech which deeply moved the council. He said that one of the failures of the schema was that it ignored poverty. Poverty should characterize the whole being and action of the church. There is an intimate link between the presence of Christ in the church and his presence in the poor. "If the Church is faithful to poverty, it will find the light which will enable it to develop the best method for preaching the whole gospel, the message of God who, for love of us, although he was rich, made himself poor."

This concern with the church's mission to serve the needs of the world led Cardinal Suenens (Belgium) to propose that one of the major tasks of the council should be to speak about such major contemporary problems as respect for the human person, responsible parenthood, social justice, economic development, the evangelization of the poor, peace and war. This was the origin of the idea for the schema on "The Church in the World," which was discussed in the third session.

Of the many conservative replies to these criticisms, that of Bishop Carli (Italy) was perhaps the most dramatic: "Many insist that we say nothing that would offend Protestants. We cannot talk of the Blessed Virgin Mary, nor of the Church Militant. We dare not mention Communism. We can hardly refer to ecumenism, and we will be outlawed if we bring up justice or chastity. Thus the council is being brought to a standstill by interdictions."

Some of the attacks by Italian conservatives speaking outside the council were even stronger. One major Italian newspaper, *Il Corriere della Sera,* printed accusations that the pope had been close to Modernism from his youth, and that he had called the council to renounce papal infallibility. Others suggested that the council intended to come to terms with Communism and sacrifice the persecuted to the persecutors.[26]

However, the general reaction of the press at the end of the first session on December 8, 1962, was enthusiastically favorable, even to a certain extent in Italy. The defeat of the conservatives raised immense hopes for the reform of the Roman Church. We shall now turn to the further progress of the council to see how these hopes will be fulfilled.

Notes

Note on sources

The full titles of the works cited in abbreviated form in the following notes are given in the "Bibliographical Appendix" at the end of this volume.

Because of the rule of council secrecy, the authors have tried to avoid using material from their own records the substance of which has not already appeared in one or more publications. However, in citing council speeches, we have not given references to these published accounts because sometimes we have used our own translations or supplemented the translations of others from our notes. Furthermore, such references would be without scholarly value because they are not based on the official acts of the council (which may not be made public for many years).

1. G. Lindbeck in Skydsgaard, *Council,* Chapter IV.

2. Cf. M.-D. Chenu, "La fin de l'ére constantinienne," *Un Concile*

Pour Notre Temps, Paris: Cerf, 1961, pp. 59-87.

3. The literature on John XXIII is already immense. A useful collection of documents is found in *Johannes XXIII: Leben und Werke,* Freiburg-Basel-Wien: Herder-Bücherei, Band 165, 1963.

4. Rynne I, 4.

5. See, e.g., *Ecumenical Press and Information Service,* Feb. 2, 1962, and in reference to *Aeterna Dei Sapientia,* Nov. 9, 1961.

6. See footnote 11, *infra.*

7. For the specific details mentioned below, of the conflict between Pope and Curia, check the indices of the books by Kaiser and Rynne. For other information regarding the preparations, see Skydsgaard, *Council,* and Laurentin, *L'Enjeu.*

8. Kaiser, p. 10.

9. Cf. "Ad Petri Cathedram" in *Acta et Documenta Concilio Occumenico Vaticano Apparando,* Rome, 1960, p. 34 (translated in H.K. XIII, 452 ff.; and D.C. No. 1308, 907).

10. E.g., G. Lindbeck, *Christianity and Crises* (22, 1962), pp. 164-168; *Lutheran World* (IX, 1962), pp. 304-317.

11. For the texts, see Z.V.K., I, pp. 28-37 and D.C. No. 1387, 1423-6.

12. O.R., Oct. 12, 1962; Rynne I, pp. 273-279.

13. Z.V.K., I, pp. 65-69; D.C. No. 1387, pp. 1407-1410.

14. Viz., "The Deposit of Faith," "The Moral Order" and "Chastity, Marriage and Virginity."

15. Laurentin, *Cross Currents,* 411 and *Bilan* I, 25.

16. S. Marsili, O.R., Nov. 4, 1962.

17. H. Fesquet, *Le Monde* (Oct. 31, 1963), p. 8.

18. Rynne I, p. 129.

19. Kaiser, p. 162.

20. Promoted chiefly by G. Tavard in America, Y. Congar in France, and J. R. Geiselmann in Germany.

21. E.g., K. Rahner, "Was ist eine dogmatische Aussage," *Schriften zur Theologie,* Einsiedeln, Benziger, 1962, pp. 54-81.

22. Rynne, p. 168, and Kaiser, pp. 149-150.

23. The greater part of the text is in Laurentin, *Cross Currents,* pp. 441-442.

24. See Robert McAfee Brown, *Commonweal,* (79, 1963), pp. 396-398; cf. *Observer in Rome,* pp. 168-171 and 205-210, *passim.*

25. Laurentin, *Cross Currents,* p. 468.

26. Rynne, pp. 220-221.

Chapter III

Paul VI Becomes Pope:
Second Session[1]

I. The Opening

Hopes were high when the council reopened, after a nine months' recess, on September 29, 1963. To be sure, there was a sense of sadness because of the death of the beloved John XXIII, which had occurred the previous June, but his successor, Paul VI, had pledged to follow in his footsteps. He had appointed four cardinals, Doepfner, Lercaro, Suenens, and Agagianian, to act as moderators in guiding the day-by-day labors of the council, and all but the last of these had the reputation of being progressive. On September 21, just before the opening, the new pope had strongly warned the curia that it could expect major reforms.[2] In his address at the initial ceremonies of the session, he in some ways went farther than Pope John had ever done on so official an occasion, especially when he asked the forgiveness of God and of non-Roman Catholics "if we are in any way to blame for the separation" (i.e. between churches).[3] Further, while the schemas that had been prepared between the sessions by the conciliar commissions did not in all respects measure up to the hopes of the progressives, they were considered, not irremediably bad, like most of the preparatory drafts, but as providing a good basis for discussion and improvement. Also, they had

47

been reduced in number from 70 to 17, which made them far more manageable.

The observers were impressed by the audience with the pope on October 17. In contrast to the previous year, one of their number, Professor Skydsgaard, addressed the pope on their behalf, and the pope's reply was a genuine attempt to enter into dialogue.[4] While Paul VI does not have the overflowing human warmth of his predecessor, there was no doubt that he (like the observers) was deeply moved by the encounter, especially when he made the unprecedented gesture of asking all of us to repeat the Lord's Prayer together with him, each in his own language.

Nor should the reception with Cardinal Bea be forgotten. The observers chose as their spokesman on this occasion the Russian Orthodox Archpriest Borovoy. This also was a sign of the more relaxed atmosphere.

Nevertheless, despite its good beginning, the second session ended on December 4 in disappointment. The constitution on the liturgy and the decree on the means of social communication were proclaimed, but the basic work on these had already been done the previous year. Only three new drafts, on the church, on bishops and the government of dioceses (later renamed "the pastoral office in the church"), and on ecumenism were discussed, but the future of important parts of these were left uncertain. The record of the session was one of the successful conservative efforts to frustrate the will of the majority. The previous year that majority had prevented the minority from imposing its will on the council. Now it discovered that this negative victory did not guarantee success for a positive program of renewal.

II. "De Ecclesia" and the Renewed Vision of the Church

In turning to the schema on the church, we are dealing with the very center of this council. The major task of Vatican II is often described as that of completing or balancing Vatican I. Because this earlier council was prematurely interrupted by the Franco-Prussian war of 1870, it defined only the infallibility of the pope and his immediate and universal jurisdiction over the entire church. It did not place these, as was originally intended, in the context of a more comprehensive doctrine of the church and the episcopacy.

Pope Paul in his opening address agreed with the many Catholics who hold that this has led to a one-sided papalist development of the Roman Church. He praised Pope John who "gathered the broken thread of the First Vatican Council" and thereby "banished the fear wrongly deduced from that Council, as if the supreme powers conferred by Christ on the Roman Pontiff to govern and vivify the Church, were sufficient, without the assistance of ecumenical councils." He added, "We look forward with great expectations and confidence to this discussion which, taking for granted the dogmatic declarations of the First Vatican Council regarding the Roman Pontiff, will go on to develop the doctrine regarding the episcopate, its function and its relationship with Peter. . . . For us personally it will provide doctrinal and practical standards by which our apostolic office, endowed though it is by Christ with the fulness and sufficiency of power, may receive more help and support, in ways to be determined, from a more effective and responsible collaboration with our brothers in the episcopate." More than this, the doctrine of the church should be explained more Christocentrically, and more attention ought to be given to all the "components of the Visible and Mystical Body . . . that is, priests, religious, the faithful [laity], and also the separated brethren who are called to adhere to it more completely."[5]

The draft of *De Ecclesia* submitted at this second session attempted to do most of these things, and it was, from the progressive point of view, vastly superior to the schema which had been briefly discussed the previous year. With major alterations and additions, it became the basis for the constitution on the church which was proclaimed at the third session.

As the fundamental ecclesiology of this constitution is discussed by Professor Skydsgaard later in this book, we shall, in reporting the debates, focus on the specific issues which received the most attention from the bishops: collegiality, the restoration of the diaconate, and the laity. However, in order to understand these discussions, we must first try to sketch certain aspects of the new vision of the church which inspired many of the bishops' speeches and which aroused the opposition of the conservatives.

According to this vision, the structure of the church is fundamentally "collegial" rather than exclusively monarchial. This implies that it is better (though not necessary) for the pope to rule the church in association with all the bishops, rather than in exalted isolation. Decentralization of the government of the church should occur. More power should be given to the bishops' conferences. An episcopal senate should be established to act as the first helper of the pope in matters which concern the whole church. Thus the order of authority would no longer be pope-curia-bishops, but, even in ordinary times when no council is in session, the pope and the bishops together would wield supreme power and the curia would simply be their executive arm. In short, the collegial vision of the church is that of a circle with the pope at the center as the locus of unity, rather than of a pyramid with the pope at the apex as the source of all power.

It is possible to apply this collegial pattern, not simply to the relation of pope and bishops, but to the church as a whole. This was done by Bishop Edelby, vicar of the uniate Melkite Patriarch Maximos IV, when he described what he called the "Eastern" view: "The Western Church has supposed that Christ established Peter as supreme head—a kind of Roman emperor in cassock . . . and then gave him apostles as colleagues, and, finally, the clergy and laity as subjects. We in the East reverse the order: first Christ calls believers to whom the preaching of the gospel rightfully belongs, then he gives them apostles, and finally chooses a head of the apostolic college so that this college will remain united."[6] In short, the bishops are the servants of the people, and the pope is the servant of the servants of God. These are traditional phrases, but now there is a great desire that they be reflected in the organizational structures of the church.

Further, as was stressed particularly by Cardinal Suenens in a notable speech,[7] the charismatic character of the church must be stressed. The Holy Spirit does not confine himself to established ecclesiastical channels, and the unexpected gifts he brings, through the laity and in other ways, must be recognized and cherished.

It is, therefore, not only the relation between bishops and pope which should become collegial, but collegiality in a sense should also prevail between priests and bishops, and between the laity and the hierarchy. While the priests were rather forgotten in this session (as a number of bishops complained), abundant attention was given to the laity. It was often said that they must exercise real responsibilities, not only in the secular domain, but also in the spiritual, theological, and administrative life of the church. A sign of this emphasis was that a number of Catholic laymen were admitted as auditors to the second session, and women were added to their number in the third.

This new vision of the church embraces not only its internal life, but also its relation to the world. The church is not a state or an army embarked upon the conquest of the nations, but it is to be viewed, on the one hand, as a loving mother and, on the other, as a pilgrim people, the humble servant of all mankind, Christian and non-Christian alike. Because the church is a sacramental sign, its duty is to symbolize and witness in all aspects of its life to a Lord who conquered through suffering, who gave his life that the world might live. The church must be more concerned with the poor and the oppressed than with the rich and the mighty. No phrase aroused more emotion in the hearts of large numbers of council fathers than "Church of the Poor" (which we mentioned that Cardinal Lercaro launched at the first session). The increasing passion for social reform came to expression time and time again, and with this, the sense that the church needs to be especially concerned with the oppressed rather than the oppressors, and with the poor, under-developed nations rather than with the rich, so-called Christian ones. Connected with this, was an insistence on openness to non-Roman Christians, as well as to so-called secular ideas and values. Those who wish to serve cannot be arrogant or defensive. Humility involves the willingness to learn from others and appreciate the good in them.

Such, then, is the vision. It is only very partially reflected in the preliminary schemas and the final constitution on the church. However, according to the advocates of renewal, it is in the light of this vision that the final texts should be read. They have opened a door to this renewed understanding of the church. To be sure, the conciliar texts do not generally exclude more conservative interpretations. If they did, they would violate the purpose of the council as defined by John XXIII when he said it should be "pastoral" and not issue condemnations either to the right or to the left. Accordingly, so the progressives say, one should understand the *De Ecclesia* as pointing beyond itself to a view of the church which is much more open and biblical than that which is explicit in the text itself. The decrees of this council do not represent a fixed position which will be simply reiterated for long periods of time, as happened in the cases of Vatican I and the Council of Trent. To be sure, it is possible that the ecclesiastical authorities will develop anxieties which will lead them to try to freeze renewal and ecumenism at the levels attained by this council. However, so the progressives assert, the changing character of our modern world and the dynamism of renewal would, in the long run, defeat such efforts. They argue that one must therefore understand *De Ecclesia,* as well as the other decrees of this council, as the beginning, not the end, of a movement which may lead farther than anyone can now foresee.

This is not the place to evaluate this view. However, we must remember that this is the typical way in which the *avant garde* thinks. Otherwise we shall fail to understand how bishops who have severely criticized schemas for falling far short of the best theological wisdom are yet generally quite content to see them promulgated.

III. Collegiality

It was on October 4, after a relatively uneventful general discussion of the schema *De Ecclesia,* and of its first chapter on the mystery of the church, that the bishops began the treatment of the central chapter on "The Hierarchical Constitution of the Church and, especially, the Episcopacy." Here the great problem was that of "collegiality."

The word was new to many bishops, and was received with puzzlement or suspicion. But the theologians pointed out that while the term might be unfamiliar, the relationship to which it refers is very old, belonging to the patristic period, and therefore of eminent lineage. This word, as already mentioned, points specifically to the view that the power of teaching and the power of jurisdiction in the church are not concentrated in the bishop of Rome alone, but they are shared by all the bishops of the church as a body, in

which body the pope is the most eminent member. The bishops
therefore are not mere messenger boys for the pope and the curia,
nor merely executive secretaries of the ecclesiastical corporation on
the diocesan level, but men who by their episcopal consecration
have responsibility and authority both for the diocese and for the
entire church. They have apostolic authority at the local level for
teaching the Gospel, administration of the Sacraments and the governing of the people of God. They also represent at the local level
the concerns of the entire church for the apostolic character of the
church and for its unity and holiness in Christ. The pope is not
to be seen over against or apart from the bishops, nor the bishops
from the pope. The authority which the pope exercises is that of
the episcopal college in union with his fellow bishops. The fact
that the pope, by definition of the First Vatican Council, exercises this power "ex sese et non ex consense ecclesiae" (by himself and not by the consent of the church) should not be understood, so argue these theologians, as though the pope were a solitary
pinnacle of power. His primacy is within the episcopal body; his
authority to act "ex sese" is an exercise of the authority of the
entire college of bishops, which comes to expression in its prime
member the pope.

This understanding of the authority of the pope and the bishops
is regarded by its advocates as a corrective to a one-sided interpretation of the decree of the First Vatican Council, one which asserts a truly Catholic concern and is consonant both with the decisions of Vatican I and traditional views of papal and episcopal
power in the church. Certain conciliar viewpoints and Gallican tendencies have been rejected as distortions or exaggerations, but the
rejection of these errors should not be interpreted as license to
plunge into diametrically opposed misunderstandings. To many, before the council, these ideas must have seemed a kind of professorial
speculation which showed knowledge of the theological and canonical details of conciliar decisions and a considerable ingenuity in
interpreting them, but gave little promise of widespread acceptance
and no possibility of influencing the thinking or decisions at Rome.
But when Pope John XXIII announced his decision to summon a
council, this kind of thinking suddenly appeared to have a gen-

uine relation to the theological and canonical realities of the situation in the church. For the very act of calling a council showed the pope to be acting with a sense of the episcopal college.

The story of John XXIII's request that a visiting bishop join him in pronouncing the benediction during a papal audience is another illustration of his conviction that he too was a bishop among bishops, and, as we have seen, Paul VI professes to be in agreement with his predecessor on this point.

Nevertheless, when the collegiality of bishops was first mentioned in addresses, there were sharp reactions to it. Some bishops objected that it threatened the primacy of the pope and should therefore not be seriously considered. Others opposed it because they considered it too recent an idea to be truly Catholic, or because they could find no basis for it in the Scriptures. The first objection obviously indicated a sensitive spot, and almost every speaker who favored the notion of collegiality insisted that it is not to be seen in opposition to the decrees of the First Vatican Council and that the primacy of the pope is in no way endangered. All firmly assert that the pope is head of the body of bishops, but urge that papal power should not be understood in legal or monarchical terms but rather in terms of the authority of the Spirit in the church which is expressed through the body of bishops with the pope as their head. Patriarch Maximos IV of Antioch (Melchite rite) emphasized that collegiality does not undercut papal primacy but corrects misunderstandings and exaggerations which have developed because of the incompleteness of the Vatican definitions. He contended that the definition of collegiality of bishops will put the authority of the pope in its proper context, so that it will no longer be "the principal obstacle to unity among Christians but will become the chief force which seeks and maintains this unity."

The charge of novelty met the reply that while the term collegiality is indeed of recent usage, the idea is very old, rooted in the Scriptures and common in the teaching of the patristic period. Bishop Bettazzi of Bologna, speaking especially for the benefit of his fellow Italians, emphasized that collegiality is neither new nor a foreign product imported from beyond the Alps, but a well established concept numbering among its advocates not only Italian the-

ologians but members of the curia and at least two popes, Urban VII
and Innocent IX.

The scriptural bases for the idea of collegiality were stressed by
several speakers, among them Cardinal Meyer of Chicago, a specialist in biblical studies. They began with the common Roman
Catholic assertion that Christ entrusted his church to the authority
of the apostles, who in turn appointed bishops to continue the exercise of apostolic authority in the church. Thus the apostolic church
as founded by Christ maintains the same structure of authority
throughout the ages. But the bishops are successors to the apostles,
not as individuals, but as a group. The pope is the successor of
Peter and thus has the primacy, but no other bishop can trace his
succession to one particular apostle. That the apostles functioned
as a group is indicated by the frequent references in the Gospels
and Acts to "the Twelve," the Apostles, the Apostles and Peter. The
power of binding and loosing is mentioned not only in connection
with Peter's confession (Matt. 16), but is clearly given to the apostles
as a group (Matt. 18). That the apostles functioned as a group is
indicated by their association with Peter at Pentecost (Acts 2),
by their summoning the whole group of disciples to name deacons
to oversee the work of charity (Acts 6:2), by sending Peter and
John to Samaria (Acts 8:14) and emissaries to Antioch (Acts 15).
When a group of bishops professed to find this scriptural basis inadequate for a theological pronouncement, a theologian pointed out
that this position is much better fortified with Scripture than the
doctrine of papal supremacy. To be sure, the transfer of this apostolic collegiality to contemporary bishops is, for the Protestant,
questionable (cf. p. 140, *infra*).

The strongest argument of the supporters of collegiality is found
in the long tradition of church councils. Long before Roman primacy was doctrinally defined, bishops met in synods and councils
to discuss the affairs of the church and decide doctrinal and practical questions. Even in present church law, the ecumenical council
is recognized as the supreme and universal power in the church.
Most of the bishops maintain that the authority they possess as a
group in council does not evaporate when the council adjourns.
They continue to have authority and responsibility, not only for

their own dioceses, but for the universal church. Just as the unity and universality of the new people of God in the New Testament are reflected in the apostles as a group, so the bishops as a group with the pope as head continue to represent the church in its unity and universality. Cardinal Suenens of Belgium put it succinctly at a press conference: "What happens to the church in Latin America is also my business."

After two weeks of discussion it became apparent that a substantial group of bishops favored the notion of collegiality. Speeches in opposition were also heard, but because they only repeated the traditional arguments, they soon began to sound threadbare and lost any power to persuade. In mid October, the four moderators proposed that four questions relating to collegiality be put to a vote to determine the sentiment of the council fathers and serve as guide to the theological commission in its revision of the schema on the church. But their competence to do this was challenged by the General Secretariat, the Board of Presidents, and members of the Theological and Coordinating Commissions. Organizationally the lines of authority in this council are seriously confused and the result was two weeks of frustration. Finally the pope was persuaded to support the moderators, and the questions were put to a vote on October 30. Over 80% voted in favor of collegiality and thus, in effect, directed the Theological Commission to revise the text of the chapter. However, as we shall see, Cardinal Ottaviani, the chairman of the Commission, proved recalcitrant, and it was not until the third session that a definite affirmation of collegiality was achieved.

The rather technical theological problem of the "sacramentality of the episcopacy" needs to be mentioned here because it provides one of the pillars of the doctrine of collegiality. *De Ecclesia* asserts that episcopal consecration confers the fullness of the sacrament of orders. This excludes one traditional view, found in germ as early as St. Jerome in the fifth century, that there is no fundamental, sacramental difference between priest and bishop, and that consecration is more a juridical than a sacramental act which, so to speak, releases powers conferred in ordination. "A priest is a bishop in chains, and a bishop is a priest unchained," to quote a witticism which circulated among the bishops in their informal discussions outside St. Peter's.[8] However, if this is all that distinguishes a bishop from a priest, why should bishops be considered the successors of the apostles in a unique way? How can one argue that because Peter together with the other apostles constituted a "college," so the pope and the bishops, but not the priests, constitute a similar supreme college? In view of these difficulties, it is necessary to affirm the sacramentality of the episcopacy in order to assert collegiality. Further, the sacramental character of the bishop's office does find support in the liturgical tradition of the early church (where, to be sure, the bishop functioned more like the head pastor of a congregation than like the present-day bishop, who is essentially the superintendent of a diocese).

It is strange that practically none of the Catholic bishops and theologians at the council showed awareness that this affirmation of episcopal sacramentality can be considered unfortunate from the ecumenical point of view. It is perhaps the only point at which this council has increased the gap between Catholics and Protestants. For the Protestant, the highest office in the church *"de iure divino"* is that of pastor, that of preaching the Word and administering the Sacraments. He cannot but regret this exaltation of the episcopal office at the expense of the pastoral one. He recognizes, to be sure, that from other points of view it does represent an advance. It increases the emphasis on the pastoral, as distinguished from the purely administrative, functions of the bishop, and, by providing a basis for collegiality, it helps balance the papal office.

IV. The Restoration of the Diaconate

During the period of uncertainty, while awaiting the vote on collegiality, other portions of *De Ecclesia* were discussed, sometimes at excessive length, with the obvious intention of filling in time until a decision was reached. One of the most hotly debated sections was a mere five lines proposing the possibility of restoring the office of the deacon as a permanent clerical order. The reason for this proposal is that the Roman Catholic Church suffers in some areas, notably Latin America and certain missionary dioceses, from a serious shortage of priests. Even with the most generous help of missionary organizations, there are not enough priests to do the necessary work of preaching, administering the Sacraments, and teaching, nor is there any prospect of an adequate number in the next decades. It is hoped that this situation can be alleviated by recruiting able laymen to serve as deacons empowered to fulfill most of the basic functions of priests except consecrating the eucharistic elements and hearing confession. Latin American and German bishops have proposed that married men be made eligible for this office.

The office of deacon has taken various forms in the history of the church. In the apostolic church the deacon was entrusted with the administration of charity. With the passage of time the character of the office changed and the deacon became the first level of the hierarchical ministry. Later the diaconate lost its identity as a special office and became merely a step on the way to the priesthood. It is the intermediate, not the earliest, stage of this development whose restoration is now being discussed.

The bishops at the council were sympathetic to the problem of their colleagues, but many resisted the attempt to restore the diaconate, particularly because of the possible inclusion of married men. Some saw in this move a threat to the celibacy of the clergy. One bishop asserted that "a married diaconate would be a wound in the sacred celibacy of the clergy." Another saw clerical celibacy as "a precious garment ever in danger of being unraveled if a single thread were to come loose." Cardinal Spellman detected the danger that vocations to the priesthood would decline in number if the diaconate were open to married men. Bishop Carraro of Verona, Italy, suggested that it would be unfair to lay institutes and lay brothers in religious communities. Another objected that the example of dissident churches which permit married clergy should be sufficient warning: the divided interests of a minister bound by family ties, the problem of support of widows, and the bad example of clergymen's children. After a succession of such addresses, Archbishop Hakim (Melchite rite) was moved to comment on the irrelevance and "triumphalism" both of the schema and the addresses. He recalled the purpose of John XXIII to make the council a genuine "Epiphany" of the church in the modern world, and regretted so much self-glorification and concentration on ecclesiastical power. He added that "the strength of the church is in the Word of God, not in self-glorification. . . . Even in this council certain observations on the possibility of married deacons in the Latin Church . . . could easily be interpreted as reflections on the Oriental Churches and as almost contempt for the many holy and zealous married clergymen in other churches."

Only the issues of papal supremacy and the place of Mary evolved stronger reactions in the second session than the proposal of a married diaconate. It was clear that for many this touched a sensitive spot, and that in detecting a threat to the celibacy of the clergy, not only a matter of discipline was at stake, but a fundamental religious value. Cardinal Ottaviani proposed as an alternative to the restoration of the diaconate that the minor order of acolyte be conferred on selected laymen and that these men be authorized to perform certain ecclesiastical functions in situations where there was a shortage of priests. Since the order of acolyte is a minor order, it does not involve the obligation of celibacy, and hence no alteration of the church's discipline would be necessary.

When the issue of the diaconate was put to a vote, at the same time as collegiality, 75% were favorable to its restoration. The final decision in the third session was to accept older, but not younger, married men into the diaconate, thus imitating the practice of the Eastern churches in reference to the priesthood, where a youth must both be and remain celibate if he enters holy orders.

V. The Laity

To those who have known only the attitudes of the Counter-Reformation to the laity, the discussion in this area at the council would be almost unbelievable. Even those acquainted with recent theological studies on the laity could not but be impressed by the solidly biblical orientation of many of the addresses, and by the boldness and imagination with which they approached the problems.

The impact of biblical studies became apparent in the mode of approach to the doctrine of the church. The schema presented to the council represented a traditional scholastic approach, but it was also strongly influenced by the newer biblical studies. The discussion on the floor was strongly in favor of abandoning the legal-juridical approach to the church as hierarchical organization and adopting an approach which treats the church as a mystery of being, illuminating various aspects of the church's life and function by biblical images rather than scholastic definitions and deductions. This involves a loss of clarity and precision but an immense gain in depth and richness as well as power of evocation. In pointing to the advantages of the new method, Cardinal Lercaro warned against too simple an identification of the organized church and the mystical body of Christ. Both terms refer to the same reality, but express different aspects of this reality, aspects which coincide only in the age to come.

The recovery of the dynamic, cosmic, and eschatological dimensions in the biblical view of the church has transformed the discussion of the place and function of the laity. No longer can it be discussed in the terms: believe, pray, obey, pay, as summed up ironically by Bishop Primeau of the United States. The starting point is rather the Christological formulation of Bishop de Smedt of Belgium: The people of God as a whole have been called and consecrated through the baptism of faith to participate in the one priesthood of the New Testament, that of Christ. The mystery of the church is the presence of Christ worshiping through his baptized people, Christ teaching through his believing people, Christ exercising his lordship over creation through the labors in charity of his people in the world. The life of the laity is thus the life of Christ in the church continuing his messianic work among and in his people.

It would be misleading to suggest that every speaker availed himself of the new approach and joined in the exultant exploration of the ramifications of the biblical images. With something approaching the regularity of a refrain, speakers would repeat the old catechetical formulas, insisting that the chief duty of the layman is to obey the hierarchy. It is notable that few of them attempted to refute the new approach; its representatives were too well equipped theologically, too eminent, and too eloquent. Several different lines of thought emerged during the council's discussion of the laity, of which the following are representative.

One approach stressed the significance of Baptism. As Cardinal Lercaro expressed it, Baptism unites to Christ, and this so firmly that no subsequent separation can undo the sacramental bond. This union implies that the Christian shares in the whole life and work of Christ, his offices as prophet, priest, and king. To be sure, Roman Catholics make a distinction between the universal priesthood of the layman and the sacramental priesthood of the hierarchy. This, of course, is necessary for them because otherwise there would be a conflict between dogma and the new approach.

Confirmation was also emphasized by many, as the sacrament of Christian maturity. Through this sacrament the layman enters upon his apostolate, sharing in Christ's priesthood, offering worship pleasing to God, and seeking to bring men to God.

The universal call to holiness was discussed by a number of speakers, for it is the theme of a special chapter of *De Ecclesia*. Holiness is not a monopoly of the religious orders but God's invitation to all men. Monks and nuns have a special and important vocation, but not a higher or holier one.

Some bishops mused on the necessity of episcopal and priestly example in holiness and lamented that the hierarchy was so absorbed in administrative matters. Cardinal Légar pointed up a new emphasis by insisting that holiness should not be described in exclusively monastic terms, since this makes holiness inaccessible to the man who must live in the world. The church should set forth the kind of holiness which is appropriate to the layman, in his married state, in his vocation, in politics, in culture, and in leisure. Others applied the same idea to the poor and those who suffer because of their Christian confession. The poor and suffering must be helped to see that God's love is addressed also to them, and that even in poverty and persecution they can respond to God's invitation to holiness. It was at times deeply moving to hear a bishop from behind the Iron Curtain interpret the call to holiness in terms of his church situation.

Clericalism and the clerical image of the church were deplored by many speakers. Great harm has resulted because men react against the cleric and suppose that they are reacting against the church. Worse yet, the notion that the layman is only a silent supporter of the work of the hierarchy has left Christianity unincarnate in the world. The present mood of the church, according to Bishop Wright of Pittsburgh, is to stress the priesthood of the laity and eliminate the vestiges of clericalism among their pastors.

In concluding this account of the discussions on *De Ecclesia* at the second session, we must note that they were accompanied by another debate, mostly behind the scenes, on the Virgin Mary. Should there be a separate statement on her, such as had been prepared by the conservative preparatory theological commission, or should she be spoken of in the context of the schema on the church, as the progressives wished?

As there is a chapter on the Marian question later in this book, we need note here only that the progressives won their point in a vote on October 29, but by the exceedingly slim margin of 1,114 to 1,074. Thus, though Mary would be considered in the church, rather than apart from it, yet the prospects were that the final document would be a compromise unsatisfactory to either party.

VI. The Schema on the Government of Dioceses
(Later renamed "The Pastoral Office of Bishops")

On October 30, the council voted to close the discussion of the schema on the church and to move on to the next item, but because of the long list of speakers who had already requested the floor, discussion of the new document did not open until November 5. Perhaps because of the overwhelming vote in favor of collegiality and the resulting confidence of the progressives, discussion now became more forthright and frank. The next two weeks were to see some of the bluntest speech of the entire council.

When discussion opened on the schema in general, a pattern at once became visible. Speaker after speaker began by asserting that the draft as a whole was good and they favored its adoption as a basis for further discussion. They then proceeded to criticize it sharply, indicating the need of extensive and thorough revision. In effect they said, "This is a good document, but it suffers from fatal flaws." It became apparent that even the members of the commission which had prepared it were very unhappy about the document. Two of them declared to the general congregations that the document was not the same one approved by the commission, one going so far as to speak of someone "tampering" with the schema. Archbishop Binz of St. Paul, a member of the commission, told a press conference that the reorganization of documents after the

1962 session of the council had transferred some chapters to other schemata with the result that the document now had no beginning, no connecting link, and no real ending, and that further it had been revised by a smaller group within the commission who were near Rome, that other members had not been consulted, and that the commission as a whole had not approved the revised document.

Procedural objections were followed by severe theological strictures. The speakers lamented the fact that the schema completely ignored the entire issue of collegiality and was therefore out of harmony with the convictions of a majority within the council. The theology underlying the schema assumed a monarchical and juridical view of papal authority and regarded bishops as little more than his appointees entrusted with limited local jurisdiction. Bishop Gargitter of Bressanone in Italy charged that the text had been altered to expound its doctrine "under the one-sided light of insistence on the rights and central organs of the Roman curia" whereas the bishops on the commission had intended that the text should "proceed under the light of basic theological principles on the episcopate."

Numerous suggestions were made as to the ways in which the document should be revised to conform to the theology of collegiality. Cardinal Koenig of Vienna proposed that the principle of subsidiarity be followed that in the hierarchical structure of the church, no responsibility should be reserved for a higher office if it could be safely entrusted to the lower one. This would mean that many rights at present reserved to the pope (and thus, for practical purposes, to the curia) should be given to the bishops, thus both relieving the log jam of business accumulating at Rome and giving the bishop more freedom to adapt himself to local situations in which he is usually far better informed than officials in Rome can be. Cardinal Alfrink of Utrecht suggested that the administrative structure of the church be modified from the existing line of authority: pope, curia, bishops. He proposed that the doctrine of collegiality be taken seriously wherein authority centers in the episcopal college with the pope as head. The new line of authority would be: pope and bishops, and then the curia as the instrument, not of the pope alone, but of the pope and the bishops in their joint responsibility for the government of the church. As these suggestions multiplied, the expectation of some action by the council grew. Reports circulated that petitions had been presented to the pope asking him to indicate what kind of action would be acceptable to him. It was reported further that the bishops favoring action on the issue of collegiality had appointed Cardinal Silva Henriques of Chile to present on the floor of the council an appeal for action by the pope. Later reports indicated that the pope had suggested that it would be better if the matter were not discussed at the council.

The place of episcopal conferences in the structure of the church also came in for much discussion. These conferences, organized on a national or regional basis, have existed in some cases for more than half a century, and serve to coordinate the work of bishops, especially in cases of problems too involved to be handled by a diocesan bishop alone. The point was repeatedly made that there are social, political, educational, and missionary problems confronting the church which are regional in character and can be handled best by men who are on the ground and understand the problems by participating in them. To refer these cases to Rome not only involves delay, which can be serious enough, but even worse, demands solutions of men who are in no position to understand the problems or the special situations which must be met in looking for solutions. Some bishops regard a certain amount of decentralization in the government of the church as imperative if the church is to move surely and swiftly enough in the complex problems facing it. The problems of the church in Latin America or the United States can be met best by men who understand the whole cultural complex of the problems by having lived in it. Events in Africa, for instance, move with such rapidity that concerted episcopal action must be rapid and informed if it is to be effective.

Another important function of the episcopal conference is the development and promotion and cooperation among bishops. Decentralization without regional teamwork might mean only a move from curial centralism to episcopal atomism. Precisely because the bishop is a member of the episcopal college and is responsible both for his own diocese and for the universal church, there must be consultation and cooperation among the bishops in a country or region. The assignment of certain well-defined if limited powers to episcopal conferences should ensure that episcopal power would be used responsibly and intelligently at three distinct levels, in relation to the pope, within the episcopal conference in confrontation with fellow bishops, and in the diocese. The bishops took three different positions respecting the granting of legislative powers to episcopal conferences. Some, like the American Cardinals Spellman and McIntyre, opposed any legislative power vested in the episcopal conference. They were reluctant to have the authority of the bishop in his own diocese invaded by the consensus of his fellow bishops. Others, like Cardinal Ritter of St. Louis, wanted to give considerable scope to the episcopal conferences, to effect greater cooperation among the bishops, and thus increase the ability of the church to work effectively in problem areas. Others, like Cardinal Meyer of Chicago, held that there were dangers in both directions, but that the conferences should have carefully defined and limited powers so that where consensus could be reached the advantages of cooperation could be obtained without the peril of interference with the administration of the local diocese.

The bishops were not satisfied, however, with addresses about changes in administrative structure: they had some concrete proposals to make about the curia's way of operating. Cardinal Frings of Cologne spoke sharply against the procedures of the congregation of the Holy Office, calling them "a source of harm to the faithful and of scandal to those outside the church." He went on to say that no group in the curia "should have authority to accuse, judge and condemn an individual who has had no opportunity to defend himself," and called for a clear distinction between the administrative and judicial procedures of the curia. He praised the loyalty and dedication of those who work in the Holy Office but insisted that "its methods should be basically revised." That Cardinal Frings was not alone in these sentiments was demonstrated by the unusual (and forbidden) interruption of his address by loud applause by the bishops.

The eagerness of the majority in the council for some kind of action to give administrative expression to the idea of collegiality soon turned to impatience, and in some, a sense of frustration. The dramatic exchange between Cardinals Frings and Ottaviani on the methods of the Holy Office was succeeded by another confrontation between the moderators of the council and Cardinal Ottaviani, this time in his role as chairman of the Theological Commission. There had been for some time considerable impatience with the slow pace of the commission, which met but once each week and seemed to be making only glacial progress in the revision of theological documents. In response to a question in the discussion, Cardinal Ottaviani made it plain that the commission had no intention of revising the theological documents in the light of the council's vote on the famous four questions. His reasons were parliamentary: the questions had been proposed by the moderators without consulting the Theological Commission, which in his view had sole authority in these matters. The questions were therefore out of order and the vote carried no binding authority. A little later the vice-chairman of the commission, Cardinal Browne, conveyed the same message in somewhat different words. The indignation of the bishops found expression in the address of Archbishop D'Souza of Calcutta, India: "Someone had said in this council that the question of collegiality has not been decided. I reply: Has not an overwhelming majority manifested its opinion? Is it not ridiculous of the minority to refuse to recognize this vote? If a few men from one commission can check the will of 2,000 council fathers, what will the residents of Rome [the curia] do when the fathers have gone home?"

Unable to resolve the tensions within the leadership of the council or to evoke action from the theological commission, the bishops could only petition the pope for action that would enable the council to give structural and theological expression to the notion of collegiality. At first there were hopes that the pope would instruct the council as to his wishes concerning a senate of bishops in Rome to assist in the governing of the church. Others hoped that the pope might prod the Theological Commission to meet more frequently and to carry out the obvious will of the majority. A letter from the pope to the chairman of the Theological Commission was reported, and while more frequent meetings did result, no other consequences were apparent during the remaining weeks of the session. The more impatient yearned for drastic action such as the appointment of new commissions, or perhaps new chairmen, or at least permission for the commissions to elect their own officers. Questions had been raised earlier about the propriety of having prefects or secretaries of curial congregations serve as chairmen of the corresponding conciliar commissions, and the hope had been expressed that this might provide procedural footing for a move to elect new commissions. But at last, after many hopes and more rumors, the now restive and impatient majority had to be satisfied with a number of minor concessions: The commissions were expanded from twenty-five to thirty members and were granted the right to elect their own vice-chairmen and secretaries. The pope's *Motu proprio* at the close of the council also gave at least some encouragement to their hopes by specifying forty powers and four privileges, previously obtainable only by application to Rome, which the bishop in charge of a diocese should now enjoy. They include the right to preach and hear confessions anywhere in the world, unless a local ordinary is expressly opposed, permission to allow priests to say mass twice on weekdays and up to three times on Sunday where necessary, permission to confirm sacred orders outside of the cathedral church and on nonliturgical days, the handling of certain marriage dispensations, and the right to permit the reading of forbidden books to those who need them for their studies or in their duties.

This, however, fell far short of establishing a senate of bishops above the curia and endowing episcopal conferences with greatly increased powers. It is not surprising that many bishops were deeply disappointed.

VII. The Schema "De Oecumenismo"

The last two weeks were taken up with a discussion of the schema which had been prepared by the Secretariat for the Promotion of Christian Unity and which dealt with the ecumenism and with the questions of religious liberty and the Jews.

The specifically ecumenical part of the schema provoked less excitement than did the other two topics. The reason for this is, not that the council considers ecumenism unimportant, but that it is so much a central theme of this council that it has been referred to frequently already from the beginning. It will be recalled that preparation for Christian union was one of the main reasons John XXIII gave for calling a council of renewal. It will also be remembered that ecumenical considerations played a large part in the debates on "The Sources of Revelation" and on "The Church," especially in the first session.

Further, the bishops were constantly aware, and often mentioned, the presence of the non-Roman Catholic observers and guests in their midst. The observers were not only physically present in St. Peter's, but were also active in many ways from the beginning of the council. They met weekly to discuss the various schemas with bishops and theologians under the auspices of the Secretariat for Christian Unity. Their comments were reported to the commissions of the council, and, on more than one occasion, points made by observers were later reflected in speeches on the council floor. Outside of St. Peter's, observers and guests frequently spoke to groups of bishops, and these groups were sometimes large.

Three of the weekly press conferences held by the official German-language council press service were given by observers or guests (Professor Cullmann in the first session, and Professors Schlink and Skydsgaard in the second).[9] There were also innumerable encounters of a more private and informal character.

For these reasons the fundamental ideas of the schema on ecumenism which would have seemed radical a year before at the beginning of the council, were now relatively familiar. As Professor Schlink discusses these later in this book, we shall here simply note that many ecumenically-minded bishops considered this first draft too cautious. For instance, while it called the Oriental communions "churches," it avoided this term in reference to the bodies which have issued from the Reformation. Cardinal Doepfner of Munich suggested that they at least be called "ecclesial communities," while Cardinal Ritter of St. Louis saw no unanswerable objections to employing the word "churches" itself.

Another point which was made a number of times was that the schema would be strengthened if it followed the example of Paul VI in his opening address of the session and acknowledged that the Roman Church has often been at fault in contributing to the divisions among Christians. Bishop Elchinger of Strasbourg went the farthest in this direction.[10] The faults have not only been moral, he said. Sometimes Protestants have recognized aspects of revealed truth more clearly than have Catholics, for example, "the dogma of justification through faith which was defined at the first council of the apostles in Jerusalem." Bishop Elchinger, to be sure, no doubt disapproves of the form which the Reformation doctrine took, but, nevertheless, it was deeply moving to hear an admission by a council father in St. Peter's that Luther's protest was in a sense necessary for the very sake of the Gospel.

This speech met with widespread approval and no public protest. Nothing better illustrates the changes in the Roman Catholic Church than the fact that when Bishop Strossmayer praised the Protestants in a considerably milder way at Vatican I, he was very nearly mobbed.[11]

Most of the opposition to *De Oecumenismo* entered, not on this first section, but on the chapters dealing with the Jews and with religious liberty. Attacks on the first of these two chapters were inspired chiefly by Catholics from Arab countries who feared that it would be interpreted, not simply as a theological declaration against anti-Semitism, but as a politically motivated pro-Israeli statement which would increase their difficulties with the Moslems among whom they live.

The most numerous and vigorous opponents of the chapter on religious liberty were those Italian and Spanish-speaking bishops who continue to favor traditional patterns of intolerance. Its strongest supporters, in contrast, were from the United States, where religious freedom has long been the national tradition, and from mission or Communist areas where the church is either weak or persecuted. Relying on arguments which have been developed most fully by the American Jesuit John Courtney Murray, they appealed to the principle of doctrinal development in order to explain how religious liberty can now be seen to be necessary even though it has not been part of Roman Catholic teaching in the past. This, it will be noticed, is a significant admission that the Catholic Church can grow in the knowledge of the truth even to the extent of reversing positions (as long as they are not dogmatically defined) which were once universally accepted.

It was not until the following year that attention focused on the theological issues involved in these chapters. In this session the opposition tried to dispose of these chapters by raising procedural questions. They argued that these two questions had no place in a schema dealing with Christian unity. Actually one of the reasons for placing them here was the purely tactical one of making sure that they would reach the floor, but their location was defended on the grounds that there is the closest of relations between the Old and the New Israel, and that a strong stand in favor of religious liberty is essential for improving ecumenical relations with non-Catholic Christians.

Despite these arguments, the opposition was so strong that it was decided to divide the schema. Only the less controversial first three chapters were discussed in detail and given preliminary approval by a vote of 1,996 to 86. They constituted the basis for the *De Oecumenismo* which was finally approved and proclaimed at the third session.

In contrast, there was great uncertainty, as the session ended, about what would happen to the statements on the Jews and religious liberty. This added to the gloom which had been generated by the impasse on decentralization and collegiality which many bishops considered essential for any thoroughgoing renewal of the Catholic Church.

In retrospect, we can see that the disappointments of the second session were in part inevitable. It is much more difficult to carry through a positive program of renewal than to defeat a minority, as was done at the first session. Many bishops were as reluctant to vote for even moderate reforms as for reaction, and they had gradually to be persuaded. Further, the administrative structures of this council are clumsy and almost necessarily produce conflict and inefficiency. These structures are the product of the conflicting aims of the curia and John XXIII, to which Paul VI added the further complications of the moderators and the Coordinating Commission. Another difficulty is that most of the key posts in the council are in the hands of conservative curial officials. This enables them, not to control the majority, but often to delay or block it.

It is often asked why Pope Paul VI failed to intervene decisively to settle these problems. Some think that he became afraid that papal power was in serious danger and so refrained from effective support of the progressives. Others believe that he avoided interfering openly with the council out of respect for its freedom and independence. Another theory is that he is a hesitant man, yielding sometimes to one side, sometimes to the other. Still another view is that the moderately progressive position he expressed in his first speeches remains unchanged, but that he works slowly and cautiously to attain his objectives in order to avoid excessive administrative disorganization or conservative disaffection.

One thing is clear, however—more and more in his speeches he has emphasized the old, especially papal primacy, even while affirming the need for the new. Yet it is perhaps impossible to know whether this represents a change in his thinking or is simply an effort to reassure the conservatives. Pope Paul remains an enigmatic figure, as we shall now see in turning to the third session.

Notes

See the "Note on Sources" appended to Chapter II.

1. Prof. Quanbeck is chiefly responsible for sections 3-6; Prof. Lindbeck for the remainder.

2. O.R. Sept. 15, 1963; Rynne II, pp. 338-346.

3. O.R., Sept. 30-Oct. 1, 1963; pp. 1364-1367; Rynne II, pp. 347-365.

4. Texts of both speeches in O.R. Oct. 18, 1963; *The Ecumenicist*, II, pp. 29-31.

5. See fn. 3, *supra*.

6. I.C.I., Nov. 15, 1963, p. 14.

7. Reprinted in Küng-Congar-O'-Hanlon, Part I, No. 2.

8. Laurentin, *Bilan* II, p. 47.

9. The text of Cullmann's conference is in Z.V.K., I, pp. 49-64; Schlink's text is in *Materialdienst des Konfessionskundlichen Instituts* (14, 1963). Skydsgaard's text appears in Hampe, pp. 382-390.

10. Küng - Congar - O'Hanlon, Part III, No. 17.

11. Dom Cuthbert Butler, *The Vatican Council:* 1869-1870, London: Harvill, Fontana, 1962 (a reprinting of the 1930 edition) pp. 236-239.

Chapter IV

The Council Continues:
Third Session

An enormous wealth of material was dealt with by the third session of the council. In the first two sessions it was comparatively easy to discover crucial points, but now, in ten weeks of the fall of 1964, everything the council has undertaken was debated or voted on with the exception of the two documents on the liturgy and the mass media which had already been completed. No new material will appear on the agenda for the fourth session announced for September 14, 1965; instead work already begun will be concluded.

Pope Paul VI's first encyclical, *Ecclesiam Suam*, can in some sense serve as an introduction to the third session. Subtitled "The Ways in Which the Catholic Church Should Accomplish Its Mission Today," this encyclical of August 6, 1964, follows the example of *Pacem in Terris* in being also directed "to the clergy and faithful of the whole world and to all men of good will." This encyclical, which continually refers to the council, outlines a program in the third part for a "dialogue of the church" which is described "as consisting of a series of concentric circles around the central point in which God has placed us." The dialogue is to be carried on with humanity as a whole (the outermost circle)—with those who believe in God, with the separated brethren, and finally, within the Roman Church itself. The fact that the encyclical got such a surprisingly meager response in the world press may be due to its very formal, distinctly curial style which not infrequently affected the clarity of the content. The one point which was unmistakable was Paul VI's strong consciousness of being pope, whereas, in contrast, his statements about atheistic communism could be given very diverse interpretations. Also left undecided is whether the dialogue is merely a new teaching method which the church uses in order to adapt to modern man or whether it involves a common search for truth.

The session opened on Monday, September 14, on the Feast of the Exaltation of the Holy Cross. Whereas a year ago Paul VI walked into St. Peter's basilica, this time he was borne to the main altar on the papal chair. There, in a dramatic and impressive way, the new decrees on concelebration contained in the constitution on the liturgy were put into effect when the pope celebrated mass together with 24 cardinals and bishops. Additional excitement greeted this session because the patriarch of Constantinople had decided to send three observers. Another noticeable addition was the presence of 15 women "auditrices" seated next to the lay auditors. Also, beginning October 15, a group of Roman Catholic priests from all over the world was present.

The first reaction of many of the observers to the pope's opening address was one of puzzlement, consternation, and disappointment. One wondered just what reasons could have motivated the pope to choose precisely the theme of the hierarchy for his introduction and scarcely to mention, or to pass over entirely, numerous other issues which, for the most part, were felt to be more urgent. One was disturbed at the way the church was unquestioningly equated with the institutional office, whose function was in turn primarily designated as being a guarantee of the unity, the ecumenicity, and the very life of the church. The repeated references to the unrestricted validity of papal primacy and the affirmation that the historical significance of the council lay in the explication of the hierarchical structure of the church was understood as a retreat from ecumenical openness. Pope Paul's statement that the church must create its ecclesiology out of its own self-awareness was similarly interpreted.

This interpretation of the opening address can be verified point for point from the text of the speech. However, it was not possible until afterwards to see that the pope intended (apparently against the background of severe controversy behind the scenes) to give the third session a focus by authoritatively expressing the desire that the question of episcopal collegiality be settled. This aim was, however, obscured by the assurances, given simultaneously to both opposing factions, that papal primacy would not be endangered nor would the function of the office of bishop be diminished.

During the first two weeks, i.e., from the 15th to the 30th of September, additional discussions of the three main themes of the previous session took place and the first six chapters of the schema on the church were brought to a vote. The material of these six chapters had already been discussed in October of 1963 and, in the meantime, had been reworked and in part reordered in view of both written and verbal suggestions for improvement from the council fathers. Already on the first working day of the session a plan for voting was distributed which provided for 10 votes on chapters 1, 2, 4, and 6; but on Chapter 3 ("On the Hierarchical Structure of the Church and in Particular on the Episcopate") 41 votes were to be taken. This shows the pre-eminent significance accorded the question of collegiality. The necessary two-thirds majority was received in all the votes on individual chapters so that by the end of September the first three-fourths of the schema on the church had been approved by the general congregation. At the same time it was decided that a separate chapter, the sixth, be devoted to those in religious orders. It was also decided that, with the consent of the pope, the newly established diaconate could be conferred on married men of mature age as well as on suitable young men, but for the latter the law of celibacy must remain in force. Along with the affirmative votes, there were a surprising number of votes made with reservations (up to 26 per cent per chapter) which the commission said it was ready to examine once more.

Chapter 7 on eschatology and chapter 8 on Mary were yet to be discussed. When the former came up it was hastily dealt with in a single sitting of the general congregation. Some council fathers felt the text lacked an adequate doctrine of purgatory, eternal damnation, and final judgment. Others held it was too individualistically oriented, lacking communal, cosmic, and *heilsgeschichtliche* dimensions. There was also no mention of the Holy Spirit as the principle perfecting the church. The three-day discussion on Mary centered on the question of giving her the title "Mediatrix of all grace." It was above all the bishops from the Latin nations who defended this maximalist title; Cardinal Frings of Germany emphasized the need for a compromise; Cardinal Alfrink of Holland rejected the title on practical grounds, and Cardinal Bea pressed for a biblically oriented Mariology. On October 20 and 29 these two chapters were approved in revised form by the general congregation. The Mediatrix title was retained in the final text, though without the additional words, "of all grace."

The work of the commission in revising the schema was mostly a matter of explaining its rejection of proposed amendments. After it had reported to the council, the individual chapters were approved, against a dwindling opposition, on November 17 and 19. The final vote on the schema was affirmative. A report on the difficulties which arose in connection with chapter 3 on collegiality will come later.

The office of bishop had already been discussed during the second session in the first part of November, 1963, under the theme "Bishops and the Government of Dioceses." Meanwhile, it was decided to enlarge that schema with material from what originally was an independent schema, "On the Care of Souls," and give it the new title, "The Pastoral Duties of Bishops in the Church." The insertions on the question of the pastoral function of the bishop (which, incidentally, doubled the size of the schema) were discussed September 18-23. Of specific concern were the episcopal tasks of teaching, sanctifying, and governing, as well as the relationship of the bishop to the clergy and the religious (exempted from his jurisdiction) in his diocese. The archaic, traditional style of the schema was sharply criticized as being wholly incommensurate with the contemporary demands of pastoral care. It ought, therefore, to be replaced by an up-to-date concrete explication of episcopal tasks. Five weeks later (November 4-6), the revised schema on the bishops came to a vote. Chapter 3 alone was approved by the general congregation, whereas 40 per cent of the votes cast by the council fathers on the first two chapters were made with reservations. This might have been because the problem of collegiality in the third chapter of the schema on the church, on which the document concerning bishops depends, had not yet been resolved.

On September 23, the pope personally participated in the mass before the general congregation in order to venerate the relic of St. Andrew before it was taken back to Patros in Greece. In 1462, when the Turks were invading, the bishop of Patros brought the head of the saint to Rome for safety and entrusted it to Pope Pius II. The return of this relic at this time, after more than 500 years in Rome, must be understood in light of the open wooing of the Orthodox Churches during this session. It was hoped that the Greeks, who to this point have been most inaccessible and have sent no observers, would be encouraged to openness toward Rome by this friendly gesture.

The themes on religious liberty and the Jews previously comprised the final two chapters of the schema on ecumenism. Now, in the last week of September, they were discussed as separate declarations. The contributions to the deliberations on religious liberty were of three types:

1. One group of conservative council fathers welcomed the demand for religious liberty only in so far as it might relieve the burden of the threatened Roman Church in communistic countries and in some of the young Afro-Asian states. At the same time they staunchly opposed granting other religions equal rights for free exercise of their faith, since the Roman Church alone possesses the objective truth and the consequent right to propagandize. Should this principle be neglected in the schema, it would lead to indifferentism; it would promote a purely subjective religiosity of conscience and cripple the mission spirit. As a result, it was demanded no less than five times that this document be set aside, or, at least, that it be wholly revised.

2. This exclusivistic attitude is supported by a strong tradition, but its opponents objected that one can claim freedom for oneself only if one is ready to grant the same to others. The conservative stance would necessarily give the non-Catholic world and governments the impression of intolerance, and would produce a reaction exactly opposite to that intended.

3. A third group was concerned about the foundations of the doctrine of religious liberty. Holy Scripture as such appeared in-

adequate because, so it was argued, these foundations must be acceptable to all men of good will. A natural law basis was repeatedly proposed. According to this, freedom of conscience is the most sacred of the human rights grounded in natural reason. Freedom of worship, in this view, is derived from the incompetence of the state in religious matters. Several North American council fathers with a real sense of mission for religious liberty finally argued from practical grounds alone. They proposed that the attempt to state the doctrinal premises be abandoned in favor of a clear and concise text. On September 25, when the discussion became repetitive, the council concluded the debate and turned to the document on the Jews.

The proposal of September, 1964, "Concerning the Jews and Non-Christians" though shorter than an earlier version, was made more inclusive through the addition of a section on "God as the Father of All Men" wherein the Mohammedans were also mentioned by name. However, it was weakened through the deletion of statements that the Jews were not guilty of the death of Christ, and that it is unjust to call them a people guilty of deicide. These omissions were strongly criticized in the council debates.

Both declarations were then presented to the Secretariat for Christian Unity for revision. Their future destiny, of which we shall speak later, was greatly influenced by powers outside of the council.

On the morning of September 29 the council fathers and the observers received a booklet printed in several languages containing confidential information about the character and procedures of the newly formed Secretariat for the Non-Christian Religions. That evening the pope held a reception for the observers in the Sistine Chapel.

On September 30 the council began work on the subject of revelation. This matter was on the agenda of the first session, but Pope John XXIII saw to it that the schema then under discussion was withdrawn (as the majority wished) and sent back for revision. What was now before the council had very little in common with that previous document. Three chapters were now devoted to the Holy Scriptures, so it was given a place of high esteem. In the directives for interpretation it was pointed out that a distinction must be made between the "Word of God" in the proper sense and the time-conditioned forms of expression used by the biblical authors. In this context, form-criticism received a positive, though reserved, evaluation.

In the debate, very strong opposition was expressed. Some demanded a greater emphasis on divine authorship and felt it out of place to speak of new exegetical principles and of a growing understanding of Scripture in the church. Others stressed the individuality of the human authors and pointed out the limits of inerrancy by referring to individual historical inaccuracies.

Substantially more problematic was the very complex concept of tradition presented in the second chapter of the schema. The conservative opposition did not charge it with being erroneous, but said it was defective. They obviously conceived of tradition in the old quantitative categories, understanding it as a sum of truths. For revelation to be complete, these truths must be added to those contained in Scripture, which by themselves are insufficient. The failure of the schema to mention this insufficiency of Scripture seemed inexcusable to the conservatives.

The progressives, on the other hand, viewed this silence about the mutual relationship of Scripture and tradition as a great opportunity. They felt it was wholly inadequate to say that truths of tradition must be added to those of Scripture to make these numerically complete. Such bald quantitative categories should be given up entirely. Instead of always emphasizing only the unchangeableness of dogma, one should speak of an organic growth and of an ever richer development of revelation in history. Since the intellect by itself is absolutely insufficient to comprehend this richness of revelation, feeling and meditation must be added. The content designated by the word "tradition" as used in the schema is this: It includes everything which contributes to living a holy life and to the faith of God's people, and everything which the church is, believes, and has. Within this plenitude, Scripture no doubt plays an essential role, but it is, so to speak, a part of tradition, and certainly not a superior entity and canon.

The five-day debate on revelation ended on October 6. On the last working day of the session, November 20, the fathers received a revised text from the commission with the invitation to submit written suggestions for improvement until January 31, 1965.

In the week-long discussion on the "Lay Apostolate" (October 7-13), a fundamental difficulty in Roman Catholic ecclesiology, which had shown up before, now became especially evident: How are the people of God and the hierarchy to be ordered in relation to one another? This question was already present in the opening papal address and then reappeared in the changes made in the structure of the schema on the church. In an earlier draft the hierarchy was placed before the people of God, but in the final text the people of God is discussed prior to the hierarchy which is then followed by the laity. Such fluctuation reflects an awareness of the problem, but no clear solution is in sight.

It is unfortunate that the schema on the laity begins with an introduction which emphasizes the place of the hierarchy. Thus, in the document which is supposed to speak of the laity, the concept of the apostolate is deduced from the office of the bishop and then, in derived form, is transferred to the laity. Therefore the objection of "clericalism" resounded no less than ten times in the *aula*. In the discussion it was stated that the laity cannot simply be viewed as miniature priests or monks whose right to existence is based on purely utilitarian considerations. It was pointed out that their present insignificance was expressed by deed as well as by word in that they themselves had practically nothing to do with their own schema. To make any progress, one would have to decide to accept the concept of a genuine mission for the people of God—a mission not deduced from the hierarchy but given them through baptism and confirmation.

Here again, the conservatives who wanted to look on the laity merely as the hierarchy's helpers whose primary task is submission were greatly outnumbered by their critics. The relator speaking for the commission obviously sympathized with the critics and requested the time necessary for a revision. Debate ended with an address in English by the American lay-auditor, Patrick Keegan. This was the first time anything like this had been done during a regular working session.

The fact that council texts with related themes were worked on independently frequently had very unfortunate results. Thus the corresponding chapters of the constitution on the church, which was not finally completed until the last day of the session, constituted the doctrinal basis for the decrees on the office of bishop and the lay apostolate, as well as for the proposals on the priests, the education of priests, and life within orders. Furthermore, without the constitution, the documents on ecumenicity and the Eastern churches, which in turn intersect one another, could not be satisfactorily interpreted. Likewise, schema 13 depends on the schema on the laity. Since these individual themes (intentionally separated completely at the beginning) were simultaneously prepared by commissions of very diverse theological orientations, it was difficult, without some clear comprehensive plan, to overcome the increasing number of inconsistencies which became apparent.

At the beginning of the second week of October many daily papers carried headlines about the "Crisis in the Council." This was precipitated by a multi-fronted attack on central points of the council by the curia. On October 9, two letters written to Cardinal Bea at the suggestion of the secretary of state, Cardinal Cicognani, were delivered by the general secretary, Archbishop Felici. They were directed against the declarations on the Jews and religious liberty. The former was to be reduced to a couple of short sentences incorporated into the second chapter of the schema on the church; it was urged of the latter that it be entirely revised once again. These things authorized by "higher authority" would be done by a combined special commission of members from the Theological Commission and the Secretariat for Christian Unity. It also became doubtful that schema 13 on the church in the present world would be discussed at all, since some very influential people thought it revolutionary and dangerous. Finally, it was rumored that Cardinal Marella had deleted the word "full" *(plena)* from the third chapter of the schema on the church (already approved by the council) where the college of bishops with the pope is designated as the bearer of "supreme and full power" *(suprema ac plena potestas)*.

The timing of the offensive was extraordinarily well chosen; on that very weekend some important progressive council fathers were not in Rome. Among those absent were the Belgian Bishop de Smedt, a prominent proponent of religious liberty, and one of the council moderators, Cardinal Suenens. The motives for the action are important since the initiative, coming precisely from the secretary of state, is indicative of a certain trend. To the previous misgivings which "churchly" interests had about religious liberty, was added the fear that the Vatican's present way of conducting politics would no longer be possible. The proclamation on religious liberty might destroy the basis for various political agreements—one need only recall, for example, the Lateran treaty of the Vatican with the Italian government. In the case of the document on the Jews, the heads of the Arab states, who persisted in interpreting it politically, were actively hostile. If such a document were proclaimed, they threatened to confiscate property, to prohibit all mission activity, and to expel all Catholic priests and members of orders. Already in the second session the council fathers from the Arab countries had assumed the role of spokesmen for their governments in protesting against the statement on the Jews. This relatively official opposition was replaced in the fall by an insidious agitation that was primarily underground. At least four anonymous virulently anti-Semitic tracts were known to be in circulation. There was evidence that in part they originated from Spanish-South American sources. There was even talk of an anti-Semitism rooted in the curia. Finally, the resistance to collegial power can be counted as contributing to the offensive. The curia had seen from the very beginning that the most dangerous threat to its own power was the rising strength of episcopal influence in the realm of church government.

The offensive was immediately countered. Already on Sunday, October 11, a dozen cardinals sent a letter to the pope urgently requesting that the rights of the council be kept intact so it could proceed with its normal work. Shortly thereafter the most prominent signers were received by the pope.

In official circles, care was taken to prevent this matter from becoming public. Neither *L' Osservatore Romano* nor the bulletins of the Vatican press, which were otherwise very complete, made any mention of these events. Rather, they were made known through the deliberate indiscretion of the Latin-American press center, whose chairman was then suspended. Not until October 21 did the committee for the council press offer an explanation which, in part, read as follows: "It is not without bitterness that the committee has had to take note that certain organs of the press, relying on regrettable and one-sided indiscretions, have published various rumors which have no basis in fact. These rumors report maneuvers which supposedly were intended to hinder the council, but which, in fact, never occurred."

The most obscure role in these affairs was played by the pope. The rumors about his behavior ran the gamut from the assertion that he himself had instigated the whole affair, to the assurance that he knew absolutely nothing about it. Officially, nothing was affirmed or denied.

None of these disturbances were mentioned in the official announcements in the *aula*, but for that very reason the private conversations in the corridors were all the livelier. When the awaited debate over schema 13 was postponed a week in favor of two other matters, there was a reaction of general surprise.

Almost without exception, the reaction to the propositions on priests discussed October 13-15 was critical. The essential objections, some of which were supported by a large number of bishops, were as follows: superficiality, lack of a theological basis, condescending tone, an overlooking of real problems, unfair demands on the priests, and an insufficient understanding of their difficult position. No one was surprised when the majority of the council rejected the draft in the preliminary vote and sent it back to the appropriate commission for complete revision. The text, greatly changed and over half again as long, reappeared on the last working day of the session in the form of a document of decrees. It was given to the fathers with the request that they submit written emendations by January 31, 1965.

The "short schema" "On the Eastern Churches" (whether it was a decree or propositions, no one could really say) was subsequently discussed October 15-20. At first it seemed that it too would get a negative response. This debate was more or less concerned with matters which could be discussed only by a small circle of experts; the other council fathers could hardly be expected to have factual knowledge and a deep understanding of the complex problems of the Eastern churches. Perhaps for that reason the schema, with the exception of a few sections, got the necessary two-thirds majority in spite of all the criticisms. Amidst indecision, most of the council fathers were obviously moved to an affirmative vote by the stirring admonitions of Bukatko, the relator for the commission.

The title of the document was misleading since it did not deal generally with the Orthodox churches, but only with those small groups which had broken off from them and had eventually united with Rome. The discussion itself was focused on four points: (1) the question of recognizing mixed marriages between Uniates and Orthodox which had been performed by the Orthodox; (2) the question of the rite to be followed by Orthodox converts, whether individuals or churches; (3) the position of the Patriarchs; (4) the *"communicatio in sacris"* between Uniates and the Orthodox, which was to a large extent approved.

The commission for the schema worked through a surprising number of amendments in less than four weeks. On the next-to-the-last working day of the council the schema for a decree "On the Eastern Catholic Churches," which was very similar to the original text, was distributed; the next day it was approved. After the vote (98 per cent affirmative), Paul VI was then able officially to promulgate the decrees at the final sitting of the session.

At the 103rd general congregation on October 16, the fathers received the "Instructions for the Implementation of the Constitution on the Liturgy" which had been approved by the pope on September 16, and is to take effect on March 7, 1965. Its release was delayed by a power struggle between the Consilium for the Implementation of the Constitution on the Liturgy, and the Congregation of Rites. A compromise resulted: the instructions are signed by representatives of both groups.

On Sunday, October 19, the festive canonization of 22 African martyrs from Uganda took place in St. Peter's. This was, in the words of *L' Osservatore Romano,* an "infallible proclamation." The pope also officially announced that he would participate in the Eucharistic World Congress in Bombay.

Except for a few brief interruptions, the council worked three full weeks (October 21—November 10) on the schema which will most likely dominate the third session, namely, schema 13 "The Church in the Modern World." Leading members of the theological and lay commissions prepared a 29-page statement on this material whose final form is yet to be determined. In a preface the schema speaks of the necessary encounter of the church with the world and seeks to recognize the "signs of the times" which show either the *"praesentia Dei"* or the *"absentia a Deo."* It is directed, in obvious parallel to *Ecclesiam Suam,* to Catholics, to other ecclesial communities, to all who believe in God, and finally to all men of good will. The first chapter, "Man's complete vocation," points out the divine task of man in relation to earthly realities. These in themselves have a high value, which in turn gives human vocation its special worth. This vocation can be adequately fulfilled only when a man acknowledges that he is a sinful creature in need of Christ the Savior of the world who has restored the harmonious unity of creation. Chapter 2, entitled "The Church Serves Both God and Man," deals with the mission proper to the church and its hierarchy and from which their relationship to temporal things is derived. The spirit of service and humility corresponds to the servant form of Christ. This spirit is not limited to the spiritual realm but extends to the entire well-being of the whole human race. The third chapter, "The Attitude of Christians to the World in Which They Live," discusses the personal relation of the individual Christian to the world. An upright, hearty, brotherly, and willing cooperation with all men is commended as a witness to Christ who lived thus among his brothers. Almost half of the entire schema is comprised of chapter 4, "The Major Tasks Confronting Christians Today." This chapter deals with the preservation of human dignity, marriage and the family, cultural progress, economic and social life, the advancement of solidarity among nations, and establishing peace.

As a kind of commentary to this fourth chapter, a 64-page supplement, the so-called *Adnexa,* was distributed. Here these practical problems are discussed in greater detail, but the importance and nature of these additions has not been clarified. They were barely mentioned in the discussion in the *aula,* and yet suggestions for changes could be submitted in writing.

During the first week, when general debate and work on the first three chapters was going on, the discussion had a very general character. It sometimes seemed that the Roman Church is now at last making a rather elementary new discovery of the world. It is becoming aware of a vast variety of things, of an intensive life, and of unimagined possibilities which have developed outside of the church. Even among the conservatives, very few showed traces of a Catholic ghetto mentality; far more were filled with a kind of optimism. They were convinced of some sort of progress in the world which the church had all too long ignored, and which she should not only affirm as quickly as possible, but actually join. This position was theologically supported by a modern interpretation of the Roman Catholic doctrine of nature and supernature whose chief exponent, Teilhard de Chardin, was often mentioned. According to this interpretation, nature is taken up and elevated by supernature, as in the case of Christ, who in the incarnation sanctified matter and in the resurrection glorified it. In like manner, the church has the right and duty to embrace and affirm earthly realities.

On the other hand, there were critics who attacked the excessive immanence, or, indeed, lack of eschatology, and the danger of an identification of the kingdom of God and earthly reality. Furthermore, the demonic reality of sin was not adequately considered, the "signs of the times" were too secular, and the theology of the incarnation was said to be too one-sided.

In the discussion, a point which the schema seems to overlook was made: There can be conflicts between spiritual and earthly powers and duties. This was illustrated by reference to the confrontation with atheistic communism. Because of this it is necessary that the church demonstrates social concern in its practice, and in its theory accept both the progress of science and its terminology. The discrepancy between faith and science has arisen "not without our guilt." Furthermore, it is necessary that all casuistry in morals be decisively rejected. The church cannot offer a ready-made solution for every single human problem but ought to appeal to the maturity and responsibility of its members. This can come about only if morality is Christocentric and breathes the spirit of love and freedom of the children of God. It must cease only to prohibit the ways that lead to damnation, and instead must make clear the paths which lead to blessedness.

On October 28 the council began to discuss individual issues. In the consideration of human dignity, several incisive speeches were made against discrimination. It was also demanded that the position of women be properly acknowledged. On the matter of "marriage and the family" the traditional Catholic doctrine of marriage expounded by Cardinals Browne and Ottaviani, presented a striking contrast to the new view now pressing for recognition. The 86-year-old Patriarch Maximos candidly raised the question whether the

Roman Church is not in fact preserving an element of Manichaeism which can be explained by a "psychosis of celibacy." The concept of love as indispensably constitutive of marriage, something taken for granted in non-Catholic circles, seemed revolutionary against the background of traditional thinking which sees marriage in terms of other goals. The problem of birth control, whose place in the discussions was greatly exaggerated by the press, was acknowledged but not acted on. In the discussion of "the development of culture," views emerged similar to those which were expressed on materialism. Interestingly, Galileo was often mentioned and became a symbolic figure for the discussion. When "economic and social life" and "the solidarity of the family of nations" were discussed, the World Council of Churches was mentioned in the *aula* for the first time. Also, the lay auditor, James Norris, spoke on the poverty in the world. In treating the last issue, "establishing peace," the wholesale pacifism of the earlier discussion was in time replaced by more refined categories. Apparently the major difficulty was to modify the distinction between a just or an unjust war (largely felt to be archaic) in such a way that it could, to some extent, apply to the atomic age.

When debate on schema 13 ended November 10, it was generally felt (as was expressed in the final words of the South American lay auditor Juan Vasquez) that the appropriate commission, with the help of laymen, would still have an immense amount of revision to do.

On November 4 one of the council secretaries requested the fathers to pray for the Pan-Orthodox Conference in Rhodes.

Shortly after the recess from October 31 to November 3 for the Feast of All Saints, the discussion of schema 13 was interrupted by the presentation of the schema of propositions "On the Mission Activity of the Church," discussed November 6-9. On November 6 the pope appeared personally for the first time to participate in part of one of the working sessions. This special event of the program was announced by the secretary general only one day before it took place.

This schema was under the direction of Cardinal Agagianian who is both the president of the Commission on Missions and the prefect of the curial congregation for the Propagation of the Faith.

After many drafts, it was reduced to a few theses. This final form, even before it reached the *aula,* was severely criticized in public speeches and interviews because of its brevity, banality, generality, and theological backwardness. Cardinal Agagianian wanted to escape this criticism by getting papal support for the schema; it was he who took the initiative for the events of November 6. In his introductory comments the pope was not content—as one might have expected from the announcements—merely to emphasize the meaning of the church's mission work, but he gave his general approval to the schema. "Therefore we think," said Paul VI, "it [the schema] will readily receive your approval even though you may judge that it could be improved and refined in a few places."

The atmosphere of the final discussion was filled with tension. Would the council refrain from criticizing and rejecting the schema because of the pope's action or would they not? After initial hesitation, the bishops forcefully expressed their disappointment over the text and their demands for a completely new version. The genuinely missionary character of the whole church, the difficult problem of adaptation, the powers of jurisdiction of the forthcoming Central Council for Evangelization, effective recruiting for mission occupations, questions of education—all of these matters were either insufficiently treated or not at all. It soon became clear that the present text could not be salvaged. This was realized by Cardinal Agagianian, who quickly decided to take the wind out of the sails of his opponents. In closing, he let the speaker for the commission thank the fathers for so strongly emphasizing mission activity. Then the commission itself proposed that the schema be entirely revised. The question was raised whether it would please the fathers that the schema be reworked in a new form by the commission. When the significance of this question had been explained for the third time, it was approved by an 84 per cent majority. Thus, in spite of papal recommendation the schema was sent back to the commission.

The final ten working days of the council can be considered from two viewpoints. On the one hand, there was the normal schedule of work; on the other, there were a number of surprising interventions which shook the very foundations of the council and wholly dominated the closing phase of the session.

According to what was scheduled, four smaller items remained to be discussed and voted on after November 10. The first three dealt with internal problems of the Catholic Church and the discussion produced no unusual contributions. These were propositions on: (1) "modern renewal of life in orders" (November 10-12); (2) "education of priests" (November 12-17); and (3) "the declaration on Christian education" (November 17-19). Each item was discussed for two or three days and then followed by an affirmative preliminary vote. A Spanish priest, Luis Marcos, gave a talk on the report concerning the "education of priests." In voting on individual sections, it became evident that the first two-thirds of the text on the religious orders would have to be revised again, but the remaining parts and drafts were approved. Nonetheless, there were still numerous proposed amendments to be examined.

On Friday, November 13, the order of the general congregation was interrupted for the festive celebration of a Byzantine liturgy in the presence of Pope Paul VI. The pope took this occasion to offer up his Tiara for the poor—an act whose meaning was not entirely clear, leaving room for all sorts of speculation.

At the end of the next to the last day, the "petition concerning the sacrament of marriage" came before the general congregation, but only one sitting could then be devoted to its discussion. The principal point of the draft was the matter of mixed marriages. The text asked that this problem be viewed in the spirit of the documents on ecumenism and religious liberty. The mixed marriage of a Catholic with someone baptized ought to be distinguished from a marriage with one who is unbaptized. To get a dispensation, the text went on to say, the Catholic partner must promise to do his best to arrange for the Catholic baptism and education of all the children. The non-Catholic partner is to be properly instructed about this promise as well as about the purposes and essential nature of marriage. Secondly, without violating the rule that the canonical form of marriage holds also for mixed marriages, the ordinary of the place (usually the bishop) should be authorized to grant a dispensation so that non-Catholic or civil marriages need not be invalid. The third section of the text on mixed marriages requires that the marriage ceremony take place in connection with the celebration of the mass. The final point recommends the abrogation of the former practice of excommunicating Catholics who marry non-Catholics. Protestants would welcome these changes, though they would also wish they went farther.

In the brief discussion it became clear that the problem of mixed marriages is not universal, and where it is a burning issue, it takes many different forms. Circumstances in the United States, for example, are very different from those in Germany. Apart from these qualifications, the suggestions of the text were affirmed without any significant resistance. It was often emphasized that the Roman Church must absolutely insist on a Catholic baptism and education for the children since these are matters of divine right. The discussion ended when the council delivered to the pope both the document and the contributions made in the discussion, with the request that, because of the urgency of the matter, he act soon in the form of a *motu proprio* on the question of mixed marriages.

Those extraordinary events which dominated the end of the session can be briefly described as an attack on the council majority by the curia (and the pope). The attackers, cleverly using the lack of time and aiming a series of rapid blows in different directions, created great confusion, and finally were victorious on point after point.

The first blow was directed against the principle of episcopal collegiality. As already mentioned, the text on the third chapter of the schema on the church was already approved in the general congregation by the end of September, though a considerable number of suggested amendments were yet to be examined. On November 12 the Theological Commission met, but the experts were excluded. The attempt to raise doubts in the mind of Paul VI concerning the dangers which the principle of collegiality might have for papal primacy had evidently succeeded. This resulted in the postponement of the distribution of reports explaining the revisions of the amendments until November 14. On November 16 the secretary general, Felici, by order of a "higher authority" read a "prefatory explanatory note" to the third chapter which contained the following points: (1) The concept of collegiality is not to be understood in a strong juridical sense as though it involves a union of equals who simply transfer their authority to the head of the college. (2) Membership in the college is not conferred simply by virtue of episcopal consecration but also requires hierarchical union with the head and members of the college. (3) The college possesses full and supreme power because it includes the pope to whom such power cannot be denied. One should not distinguish between the totality of the bishops on the one side and the pope on the other, but rather only between the pope alone and the pope in union with the college. The pope is to proceed according to his own judgment in the shaping, promotion and approval of collegial activity. (4) Only the pope can freely exercise the full power. The college, to be sure, always exists but does not continually have full actuality; rather it acts collegially, in the strict sense of the term, only from time to time and then never without the consent of its papal head.

A summary interpretation of this text can only come to the conclusion that through a number of juridical limitations—not so easily understood in their details—the college of bishops has been degraded to nothing but an instrument of the pope. He can use it to express and exercise his full power in case he does not wish to exercise this by himself.

During the next day's vote on the amendments, there was absolutely no mention of this explanatory note. Almost 98 per cent once again approved the text of the third chapter, including the 31 changes made in the meantime.

The final vote on the dogmatic constitution *De Ecclesia* took place on November 19. Before the vote the secretary general reminded the fathers once again of his announcement concerning the note. This vote, like the public vote prior to papal approval, must be understood in view of that announcement which, because of its importance, was printed once again, but this time on a separate sheet. The note was described as having permanent validity and as belonging to the acts of the council. All these momentous preliminaries made no change in the final results—of 2,145 fathers, 2,134 voted for the constitution, 10 voted against it, and one vote was invalid. In the public vote there were but 5 opposed.

The second blow was directed against the "Declaration on Religious Liberty" whose fate we have followed until it was jeopardized in the second week of October. Those who claimed no damage was done at that time are shown to be wrong in so far as the Secretariat for Christian Unity had to submit the text which it had already revised by October 24 to five members of the Theological Commission for examination. An agreement was reached on November 9; on November 17 the new text was distributed, and a vote was announced for November 19.

On November 18 the secretary general, speaking on behalf of the presidents, said a number of fathers had requested further discussion of religious liberty since an entirely new text was up for consideration. The unrest caused by this announcement was immediately allayed as Felici went on to say that a preliminary vote would come the following day to determine whether the council wished to vote immediately on the document or not. None doubted that the majority preferred the former.

On November 19 Cardinal Tisserant, chairman of the council presidents, announced that, contrary to yesterday's announcement, there would be absolutely no vote on religious liberty during this session. It was stated that the presidium had the right to make this arrangement and did so in order to give the fathers opportunity for thorough study and mature reflection on the document so they might suggest improvements which could be submitted until January 31, 1965. Today only the report would be read. This was done in stirring tones by Bishop de Smedt. The loud and sustained applause which he received was unlike any that had occurred before. On the same day the pope was given a letter with the urgent request that religious liberty be voted on during this session. This letter, initiated by North American bishops, was signed by some 1,000 to 1,400 council fathers. But the attackers were unshaken: On the next day at the final setting of the general congregation, Cardinal Tisserant, speaking on behalf of the pope, pointed out that the decision to postpone the vote was made by the Council of Presidents in accordance with the rules of order of the council. He said the schema on religious liberty would be dealt with during the fourth session and, if possible, as the first item of business. In his closing address, the pope said it was only because of the lack of time that the schema on religious liberty could not be further discussed during this session. It would, however, be completely aired during the fourth session. Yet, in view of the fact that the vote was delayed, we may say that the second blow had accomplished its purpose.

The third and perhaps most momentous blow was aimed against the *Decree on Ecumenism.* Its individual chapters had been approved between October 6 and 8; the subsequent revision of the amendments was then overwhelmingly approved November 10-14. The text was thus ready for promulgation a full week before the end of the session. However, it was not mentioned again until November 19. The secretary general announced that on the following day a vote would be taken on the schema which now would include 19 changes. "In addition to the revisions made on the basis of the amendments suggested by the council fathers, the following improvements were inserted by the Secretariat for Christian Unity to clarify the text. In so doing, the Secretariat accepted friendly suggestions expressed by higher authority." After saying this, Felici raced through the 19 changes so fast that no one could possibly catch their significance. Most of the members of the Secretariat were completely surprised by the announcement, for now they heard for the first time about the *"clarificationes"* they supposedly had made.

Through this maneuver the council came to feel that a "higher authority," at any time and how it pleased, could change a text even though it had been approved by the council. The sheet of amendments handed out later clearly revealed that among numerous insignificant stylistic modifications there were also changes in the content of the text itself. Now conversion and ecumenism are instances of the "marvelous ways of God" and are not, as stated before, "inspired by the Holy Spirit." Previously the text stated that the people of God "remains liable to sin during its earthly pilgrimage" but now it only says that it is "in its members liable to sin." The Church as such does not feel susceptible to sin! It is no longer enough to say that the Protestant churches, according to Catholic faith, "have not preserved the full reality of the eucharistic mystery," but now it must be explained that this means "the proper and full substance of the eucharistic mystery." The most disastrous change and the one which most distressed the observers was this: concerning the Reformation churches the text had stated, "Moved by the Holy Spirit, they find God speaking to them in the Holy Scriptures in Christ." This statement was corrected in three places. The first clause now reads "while invoking the Holy Spirit," thus raising a question regarding the previously granted presence of the Holy Spirit in Protestant Scripture study. Further, it is no longer stated that they thus find God: "find" has become "seek." Finally, in the Latin, "quasi" is inserted in such a way that one may translate either, "they seek in these very Scriptures God *as* he speaks to them in Christ," or "*as if* he speaks to them in Christ." The standard English version follows the first reading, but this leaves too little room for that uncertainty which the change clearly intended to impute to the non-Catholic reading of Scripture. At the same time, it would be exaggerated to translate "as if."

Until this time the texts and amendments had been voted on separately, but now this possibility was excluded. The only alternative was either to accept the altered text or vote against the *Decree on Ecumenism.* Only 75 fathers did the latter, and but 11 opposed it in the public vote taken November 21

Those who felt the brunt of these blows were by no means apathetic. Anger, grief, indignation, and dejection hit what was for the council an all-time high on November 19. Perhaps the worst bitterness arose because certain lesser powers continually referred to some "superior authority" which never put in an appearance. But as one commentator said, it took but one night to quieten the hearts. Resistance has no tradition in the Roman Church. So the third blow of the attacker found its mark.

It was mildly comforting for some that on November 20 the fathers voted on the declaration on the Jews, now entitled "The Attitude of the Church Toward Non-Christian Religions." In his official presentation of the schema, Cardinal Bea said that in order to avoid any political misinterpretation, it was to be regarded as a supplement to the constitution on the church. This newly formulated document specifically mentions Buddhism, Hinduism, and Islam among the non-Christian religions, and then deals with the Jews in a fourth section. This section was now more complete and more

biblical than in the draft discussed some weeks earlier. The schema
was approved by an 83 per cent majority, but 242 bishops voted
with reservations which the Secretariat then had to review.

The final public session took place on the Feast of Mary's Presentation in the Temple. The pope appeared on the papal chair and
concelebrated the mass with 24 bishops from dioceses where the
most famous Marian shrines are located. Then came the public
vote on the promulgation of "The Constitution on the Church" and
the two decrees "On Ecumenism" and "On Eastern Churches." The
concluding papal address focused on two major themes: papal primacy, which is buttressed by the principle of collegiality, and the
Virgin Mary. The pope said, "Therefore we declare to the honor of
the Holy Virgin and for our comfort that Holy Mary is Mother of
the Church." In so doing thus he attributed to Mary a title which
the council itself had avoided using in its texts. He called the chapter on Mary the high point and crown of the constitution on the
church and concluded his address with a hymn to the Holy Virgin.
Before that, however, he announced his intention to send a golden
rose to the Marian shrine at Fatima. This gesture was understood
as an attempt to appease the Portuguese who, because of the Goa
situation, strongly disapproved of the pope's trip to India.

That afternoon the pope attended a Marian Feast at Saint Mary
Major. Cardinal Confalonieri read a eulogy to Mary in which the
new title "Mother of the Church" stood in the very center. Only
about 400 fathers participated in this feast.

The bishops left Rome without knowing the exact date for the
final session of the council. At the beginning of January it was officially announced that it would begin on the 14th of September.

EDITORIAL EPILOGUE
The Future of the Council

As this is being written, some months after the close of the third session, different explanations are being offered for the four blows against the council described above by Dr. Dietzfelbinger.

Some Catholic and most Protestant commentators believe that the pope has become disturbed by the reforming ferment in the council, and that he has decided, at the very least, to dampen it. This, if true, means that further major advances will be hindered and the practical implementation of the reforms already decreed will be slow.

However, there are others who argue that the pope was motivated primarily by the desire to maintain the principle of conciliar unanimity. He did not wish, it is said, to ride roughshod over the minority as was done at Vatican I. Those who hold this view grant that the pope's behavior was anti-collegial, interfered with the independence of the council and undermined the confidence of many bishops in his leadership. Nevertheless, they hope that this will prove to be an unfortunate interlude rather than a foretaste of the future.

Whichever theory is correct, some fairly definite things can be said about what will happen at the fourth session in the fall of 1965. Eleven documents, some short and some long, will be discussed and, according to present plans, final action will be taken on all of them. Five of these will probably be approved in much their present form, while the final shape of the six others is still uncertain.

Four have already been approved in preliminary votes, viz., the drafts on revelation, non-Christian religions (including the Jews), the formation (or education) of priests, and on Christian education. As is pointed out elsewhere in this book, the first two of these are theologically significant and do involve some progress. The third, on the formation of priests, will prove helpful to the degree it is put into practice. The fourth, on Christian education, does not resolve any of the basic problems centering around, for example, Catholic schools in places like the United States, but at least it is not likely to do any harm.

The fifth document whose future seems assured is that on the crucial subject of religious liberty. Even those conciliar experts who are, in general, pessimistic about the future agree that the conservative minority will not again be able to delay this declaration as it did at the end of the third session. Their confidence is based, in part, on the strong feelings of the majority of the bishops in favor of religious liberty and, in part, on the clear support which Pope Paul VI has in the past given to this principle.

Among the six documents which are being drastically revised in preparation for the fourth session, the two on the priesthood and on the religious life do not seem likely to propose any major reform, even though they may suggest the need for these.

In contrast, the schema on missions may contain important proposals for cooperation between Catholic and non-Catholic missions as well as for the reorganization of the Catholic missionary effort. This clearly would be of great moment for Protestants, but it is still too early to say anything definite.

What happens to the draft on the lay apostolate will be watched with great attention by multitudes of Roman Catholics. If it fails to give concrete expression to what, for Catholic theology, is the revolutionary doctrine of the "general priesthood" of all believers as this is found in the *Constitution on the Church,* it will be a grave disappointment.

Of even greater significance for the internal life of the Roman Church is the schema on the government of dioceses. This will in part determine the degree to which the principle of collegiality, affirmed in the *Constitution on the Church,* is put into practice. It will almost certainly contain proposals for the reform of the curia, for a bishops' senate and for strengthening episcopal conferences. These will, in effect, take the form of "petitions" to the pope, for he alone has the power to enact these changes. It is important that the recommendations be strong because it is most unlikely that the pope will do more than the council requests (although, it must always be remembered, he may do considerably less).

The last item of outstanding business is the famous schema 13 on the church's presence in the modern world which is discussed in Chapter X of this book. Many bishops hope that it will be one of the great documents of the council, equal in importance to the constitutions on the liturgy and the church. If successfully formulated, it may prove even more significant for relations with those outside the Roman Church than the decree on ecumenism. If a failure, it will probably do no lasting harm, though it will be a resounding disappointment especially to many Catholics.

As can be seen from this outline, the progress of the Second Vatican Council up until now has aroused hopes for substantial additional accomplishments in the fourth session, especially in the concrete application of reforms which have already been approved as a matter of theological principle. The consequences will be grave both for the Roman Catholic Church and the ecumenical situation if these hopes are dashed because of the passivity of the progressive majority or because of papal opposition. Nevertheless, even if this occurs, much has happened which seemed impossible three years ago and which will have a profound effect on both the Roman Catholic and other Christian churches in the years to come.

Part II
Evaluations

Chapter V

Renewal of Worship: De Sacra Liturgia

I

Relation of the Council to the Liturgical Movement

"Signum providentialium dispositionum Dei super nostra aetate"

"The liturgical movement has caught fire like a sign of God's providential care for the present time. It is like an eruption of the Holy Ghost into his church in order to bring men closer to the mysteries of faith and riches of grace which stream from the active participation of the faithful in the liturgical life." It was with these words that Pope Pius XII greeted the international Liturgical Congress which was held at Assisi in 1956.[1] The Second Vatican Council's Constitution on the Sacred Liturgy recalls this evaluation of the liturgical movement.[2]

The Roman Catholic Church was characterized, on the eve of the council, by two great movements, the biblical movement and the liturgical movement.[3] The liturgical work of the council is unthinkable without this background. As we shall see, it involves a positive recognition, not only of the theological research which lies behind these movements, but also of the specifically pastoral liturgical efforts which are connected with this research. An observer remarked on the basis of the first chapter of the constitution that "there can

101

be no doubt that the general principles of the schema are nothing short of revolutionary—at least to Protestant eyes."[4] This judgment also applies to the entire constitution. That this is so, however, must be credited to the liturgical efforts of this century.

To be sure, what is generally called the "liturgical movement" started over a hundred years ago.[5] However, in the last century it suffered from an execessively "romish" and "papalist" character, but this can no longer be said.[6]

Pius X pushed the movement in a direction which proved fruitful, and later popes further advanced it. This phase was in a sense concluded by the Pius XII encyclical, *Mediator Dei* (1947).[7] Because the council's constitution to a certain extent builds on the principles and practical recommendations of *Mediator Dei,* we shall find it highly informative to compare the two documents at important points.

The new constitution is related to a concrete liturgical situation which was molded by the reforms of the Council of Trent and of the post-Tridentine period. While Trent decided on the revision of the liturgical books, this revision was actually not accomplished until later through papal measures.[8] In this way standardization was achieved, and even in the last century it was still seriously supposed that the way to manifest the unity of the Church of Jesus Christ was to make the Roman liturgical norms supreme everywhere.[9] A very different way of realizing this goal is made possible by the present constitution when it strives to contribute "to the unity of all who believe in Christ" (No. 1) through the renewal and cultivation of the liturgy.

The way in which Protestant theology should evaluate the newly opened path of liturgical development in the Roman Church will become clear in the course of our presentation. Something, however, can be said immediately. Just as the Council of Trent occasioned a new liturgical epoch within the Roman rite, so the Second Vatican Council will doubtless have a comparable effect. Even though it shows a concern to assure continuity, the fundamental principles of this constitution bring the Tridentine period to a conclusion, at least in reference to the concrete shape of the liturgy. Whatever may be done in detail by a postconciliar commission, still a fundamental liturgical reform will occur.

The Protestant Christian will recognize some of the crucial concerns of the Reformation, not only in the liturgical principles, but also in liturgical practice. Nevertheless, it is necessary to warn against thoughtlessly concluding that Reformation influences are present. Rather, the decisive influences come from the liturgical movement itself. The fact is that this movement has been nourished by "ressourcement," that is, by the return to the Bible and the patristic sources. It is from these sources that both the Reformation and the liturgical movement stem, and consequently it is not surprising that they have resemblances in faith and forms of spiritual life. Yet it is important for the Catholic Church that it has drawn from a direct encounter with Scripture and the apostolic-patristic tradition. This should be cheerfully conceded by evangelical theology, even though in some individual cases—for instance, in exegesis—connections with evangelical theology can be discovered. This direct recourse to the sources deprives us of any human honor, and so the evangelical churches should be ready to agree with Pius XII by praising the Holy Spirit alone for the liturgical renewal which has been given us in our day.

II

1. Relation Between Soteriology and Liturgy
"Opus nostrae Redemptionis exercetur"

In one of the secrets the Catholic Church prays, "Let us worthily partake of this mystery, so that the work of our salvation may be accomplished as often as the memorial of this sacrifice is made."[10] It is in reference to this prayer that the liturgy is defined by the present constitution (No. 2). A *heilsgeschichtliche* characterization of the liturgy is thereby suggested, i.e. the liturgy is to be looked at in connection with the history of salvation.

In recent times this view of the liturgy has become current in opposition to a technical, juridical study of the liturgy as a mere matter of rubrics. This view also opposes an aesthetic and "archeological" concern with the liturgy.[11] To be sure, research in the history of the liturgy is not devaluated, but is rather pursued as of decisive importance. Yet the liturgy itself is inserted into the succession of the mighty acts of God *(magnalia Dei)*.[12] In it God continues his saving work until, with the return of his Son, he and his people enter their eternal rest and the earthly liturgy is transformed into the heavenly.

This *heilsgeschichtliche* understanding of the liturgy has a biblical basis, and it also corresponds to what has become, to a large extent, the standard view in Protestant theology.[13] However, immediately after noting this correspondence, it must be observed that the way in which the liturgy is placed in the history of salvation raises the central controverted questions. What is the relation between Christ's once-for-all redemptive act upon the cross and the Lord's Supper which continues even until today? It is no exaggeration to say that it is precisely in answering this question that the division in the Western Church has been greatest. The Reformation attack upon the mass was, for the Roman Church, an attack upon the present reality of God's redemptive work.[14] Conversely, it was because the Reformation saw the mass as a threat to the uniqueness of the sacrifice upon the cross that it so adamantly rejected it.[15]

The Protestant theologian will therefore carefully examine the constitution on this point, and must then ask whether it is possible to clarify the issue, and how this can be done.

It must be noted in this connection that the dogmatic material in the constitution is sparse. The few expressions which can be used to answer our question are simply hints pointing in the direction of traditional doctrines. While the *heilsgeschichtliche* context is assured, the fuller understanding of what this involves must be drawn from the declarations of the magisterium. In other words, nothing is changed in what the Council of Trent said about the nature of the sacrifice of the mass. Naturally, on the basis of Catholic presuppositions, nothing else can be expected. It must therefore be concluded that, in the opinion of the council fathers, the description of the liturgy *agrees with the essential doctrines of the past*. The characteristic dogmatic accents and provisions of this constitution are basically, not "novelties," but "renovations" which logically follow from Catholic dogma. The dogmatic points which the constitution stresses show us what it considers to be of chief importance.

Our reconciliation has been accomplished and fulfilled in the incarnate Son of God, Jesus Christ, and especially in his death and resurrection *(paschale mysterium)* (No. 5). That is (as also follows from Catholic doctrine), the continuing work of our Savior adds nothing to his unique work in so far as this latter refers to the salvation which has been given, and to the reconciled will of God.[16] The central Christian proclamation is here firmly maintained because Christ's redemptive work is described in prevailingly biblical terms.

It is the presence of Christ in the liturgy which produces the identity with the sacrifice on the cross. In dependence on Trent, this identity of the sacrifice of the mass with that on the cross is portrayed in reference both to the offering priest and the gift which is offered (*Denz.* 940). This presence of Christ in the person of the priest and in the eucharistic elements is, so to speak, only phenomenologically described and is not precisely defined (No. 7). It is apparently more important for the constitution to affirm the factuality of the identity than to clarify its connections with the history of salvation. We must leave open the question of whether this suffices for the Protestant theologian. In any case, it does not necessarily close the road to an evangelical understanding. It is in accordance with good biblical teaching to say that "the liturgy is the exercise of the priesthood of Christ" (No. 7). Everything depends on how this is interpreted.

The particular concept which is here made central both for the eucharist and for the cross of Jesus Christ is that of *sacrifice*. The one offering on the cross continues in the eucharist (No. 47). Once again, however, it is not said in what sense that offering endures even until the Second Coming. Trent defined that offering as a propitiatory sacrifice, and expressly rejected the Reformation view that it was simply a sacrifice of praise (*Denz.* 948, 950-1). This characterization is also presented by *Mediator Dei* in strongly formulated terms.[17] Naturally, all this must be remembered even though the constitution does not itself develop the notion of sacrifice.

At one place the *concept of representation* emerges (No. 6, cf. *Denz.*, 878, 938). It will be recalled that this is the concept used by traditional Roman Catholic dogmatics to describe the connection between the mass and the sacrifice of the cross. Today this concept is often made primary in the belief that it meets the traditional Protestant criticism. By using it one avoids speaking of a "repetition" of the sacrifice of the cross, and instead emphasizes the presence of that sacrifice in the mass. Up to this point there is no disagreement with evangelical teaching. For this reason, certain Lutheran theologians for whom the real presence of Christ in the sacrament appears important have approved and adopted this concept.[18]

However, the Catholic concept of representation goes farther. It is particularly relevant to the ministerial office.[19] The priest does not only represent Christ in his own person, but he also makes Christ present in the Sacrament through the consecration. Again, these connections must be kept in mind.

The same holds for the concept of *memorial,* which is a notion parallel to that of representation (No. 7). Even though this is not intended, still both concepts make it easier to think of the sacrifice of the mass as having a certain existence of its own in relation to the sacrifice of the cross. The active agents in the memorial of the mass are Christ *and* the church. This "and" can be given a *heilsgeschichtliche* interpretation, but in Catholic theology it designates the basis for the "cooperation of the church" in the continuing redemptive work of Christ, i.e. chiefly in the liturgy.[20] In the present context "cooperation" does not refer to any contribution on the part of individuals to their salvation, but only to the fact that it is through the hierarchy that the sacrifice comes into existence as an objective work *(opus operatum).*

While it is true that the Tridentine *repraesentare* does leave a great deal open,[21] still it does make clear that the sacramental hierarchy has the power to make present the sacrifice of the cross in the mass. All this is derived from Christ's words of institution, "*Do* this in remembrance of me" (*Denz.,* 949). Even though Protestant theologians may find Luther's interpretation of "remembrance" as "proclamation"[22] too narrow and wish to enlarge this with the sacramental "doing," still, from their point of view, the Lord's words at this point cannot be understood as founding a hierarchy.

This, however, should not obscure the fact that what the constitution everywhere emphasizes is the presence of Christ in the liturgy. He is present in all of its parts. It is true that his presence "in the person of his minister," is first named, and that he is said to be present "especially under the eucharistic species" (No. 7), but the nature of this presence is not defined. Nowhere is transubstantiation mentioned. In one of the places where the presence of "the mysteries of redemption" in the worship of the church is described, it is said that they are "*in some way* made present for all time" (No. 102). No doubt the intention here is simply to avoid a precise statement in order to leave room for various theories (such as that of Dom Odo Casel) regarding the way in which divine realities become present in worship. Yet, if one is to believe a leading Roman Catholic theologian, the dogma of transubstantiation itself affirms, not *how*, but only *that* Christ is present.[23] In accord with this phenomenological approach, it is the fact of Christ's presence which is emphasized and the particular dogmatic specifications of the nature of this presence recede into the background.

In short, the approach to the liturgy in terms of *salvation history* is everywhere present in this constitution. Yet the brief dogmatic allusions must also be understood, and it is for this reason that we have mentioned a few of the magisterial pronouncements to which they refer. However, even after this is done, a great deal of room is left for further theological interpretations.

Indeed, so far we have noted only one point of a clearly controversial character: A hierarchy is necessary in order to make the liturgy possible. This, however, is important. A hierarchical-institutional conception of the liturgy is in irreconcilable conflict with one derived from the history of salvation.

Is this conflict perhaps the explanation for the astonishing omissions in the constitution regarding the role of the Holy Spirit? Not only is the Holy Spirit scarcely mentioned,[24] but there is no indication of the *place* of the Holy Spirit in the history of salvation. Instead, the reality of the church is spoken of analogically as the continuation of the incarnation. It is viewed, not in terms of the mighty acts of God in the history of his people, but in terms of Christ's sending of the apostles into the world, and the consequent establishment of a hierarchy which has received the Savior's commission to adminster the continuing work of redemption. The hierarchy is the extension in history of our Lord's humanity. The liturgy can therefore be thought of without Pentecost, but this is impossible from a *heilsgeschichtliche* perspective.

It is therefore not accidental that there is no reference to one of the fundamental aspects of the liturgy, to the *koinonia* in the body and blood of our Redeemer. This is *koinonia* in the Holy Spirit. In it, Christ, as present in the here and now, actualizes a participation *(koinonia)* in the redemption which he has wrought. It cannot be reduced simply to fellowship among Christians. Rather, since the ascension of our Lord, and in the power of the Holy Spirit, it is a spiritual reality among us. This participation in the work which Christ did in history is what constitutes the church. The hierarchy is not primary, even if it is traced back to Christ's commission. Rather, what is primary is the gift of the Holy Spirit and the foretaste through this gift of the coming glory of God's people at Christ's return.[25]

If this *koinonia* in the Holy Spirit had been placed at the center, then the *heilsgeschichtliche* view of the liturgy would have been better preserved.

2. The Active Participation of the Faithful
"Christus Ecclesiam sibi semper consociat"

The absence which we have noted of this fundamental liturgical category of the *koinonia* of the Holy Spirit has especially weighty consequences at one point. It has these consequences in reference to the active participation of the faithful in the liturgy, that is, in reference to what is the major concern both of the contemporary liturgical movement and of this constitution. Post-Tridentine Catholic theology viewed the Reformation as endangering the work of salvation which is continued in the church through the priestly office. It was this which it was chiefly concerned to protect. It neglected that which was and remains the chief interest of the Reformation, namely the active participation of the faithful in the redeeming work of Christ.[26] However, the reforming decrees of Pius X brought this aspect to the fore once again, and since then it has dominated liturgical discussions. Not only does it represent the major liturgical problem of the day,[27] but it also raises dogmatic problems which are as yet unsolved and must be worked on further.

According to the constitution, active participation springs from *the very nature of the liturgy* (Nos. 14, 27). Christians are a *royal priesthood*, and this means not only that they have a right to participate actively in worship, but that this is their proper office. Here again we encounter a completely biblical and evangelical theme. Our only question is whether it is consistently carried through in the constitution.

In answering this question, we must first note that the theme of active participation is associated in this constitution with that of the church as the mystical body of Christ. Just as every member of the body has a particular role, so it is emphasized that every one who participates in the liturgy does so *in accordance with his own liturgical office* (Nos. 26, 28). Hierarchy and people are carefully distinguished, even though each one who participates exercises his own genuine liturgical function.[28] The hierarchic nature of the liturgy is also carefully distinguished from its communal nature (No. 26). It seems that active participation is something different for the people and for the liturgist. "Participation," in other words, does not refer to what is common to both, namely, the sharing through faith in the redeeming work of Jesus Christ made present in the liturgy. It does not refer to the biblical *koinonia* in the Holy Spirit, in which liturgist and people alike are simply recipients. It is true, of course, the liturgist, as minister of Jesus Christ, does act in Christ's name. It is as the instrument of the head of the church that he administers the Sacraments. But as participant in the holy liturgy of the heavenly high priest he is called to active, that is, believing, reception of the heavenly gifts. Nothing is said of this in the constitution, although there are tendencies within Catholic theology[29] which make apparent the necessity of this distinction between the office of the priest, which does not depend on his belief or unbelief, and his situation as a person standing in the relationship of faith. From the evangelical viewpoint, it is only the latter which is the basis for active participation in worship.

In this connection, *faith stands in the center* for the evangelical theologian. The constitution, in contrast, remains traditionally Roman Catholic by using the concept of faith to refer, not to a living sharing in salvation, but to the disposition which prepares for the reception of the Sacraments (Nos. 9 & 11). When speaking of this living sharing in salvation, another concept is employed, that of "cooperation." What is meant by this?

Once again we must refer to the *corpus Christi mysticum*. It is in the context indicated by this phrase that the constitution uses the notion of cooperation. Christ, as head of the church, does not accomplish his work for himself. "Christ indeed always associates the Church with himself in this great work wherein God is perfectly glorified and men are sanctified" (No. 7:2). Because of the fall into sin, men can no longer rightly honor God. It is only through Christ's redemption that mankind's true *liturgia* becomes possible. And this possibility arises from the fact that Christ, as head of the church, worships the Father together with those who are the members of his body. Thus worship is primarily an activity whereby men present their homage to God in and through Christ. In doing this, they are themselves sanctified.[30] They become cooperators with grace, because it is in this collaboration between Christ and his people (the church) that grace becomes efficacious (No. 11). It is in this sense that active participation in worship signifies the cooperation of the faithful with Christ.

It is perhaps appropriate in this connection to recall a citation from Pius XII's encyclical *Mystici corporis* (1943). It describes how Christ, the Head, is helped by the members, especially by their prayers, because head and members together constitute a mystical unity. "Further, as our Saviour himself rules the church in an invisible way, he wills the members of his mystical body to help in accomplishing the work of redemption. . . . Although in dying on the cross, he bestowed the immeasurable treasure of salvation on his church without it in any sense collaborating, yet in reference to the distribution of this treasure, he not only shares with his immaculate bride the work of salvation, but he wills that it even in a certain sense come from her activity" (*Denz.*, 2287).

This passage is quoted in the encyclical *Mediator Dei* in a context which describes the active participation of the faithful. There it is said, "In order that each sinner may be washed clean in the blood of the lamb, the collaboration of Christians is needed. While, speaking universally, Christ has reconciled the entire human race with the Father through his bloody death, yet he has willed that in order to obtain the fruits of salvation gained on the cross, all should be drawn and led to the cross by the Sacraments, and especially by the eucharistic sacrifice. By this active and personal participation (*actuosa singulorum participatione*), just as the members come to resemble their divine head ever more closely, so also the saving life flowing from the head is communicated to the members in such a way that we also can repeat the words of St. Paul, 'I have been crucified with Christ; it is no longer I who live, but Christ who lives in me' (Gal. 2:20)."[31]

These texts help us to understand the constitution on the liturgy. The Protestant reacts unfavorably to its coupling of active participation with cooperation. He is immediately inclined to assume that behind the exchange of the concept of faith for that of cooperation, there lies the old struggle of works-righteousness against the righteousness which comes through faith. This should not be assumed too easily, however, as the above texts indicate. *In the first place,* it is underlined that redemption through the cross is exclusively the work of Christ ("without it"—the church—"in any way collaborating)." Thus the activity of believers is explained in terms of the history of salvation, because their activity in the liturgy is related, not to the deed by which Christ has redeemed mankind, but to the distribution of the fruits of this deed in the here and now. *Secondly,* cooperation is a matter of being made like unto Christ. He is the active agent ever working in the hearts of believers. In the words of the constitution, "by baptism men are plunged into the paschal mystery of Christ; they die with him, are buried with him and rise with him; they receive the spirit of adoption as sons 'in which we cry: Abba, Father' (Rom. 8:15), and thus become true adorers whom the Father seeks" (No. 6).

Catholic theology has often objected to the Reformation emphasis on faith in reference to the Sacraments.[32] In the scholastic schematism *fides* is the subjective condition for the reception of grace, for the efficacy of the Sacraments. From this perspective, a strong emphasis on faith seems to minimize the objective reality of the redemption present in the Sacraments. However, this objection involves a basic misunderstanding of the Reformation concept of faith. For the Reformation, faith is the gift of the Holy Spirit by which men are drawn into the work of redemption through the means of grace.[33] It is participation in the redemption offered through the Sacraments.

The reaction of Protestant theology against the idea of human cooperation has been equally strong. Yet in attacking this notion, it does not intend to deny that faith is an active thing which over-powers man and places him under the lordship of Christ.[34] It avoids the concept of cooperation, which has been used without the neces-sary precautions by Catholic theology, but this does not at all mean that God alone is active in such a way as to make man wholly pas-sive.[35] Protestant theology also recognizes a genuine sanctification of human beings springing from the only "work," i.e. from faith. In view of these considerations, it must be asked whether these two apparently conflicting positions are only terminologically dif-ferent, or whether there is a substantive disagreement at this point grave enough to justify the division of the church.

In dealing with this question, the first thing is to clarify the re-spective functions in active participation of what the Protestant calls "faith" and the Catholic calls "cooperation." An investigation of this problem would show that, for the Protestant, "active" participa-tion is primarily a reception of the gift of salvation. It is the hearing of the Word and an eating and drinking of the sacramental body and blood of Christ. It is only after speaking of reception in faith that Protestant theology deals with the activity of believers in the offering of prayers, of the sacrifice of praise and of their own selves.[36] Because of this perspective, the question arises for the Protestant of whether the Catholic doesn't speak "too quickly" of active participa-tion, i.e., before he has properly considered faith. The Catholic, on his side, will ask whether the Protestant doesn't speak "too slowly" of the fruits of faith. And it must be admitted that exclusive insist-ence on faith as receptive can contribute to a passivity which fails to give enough place to the life of faith.

These questions regarding the foundations for active participa-tion in the liturgy must first be dealt with in order to supply a new basis for the interconfessional discussion of these matters.

The constitution on the liturgy urges that "those who have faith in Christ, when present at this mystery of faith, should not be there as strangers or silent spectators" (No. 48). However, mere activity is not enough. Christ is the one who supplies the inner reality cor-responding to the outer behavior. Everything comes from his and his high-priestly prayer, so that it is he who must create agreement between the inner and the outer. It is only when faith is active that the self-offering, the co-offering of the faithful in the liturgy (No. 48), becomes, not simply a ritual performance, but the expression of that dying and rising together with Christ which is received in Baptism. Only thus does active participation become more than studied gestures or mere lip service.

Further, active participation must begin, and be ever renewed, in the hearing of the Word. It must constantly nourish faith through the reception of the Sacrament. These affirmations are fundamental to the evangelical position. We must rejoice that the constitution makes them, thereby adopting and strongly supporting the new approach of the liturgical movement. We shall later say more about this emphasis on the Word. Here we shall simply note one point at which it is not adequately developed.

The constitution refers to the need for the religious instruction of the faithful. In itself this is praiseworthy, but the approach is pedagogical, rather than existential. In order to understand why this is so, let us review the argument. The constitution quite rightly asserts that active participation is required by the very nature of the liturgy because Christians are, through baptism, a royal priesthood. This emphasis on active participation is an acknowledgment, so to speak, that the Reformers were justified in complaining that the scholastics were concerned only with works and not with faith. Now, however, this new approach is interfered with by a rather technical use of the notion of participation according to which faith is thought of scholastically as a disposition. Consequently the genuine evangelical concept of faith as the permanent basis of participation is obscured. From this arises the pedagogical, rather than existential, character of the references to the need for religious instruction. It is forgotten that the success of catechetics and religious education in bringing the faithful to truly active participation is not dependent on whether they are well trained and take an outwardly active part in the liturgy, but on the genuine proclamation of faith. It is this which, without any "cooperation" from us, makes the redeeming work of Christ efficacious for us in order that we, with him as our living Lord, may enter into active faith. It is Christ who makes his life work in and through us. Our cooperation is that *he* works in *us*.

3. Basic Structure of the Liturgy
"Liturgia verbi et Eucharistica"

So far we have considered the nature of the liturgy in general. Now we must turn to the fundamental structure of the liturgy into which the principles which we have examined are woven. There are two basic forms of the liturgy, the mass and the daily office. Of these, the mass is the more important. While it can be said of all liturgy that it is "the summit towards which the activity of the church is directed at the same time that it is fount from which all her powers flow" (No. 10), still this applies particularly to the mass.

The constitution describes the basic structure of the mass in this way: "The two parts which, in a sense, go to make up the mass—viz., the liturgy of the word and eucharistic liturgy (liturgia nempe verbi et Eucharistica)—are so closely connected with each other that they form but a single act of worship" (No. 56). The Protestant must note with thankfulness that the Word of God is here given its fitting place. Through this statement of the constitution, the highest teaching authority in the Roman Church accords recognition to certain tendencies in recent Roman Catholic theology.[37] Naturally the fact that the Sacraments have their own particular importance is also emphasized (No. 6), but in view of the one-sidedness of a certain modern "theology of the Word," this also will be welcomed by Lutherans.[38]

The Constitution stresses that Christ is present in the Word (No. 7).[39] Consequently, Holy Scripture is of the highest importance for the liturgy (No. 24): "The treasures of the Bible are to be opened up more lavishly, so that richer fare may be provided for the faithful at the table of God's Word. In this way a more representative portion of Holy Scripture will be read to the people in the course of a prescribed number of years" (No. 51, cf. 35:1 and 92a). It will be possible in the future to give these readings in the mother tongue with the approval of competent authorities (No. 54). If this happens soon, more place will be given to the reading of the Bible in the Catholic mass than in many Protestant churches. An astonishing development![40]

Preaching also "is to be highly esteemed as part of the liturgy itself" (No. 52 & 35:2). While it will still be possible to celebrate mass without a sermon, this should not occur on Sundays or festivals unless there is a serious reason *(ibid.)*. Further, special "Bible services should be encouraged" (No. 35:4).[41]

What are the reasons for giving this new place to preaching in the liturgy? On the one hand, we naturally find present the scholastic conception of preaching as a preparation for the reception of the Sacrament—an idea which endangers the view of preaching as a saving act of God (No. 9:2, but *in contra* cf. No. 6). The Sacrament is given precedence in such a way that there is too little recognition of the saving gift of Christ through preaching.[42] However, the constitution also reflects a kerygmatic-*heilsgeschichtliche* outlook which may, in fact, constitute its fundamental approach in this matter. In one place it is said that the fundamental character of preaching "should be that of a proclamation of God's wonderful works in the history of salvation or in the mystery of Christ ever made active and present within us" (No. 35:2, cf. 6 and 52). This provides a role for preaching which is not simply that of giving an invitation to a higher (sacramental) level of fellowship with God, but which is itself the proclamation of what is essentially given in Baptism and the Lord's Supper, viz., the incorporation into the death and resurrection of the Lord and the fellowship of the body and blood given and shed for us on the cross. In this way Reformation and recent Catholic tendencies rejoin the conception of preaching which is that of the Bible and the early church. Both desacramentalization and a deemphasis on preaching are opposed, and the balance between "word" and "work" in the means of salvation is maintained.[43]

This renewal of preaching in Catholic worship is a natural result of the emphasis on active participation. This same emphasis leads to insistence on the importance of *partaking of the body and blood of Jesus Christ,* that is, on Communion. As in the case of preaching, we are here confronted with one of the traditional points of dispute between the confessions. For the Reformers, a mass without congregational Communion was reprehensible. Luther considered the medieval practice of private masses as the reason why the mass was understood exclusively as a sacrifice offered to God by the church. His attack on the mass must be viewed as primarily an attack on private masses and on the associated notion of sacrifice.

This was the point at which a line had to be drawn. In comparison, even the question of Communion under both kinds was, to a certain extent, secondary.

The Council of Trent rejected the Reformers' criticism of private masses on the ground that the Communion of the priest gave these a communal character (*Denz.*, 944, 955). The Roman Catholic Church is therefore dogmatically bound to private masses, even though it finds it difficult to justify them. Yet, despite the unchangeable, dogmatic definition, the communal character of the liturgy has been convincingly presented in recent times. The dogmatic difficulty has been dealt with by viewing the private mass as the exception, rather than as the normal case which exhibits the total character of the mass.[44] Further, Trent does say that Communion is desirable, and this provided Pius X with a starting point for his recommendation of daily Communion.

The council carries this development farther. It says that the order of the mass should be revised in order that "active participation by the people may be more easily achieved" (No. 50). This desire applies also to Communion: "That more perfect form of participation in the Mass whereby the faithful, after the priest's communion, receive the Lord's body from the same sacrifice, is strongly commended" (No. 55). In harmony with this, the general principle is laid down that communal rites are to be preferred to individual and "quasi-private" ones (No. 27). The logical conclusion would seem to be that private masses should disappear, but the constitution guards against this by affirming "the public and social nature of every mass" (*ibid.* & No. 57:2.2). Thus we have here a theological position according to which privately celebrated masses are still possible, but communal ones appear as most appropriate to the nature of the mass. This represents a considerable difference, not only from Trent, but from more recent magisterial pronouncements.[45] An approach is made to the congregational worship for which the Reformation strove when it is said that the sense of community of the parish should be encouraged by the communal celebration of the mass (No. 42:2). When we further remember that the rubric "Missae privatae" has been eliminated since 1953,[46] it is possible to ask whether *an epoch in the history of the mass has come to an end.* To be sure, the phenomenon of what Luther called a "Winkelmesse" is still both dogmatically and practically possible,[47] but this is being increasingly displaced by communal celebration. Liturgical research is giving powerful historical and dogmatic support to this development.

Protestants must ask, to be sure, whether the theory of the sacrifice of the mass still doesn't leave everything unchanged. It need only be remembered, however, that a rite for which Communion is an essential element will *liturgically* counteract the one-sidedness of the concept of sacrifice. Theological consequences will have to be drawn from this emphasis in practice on the reception of the gift in Communion. The decisive factor is that the multiplication of masses, which Catholic theology at one time represented as producing an objective increase of grace, now appears as erroneous. Now instead, it is understood that greater honor is done to God when his people share in the sacrifice of the cross present in the Supper.[48] This was also the position of the Reformation, and consequently the discussion regarding the mass must enter into a new stage.

What the constitution has to say about *concelebration*[49] is also important for developments in this direction. Not only can masses on special occasions, such as Maundy Thursday, be celebrated in this form, but bishops may also give permission for the celebration of a communal Sunday mass by all the clergy of a parish (No. 57:1, 2a). This creates the possibility of a development which places the communal mass at the center of congregational life, as it is even to this day in the East, and as was desired by the Reformation.[50]

The topic of Communion under both kinds was also considered by the council. Despite the practice of the Eastern uniate rites, to which any Catholic can have access,[51] and despite the objections—voiced by the Reformation—which point out that it is against our Lord's words of institution to deny the cup to anyone, this council did not make courageous changes. The possibility of Communion under both kinds for the laity is illustrated only by reference to the newly ordained, newly professed, and newly baptized (No. 55). There is, however, nothing in this constitution or in dogma (*Denz.*, 930-932, 934-936) to prevent the indefinite increase of the circumstances in which this is practiced. Pressing in this direction is the rediscovery in contemporary Roman Catholic theology of the *eucharist as a*

meal[52]—a point well known to the Reformation. In participating in
the Lord's Supper, the congregation not only shares in the fruits of
the sacrifice on the cross, but it also has a foretaste of the heavenly
banquet.

Prayer is also part of the basic structure of the mass, as of every
liturgical action. Prayer is the congregation's answer to God's address: "For in the liturgy, God speaks to his people and Christ is
still proclaiming his gospel. And the people reply to God by both
song and prayer" (No. 33).[53] The hierarchical structure of Catholic
worship implies that "the prayers addressed to God by the priest . . .
are said in the name of the entire people and of all present" *(ibid.)*.
Faith is nourished through such prayer so that the worshipers can
render to God their spiritual service. Indeed, they become *"co-
offerers,"* for they are included in the high-priestly prayer "which
Christ himself, together with his body, offers to the Father" (No.
84). Here is another place in which the already discussed cooperation of the faithful with their Redeemer is expressed. "He joins the
entire community of mankind to himself, associating it with his own
singing of this canticle of divine praise" (No. 83). The worship of
the congregation resounds daily in the divine office, even though
until now this has been chiefly a prayer of the priests and the religious. However, according to the constitution, it is possible that
the laity also will be given opportunity to participate in the daily
office.

The constitution has decreed that the "Prayer of the Faithful"
(corresponding to the Lutheran and Anglican "Prayer of the Church")
should be restored to the mass (No. 53). This fulfills a widespread
desire often expressed in the liturgical movement. As an intercession,
this prayer is especially suited to active participation because it provides place for the people to add their voice between the various
petitions. This unquestionably represents an enrichment of Catholic
worship.

The question of how the *canon* of the mass is to be brought into
harmony with the principles of active participation is of special interest to Protestants. No provision is made for substantial changes in
this central portion of the mass, which was given special protection
by Trent (*Denz.*, 942, 953). This does not mean, however, that a
revision of the Roman Missal would not also lead to a consideration

of the restructuring of the canon. From the Catholic point of view, certain changes would clearly be desirable if one is to take account of the recommended liturgical practice of the communal mass.[54] Nevertheless, because this is the most sensitive point of the Roman Catholic theology of the mass, it is not likely that major alterations will be made in the canon, even though they are possible according to the constitution. What must come first is a new interpretation of the canon.[55]

4. The Adaptation of the Liturgy
"Ad nostrae aetatis necessitates melius accommodare"

"The liturgy is made up of immutable elements divinely instituted and of elements subject to change. These not only may but ought to be changed with the passage of time . . ." (No. 21). Thus the constitution affirms a basic freedom for the reshaping of the liturgy. This affirmation is grounded in earlier papal pronouncements.[56] Yet, quite apart from the fact that the canonical regulation of possible changes is entirely reserved to the hierarchy (the Holy See and the bishops), there are considerable restrictions on the use of the freedom. The decisive question is how to distinguish rightly between the immutable elements instituted by our Lord and those which the church is free to alter. In view of the Tridentine decision that the question of Communion in one or both kinds is subject to the church's decision (*Denz.*, 931), it seems difficult to specify any particular element as of "divine" institution. Yet, in practice, the Roman Church seems to consider the shape of the liturgy much more unalterable than this decision seems to imply.

The council rightly felt that the post-Tridentine uniformity of the Roman liturgy needs revision. Its dominance for a period of 400 years makes it impossible for the church to respond to the pastoral-liturgical needs of our times. One of the objectives of the constitution, consequently, is "to adapt more suitably to the needs of our times those institutions which are subject to change" (No. 1).

The first step in this adaptation ("accommodatio," "adaptatio") is to give to those non-Latin rites recognized by Rome "equal right and dignity." It is guaranteed that the church "wishes to preserve them in the future and foster them in every way" (No. 4). This principle,[57] which was supported by John XXIII, made it possible at the council to celebrate the liturgy according to the different Eastern and Western rites. This was a noteworthy symbolic protest against the exclusive supremacy of the Roman mass. The very existence of this diversity of rites constitutes the beginning of "adaptation." The history of the liturgy in which the different types of worship service have developed serves as both a guide and a support for the adaptation of the liturgy to the customs and traditions of different peoples and of different times.[58]

It would not be correct to suppose that this demand for adaptation has not arisen until in recent times, as a result, for example, of the growth of missions. To be sure, the conditions which the liturgy encounters among peoples of non-Western culture make the demand particularly acute. The Western forms and modes of expression which have created the Roman liturgy—and, indeed, Western liturgies in general—are different from those of other continents. However, the need for new forms is also present in the West. Both in mission lands and the dechristianized Occidental countries the requirements for effective evangelization confront the church with the same challenge.[59]

Adaptation will make easier the active and communal participation of the faithful in the liturgical actions. This will happen only if the liturgical forms are revised in such a way as to meet the requirement that "the Christian people, so far as possible, should be enabled to understand them easily" (No. 21). "They should be within the people's power of comprehension, and normally should not require much explanation" (No. 34).

This also raises the problem of the use of the *vernacular* in the liturgy. Again we encounter demands which were made by the Reformation and carried out in Protestant churches. The Catholic Church is bound on this point by the decisions of the Council of Trent (*Denz.*, 946, 956). In practice this has meant the almost exclusive employment of Latin. Only because of the liturgical movement has it become possible once again to discuss the use of the mother tongue.[60] According to some recent research, Trent's goal was not to establish the exclusive supremacy of Latin. It intended simply to speak against the notion that the vernacular is obligatory and to resist Protestant principles which, in the opinion of the council, were necessarily connected with the use of the vernacular.[61]

The constitution proposes to keep Latin as the general liturgical language. However, it no longer reflects the fear which was present at Trent that strange doctrines might creep into the Catholic faith through the use of the vernacular. Rather, it recognizes that the vernacular can greatly strengthen participation in worship (No. 36: 1-2). Thus the use of the vernacular in the liturgy is viewed as depending on considerations of prudence. The mother tongue is to be employed in the scriptural readings, general prayers, and those parts of the liturgy especially pertaining to the people—hymns, responses, etc. (No. 54). In the other Sacraments and the sacramentals, where the vernacular is already common, further extensions of its use are made possible (No. 63). Permission can even be obtained to say the daily office in the mother tongue by "those clerics for whom Latin constitutes a grave obstacle to their praying the office as it should be prayed" (No. 101:1). As it has long been complained that Latin often is such an obstacle, there is no doubt that this possibility will be much used, not only in mission lands but also in other parts of the world.

Thus the constitution has taken a middle way in this matter of the vernacular. It had, on the one hand, to assure the conservative bishops that the classic language of the Roman rite would be preserved, while, at the same time, it was necessary to open the doors to the efforts to transform the liturgy from a remote and inaccessible ritualism into something which could really be appropriated by believers.[62] There is no doubt that a major renewal of Roman Catholic worship is to be anticipated through this greater employment of the mother tongue. Permission will be granted to move from experiments to the entire use of the vernacular.

If the liturgy is quickly adapted to that which is, after all, the most important aspect of a people's cultural heritage, its language, then a further step can be anticipated: *the assimilation of the customs* and usages of the different peoples into the liturgical life of the church. The fundamental principle is that "grace does not destroy nature, but perfects it." Since uniformity is not obligatory, the church "respects and fosters the genius and talents of the various races and nations. Anything in these peoples' way of life which is not indissolubly bound up with superstition and error she studies with sympathy and, if possible, preserves intact. Sometimes she

even admits such things into the liturgy itself, so long as they har-
monize with its true and authentic spirit" (No. 37). A basic principle regarding a very delicate matter is thereby expressed. Christian missions among the heathen have suffered greatly from the ab-
solutizing of Western culture and of its liturgical and artistic forms.
On the basis of religious opposition to heathenism, the natural, popular forms of expression of non-Christian peoples have also been rejected. It has been forgotten how much the Western Christian cultural heritage has taken over from the Greeks and the Romans.
In view of the situation of the younger churches in Asia and Africa,
it is today absolutely necessary to take to heart this lesson from
church history. The constitution provides that the Roman ritual be
revised in order to provide for the more adequate expression of
local usages and customs in the case of marriage (No. 77), burial
(No. 81) and initiation rites (No. 65). Native musical traditions
should also be given greater room and even adapted in the church
liturgy (No. 119).[63] The same holds for different types of plastic
art, including modernistic ones (No. 23). Bishops' conferences "are
empowered to adapt . . . to the needs and customs of their different
regions . . . the materials and styles of church furnishings and vest-
ments" (No. 128). While it is admittedly difficult to put such a program into practice, its purpose is to penetrate the various cultures
with the "Spirit of the Liturgy" (No. 37) which is itself nourished
by Holy Scripture (No. 24). It is to be assumed that churches in
mission lands will warmly welcome these measures and be encouraged to make energetic adaptations of the liturgy to the various cultural heritages.

This kind of liturgical adaptation is not easy. It is therefore proposed to begin with experiments before making definitive changes
(No. 40). Liturgical renewal must proceed as an organic development which takes account of already existing conditions and thus
leads without undue forcing to the new. Yet the problems are such
that a certain degree of radicalism cannot be avoided.

A revision of the liturgical books is also envisaged (No. 25). The
directives which will apply to this revision are evident from what
has already been said. There is no doubt that the postconciliar commission which will do this work has the possibility of fundamentally
reshaping the Roman rite. Whether it will wish to do so, or whether

it will be limited by papal instructions, is a question for the future.

The council's wish is clear: "The rites should be distinguished by a *noble simplicity;* they should be short, clear and unencumbered by any useless repetitions; they should be within the people's powers of comprehension, and normally should not require much explanation" (No. 34). It remains to be seen how radically the order of the mass will be reshaped in the light of the requirements that the rites "be simplified" and that they "be restored to the vigour which they had in the days of the holy Fathers," or to what extent changes will be inhibited by the admonition that "due care be taken to preserve the substance" (No. 50). If there is to be a discussion between the churches regarding an ecumenical liturgy,[64] then this council's decisions, whose flexibility leaves nothing to be desired, will have to make possible new experimental eucharistic orders which go beyond anything which now actually exists. The degree to which Rome is ready to venture on this road does not depend on the liturgical experts. It is the hierarchy which will make these decisions; that is, first the bishops and bishops' conferences which are given considerable authority in these matters by the constitution (No. 22), and, secondly, the Holy See, which retains a veto power.

There is no doubt that the Second Vatican Council has turned away from Roman uniformity to liturgical diversity, and thereby also from papal centralism to a partial recognition of the rights which the bishops originally had. The possibility has been opened for a development which will be the opposite of that during the post-Tridentine period. It is sufficiently clear from what has been said that this possibility involves, not only a hierarchical, but an evangelical renewal of Roman Catholic worship.

III

The Reciprocal Causality of Liturgy and Dogma
"Ut legem credendi lex statuat supplicandi"

Our analysis of the Second Vatican Council's constitution on the liturgy has also thrown light on the dogmatic presuppositions of the liturgical renewal. We see illustrated the interactions of liturgy and dogma in the life of the church.[65] This constitution is unthinkable apart from certain new dogmatic developments in the Catholic Church. These in turn, however, draw from the recovery by recent research of the immense liturgical treasures of the early church which are of dogmatic relevance.

Trent focused on dogmatic considerations regarding the mass. Vatican II has moved in another direction and has placed the pastoral-liturgical aspect in the foreground. Surely the old principle, "ut legem credendi lex statuat supplicandi" (the rule of prayer determines the rule of faith) will once again prove to be valid.[66] Only recently, Roman Catholic history has given us an illustration of how extraliturgical piety has led to a new dogma (viz., that of the Assumption of Mary). It is true that neither this constitution nor *Mediator Dei* sweep aside those many pious practices, so unintelligible to a Protestant, which can scarcely be harmonized with Holy Scripture and with the Sacraments instituted by our Lord. The constitution simply seeks to order them in such a way that they are in "accord with the sacred liturgy, are in some fashion derived from it and lead the people to it, since, in fact, the liturgy by its very nature far surpasses any of them" (No. 13). At least this does constitute an attempt to set a liturgical limit to the exuberance of Catholic popular piety. It does clearly set forth the genuine center of the life of Christian worship.

We have seen which aspects of the liturgy are now being newly emphasized: the renewal of the use of Scripture in the liturgy, the proclamation of the mighty acts of God, the active participation of the faithful in worship on the basis of their Baptism and, especially, the restoration of Communion in the eucharistic celebration. As every heir of the Reformation will easily see, these are precisely the elements which are fundamental for evanglical liturgical life. For this we must rejoice. Nevertheless, our analysis of the dogmatic presuppositions of the constitution has shown that this kind of liturgical practice poses problems for Catholic dogmatics which have not yet been solved. This is evident in regard to the relation between the once-and-for-all sacrifice on the cross and the celebration of the present Lord in the eucharistic memorial. It is also evident in the failure to recognize clearly that the participation of the faithful in liturgical acts in a sharing through faith in God's saving acts. The

Gospel requires us to continue to raise these questions. But now they have become questions which are directed at Catholic dogmatics by liturgical practice itself as this has been legislated by this constitution.

This provides a new basis for discussion between the churches. It is true that the "theology of the sacrifice of the mass" and the "cooperation of the church" contain elements which need to be criticized by Protestants, but now the concrete practice of the worshiping community provides powerful arguments against the lack of dogmatic clarity at these points. Through a genuinely evangelical "lex supplicandi," the Roman Catholic Church must come to master its "lex credendi." This is the new situation which has been created by the constitution. It also affects the Protestant theologian. He is called upon to listen and to accept in the freedom of faith those questions which are asked of him on the basis of the Word of God.

Notes

1. In this chapter, references to the following sources are given in the text itself: *The Constitution on the Sacred Liturgy*, tr. C. Howell, Cirencester, England, Whitegate Publications (available also in a slightly different translation from the Paulist Press, Glen Rock, N. J.), is referred to simply by number, e.g., "No. 1"; H. Denzinger, *Enchiridion Symbolorum, definitionum et declarationum de rebus fidei et morum*, 30th ed. (in English: *Sources of Catholic Dogma*, tr. R. J. Deferrari, St. Louis, 1957), is cited in the form of, e.g., "Denz., 950."

2. J. Wagner (Editor), *Erneuerung der Liturgie. Akten des ersten Internationalen Pastoralliturgischen Kongresses zu Assisi*, Trier, 1957, p. 344.

3. G. A. Lindbeck, "Roman Catholicism on the Eve of the Council," *The Papal Council and the Gospel* (ed. K. E. Skydsgaard), Minneapolis, Augsburg, 1961, pp. 61 ff.

4. G. A. Lindbeck, "Liturgical Reform in the Second Vatican Council," *Lutheran World* X, 1963, p. 161.

5. For the 19th Century, see O. Rousseau, *Histoire du mouvement liturgique*, Paris, 1945.

6. For the later development, see E. B. Koenker, *The Liturgical Renaissance in the Roman Catholic Church*, Chicago, 1954.

7. For the relevant papal documents, see A. Bugnini, *Documenta pontificia ad instaurationem liturgicam spectantia*, Vols. I-II, Rome, 1953-59.

8. J. A. Jungmann, "Das Konzil von Trient und die Erneuerung der Liturgie," in: Georg Schreiber (Editor), *Das Weltkonzil von Trient*, Vol. I. Freiburg, 1951, pp. 325 ff.

9. This ideal of the initiator of the Benedictine movement in Solesmes, Dom Guéranger, is today generally criticized. E.g., Herman A. P. Schmidt, *Liturgie et langue vulgaire*, Rome 1950, pp. 188 ff., and L. Bouyer, *La vie de la liturgie*, Paris, 1960, pp. 76 f.

10. *Missale Romanum,* 8th Sunday after Trinity.

11. For example in the fundamental work by C. Vagaggini, *Theologie der Liturgie,* Einsiedeln, 1959. (An abridgment of this work has appeared in English: *Theological Dimensions of the Liturgy,* Collegeville, Minn., 1959.)

12. J. Daniélou, "Sacrements et histoire du salut," in *Parole de Dieu et liturgie,* Paris, 1958, pp. 26 f.

13. See especially P. Brunner, *Zur Lehre vom Gottesdienst der im Namen Jesu versammelten Gemeinde,* in *Leiturgia. Handbuch des evangelischen Gottesdienstes* Vol. I., Kassel 1954, and V. Vajta, *Luther on Worship* (tr. U.S. Leupold), Philadelphia, 1958.

14. This opinion is still maintained, even though today Roman Catholic research largely concedes the existence of the abuses regarding the mass in the Middle Ages.

15. V. Vajta, *op. cit.,* pp. 54 ff.

16. K. Rahner, *Die vielen Messen und das eine Opfer,* Freiburg, 1951, pp. 55 f.

17. Bugnini, *op. cit.,* Doc. 41. No. 72.

18. Most recently, P. Meinhold and E. Iserloh, *Abendmahl und Opfer,* Stuttgart, 1960, pp. 70 f. M. Lackmann rightly says in this same volume that it is doubtful that Protestant and Catholic theology mean the same thing by this concept of *repraesentatio* (pp. 126 ff.).

19. P. E. Persson, *Kyrkans ämbete som Kristus-representation,* Lund, 1961, has recently shown this with convincing clarity. Cf. also his shorter study, *Roman and Evangelical; Gospel and Ministry,* Philadelphia, 1964.

20. M. Schmaus, *Katholische Dogmatik,* Vol. IV, 1 (5th Ed.) Munich, 1957, pp. 326 f.

21. So J. Pascher, *Eucharistia,* Freiburg, 1953, pp. 24 f.

22. For references, see V. Vajta, *op. cit.,* pp. 82 f.

23. K. Rahner, *Die Gegenwart Christi im Sakrament des Herrenmahles,* in Th. Sartory (Editor), *Die Eucharistie im Verständnis der Konfessionen,* Recklinghausen, 1961, pp. 345 f.

24. In the present context, only the concluding words of No. 6 (per virtutem Spiritus Sancti) are relevant.

25. Eschatology in general is not sufficiently emphasized in this constitution. Outside of a reference to the relation of the earthly and heavenly liturgies in No. 8, scarcely anything is said.

26. F. X. Arnold, "Vorgeschichte und Einfluss des Trienter Messopferdekrets . . .", in F. X. Arnold— B. Fischer, *Die Messe in der Glaubensverkündigung,* Freiburg, 1953, pp. 115 ff.

27. C. Vagaggini, *op. cit.,* p. 194.

28. This statement in No. 29 holds only for those members of the laity who have a particular function in the liturgy, not for all people.

29. K. Rahner, *Die vielen Messen,* pp. 73 f.

30. This basically Thomistic concept of worship as "glorificatio Dei— sanctificatio hominis" shapes both *Mediator Dei* and the constitution.

31. Bugnini, *op. cit.,* Doc. 41, No. 77.

32. E.g., canon 4 of the VII. session of the Council of Trent. *Denz.,* 847.

33. Cf. E. Thestrup Pedersen, "Troen og sakramentet," *Evangelium og Sakramente. Festskrift til K. E. Skydsgaard,* Copenhagen, 1962, pp. 98 f.

34. Cf. Vajta "Reformation und Gottesdienst," *Ökumenische Rundschau,* XII (1963) pp. 137 ff., esp. 139 f, 144 ff.

35. Cf. E. Stakemeier, "Trienter Lehrentscheidungen und reformatorische Anliegen," *Das Weltkonzil von Trient* (ed. G. Schreiber) Vol. I, esp. pp. 100 f.

36. This line of thought is beautifully developed in Luther's "Sermon von dem hochwürdigen Sakrament des heiligen wahren Leichnams Christi" from the year 1519 (WA 2,742-758).

37. The "ministerium predicationis" (No. 35:2) is today being emphasized in a new way by the Roman Catholic Church. Cf., e.g., the lecture of Cardinal Bea at the Congress in Assisi (J. Wagner, *op. cit.*, pp. 130, 148).

38. Cf. R. Prenter, "Den dogmatiske aktualitet af 'De captivitate Babylonica,'" *Festschrift für K. E. Skydsgaard*, Copenhagen, 1962, esp. pp. 206 f. and 226, and "Die Realpräsenz als die Mitte des christlichen Gottesdienstes," *Gedenkschrift für W. Elert,* Berlin, 1955, pp. 307 ff.

39. This passage of the constitution is taken almost word for word from *Mediator Dei* (Bugnini, Doc. 41 No. 20) with one exception: The presence of Christ in the Word is not mentioned, and is first spoken of in the constitution. Clearly this is an important addition.

40. For the readings, see No. 92, where readings from the Fathers and stories of the saints are also spoken of.

41. These are of greatest importance in mission lands and other areas where there is a shortage of priests. Cf. J. Hofinger and J. Kellner *Liturgische Erneuerung in der Weltmission,* Innsbruck, 1957, esp. pp. 204 ff. and pp. 238 ff.

42. Cf. K. E. Skydsgaard, *One in Christ* (tr. by A. C. Kildegaard), Philadelphia, 1957, pp. 159 ff. for a good statement of the relative importance of preaching and the Sacraments in the Reformation and Roman Catholic traditions.

43. Cf. V. Vajta, *Luther on Worship,* pp. 70-75.

44. For the historical aspect, see J. A. Jungmann, *Missarum Sollemnia,* Vol. I., (3rd Ed.) Vienna, 1952, pp. 279 ff.; for dogmatic considerations,

see M. Schmaus, *op. cit.,* p. 382 and J. Pascher, *op. cit.,* pp. 32 f.

45. *Mediator Dei,* Bugnini Doc. 41, Nos. 111-114.

46. *Instructio de musica sacra et de sacra liturgia* (1953), Bugnini, Doc. 84, No. 2.

47. The system of mass stipends was, for example, not abolished by the council. Everything allowed by Trent is still possible, even though improvements have been made.

48. *Confessio Augustana,* Art. XXIV, 23-24, and *Apolog,* XXIV, 13. Cf. K. Rahner, *Die vielen Messen und das eine Opfer,* esp. pp. 36, 55 f. and 77. K. Rahner's presentation represents only one of the possible Roman Catholic positions. Pius XII, e.g., energetically represented the traditional opinion. Cf. Bugnini, Doc. 63, esp. No. 4, and Wagner, *op. cit.,* pp. 350 ff.

49. For the history of concelebration, see J. A. Jungmann, *op. cit.,* Vol. I. pp. 258 ff. The theological problematic is indicated in C. Vagaggini, *op. cit.,* pp. 443, esp. fn. 54, where references to the literature are given.

50. *Conf. Aug.,* Art. XXIV, 34 & 40, and *Apol.,* XXIV, 6.

51. *Codex Iuris Canonici,* can. 866.

52. P. Parsch, *op. cit.,* pp. 34 ff.; J. Pascher, *op. cit.* pp. 31 ff.

53. This formulation appears as a happy accident when it is compared to the much-cited words of Luther at the dedication of the church in Torgau: ". . . may nothing else happen here than that our beloved Lord himself speaks to us through his holy Word, and we in turn speak with him through prayer and praise" (WA 49, 588:15).

54. H. Küng, *The Council in Action,* New York, 1963, pp. 135 ff. He says, "Any reform which stops short at the Canon and does not attempt to provide the Eucharist and the words of institution with the new form of expression which they need would be,

for non-Catholic Christians as well, a superficial reform" (p. 143).

55. Luther still sought for this in 1521 in *De captivitate Babylonica*.

56. *Mediator Dei*, Bugnini Doc. 41, Nos. 49 and 58.

57. Already expressed by Pius XI in a *Motu proprio* (Bugnini, Doc. 23).

58. E.g., in Hofinger—Kellner, *op. cit.*, pp. 13 ff.

59. *Worship and the Church's Mission and Unity*, A Report of the Third Indian Conference on Worship, Bangalore, 1960, pp. 13 ff.; and *Report of the Theological Commission on Worship* (to the 4th World Conference on Faith and Order in Montreal, Canada, 1963), Faith and Order Paper No. 39, Geneva, World Council of Churches, esp. p. 39, point 3.

60. A summary statement of the new situation is found in H. Küng, *op. cit.* pp. 122 ff.

61. Cf. H. A. P. Schmidt, *op. cit.*, pp. 153 f. and 174 ff.

62. The situation is reminiscent of the introduction of the vernacular in the Reformation. Then also Luther and the Lutheran Confessions were in favor of a restricted continuation of the use of Latin wherever suitable conditions prevailed. Cf. Apology, Art. XXIV, 2-5.

63. Cf. Hofinger—Kellner, *op. cit.*, pp. 305 ff. The problem of the adaption of native musical traditions to the music of worship is dealt with in a noteworthy monograph by H. Weman, *African Music and the Church in Africa*, Studia Missionalia Upsaliensia 3, Uppsala, 1960.

64. H. Küng, *op. cit.*, pp. 112 f., thinks that it is in accordance with the liturgical movement to draw closer to the example of the Last Supper of our Lord before his death. This would naturally be of ecumenical importance.

65. Cf. my essay "Creation and Worship," *Worship and the Acts of God*, (Ed. W. Vos), Nieuwendam, 1963, esp. pp. 29-34. This also appeared in *Studia Liturgica*, 1963.

66. Denz. 139 and 2200. *Mediator Dei* (Bugnini, Doc. 41, Nos. 44-47) deals with this principle.

Chapter VI

The Bible in the Council

I. The Biblical Renewal as Preparation
for the Council

Is the renewal of Catholicism which is taking place through this
council a renewal through the Bible? We must say "no" to this
question if we think in terms of the exclusive role which the Bible
played in the 16th century Reformation. As we shall see, no internal reformation of Catholicism can in that sense be a renewal
through the Bible. It is true that most Catholic reforming movements in the course of church history have been inspired by the
Bible. Nevertheless, according to the Catholic conception, the
church can never be judged by the Bible as if this were a tribunal
standing over against the church; it is only the church as such
which can interpret the Bible. Yet, although the present council
also, as we shall see, could not change this theory, still the Bible by
its own intrinsic energy has, so to speak, asserted itself as a renewing power and inspired more strongly than ever the contemporary
movement of reform. There has been scarcely any previous council
in which the effort to give the conciliar texts a biblical foundation
has stood so much in the foreground.

One can even say that without the intensive Catholic biblical
studies of the last decades the present council is scarcely imagin-

able. We ought not to forget that the ecumenical dialogue began as a conversation between biblical exegetes before it became a dialogue between theologians in the stricter sense of the word.

The ecumenical studies of the last thirty years have been intimately connected with the renewal of Roman Catholic biblical studies. It is no accident that it was a first-rate biblical scholar, formerly professor of Old Testament and rector of the Biblical Institute at Rome, the present Cardinal Bea, who was placed at the head of the Secretariat for the Promotion of Christian Unity whose role for the present council it is impossible to exaggerate. The changed orientation of the Roman Catholic Church in regard to biblical studies has fostered scholarly exchanges between Catholic and Protestant exegetes, and these exchanges, in turn, have intensified exegetical work. In those professional societies whose membership embraces Old Testament and New Testament scholars of the different Christian confessions, discussion is no longer limited to questions of purely textual and literary criticism and, on the personal level, it has entirely lost any unnecessarily polemical character, giving rise to a truly fruitful collaboration. Further, contacts are more and more frequently being established even outside the framework of these societies. The development which has taken place in this respect is indicated by the fact that exegetical divergences in the area of biblical studies no longer correspond to the distinction between Catholic and Protestant exegesis. Many of the exegetical issues now under discussion cut across confessional lines.

The biblical renewal was inaugurated especially under Pius XII. In view of the tendency to look only at the negative aspects of this pontificate, we should not forget one of its great merits, the promulgation of the encyclical *De Divino Afflante Spiritu* (1943). Certain personal memories of the present writer are connected with this text. A little after its publication, the essential passages were read to me at the Biblical Institute of Rome by Cardinal Bea, who was at that time rector. I also remembered witnessing the sense of liberation which the encyclical produced among Catholic exegetes who previously had had to carry on their work under conditions which were often very difficult. It is true that, despite these difficulties, the Ecole Biblique in Jerusalem and Biblical Institute in Rome had already for a long time been able to provide significant exegetical contributions, at least in certain areas. Nevertheless, it is especially since the promulgation of this encyclical that Catholic biblical studies have made a remarkable advance as witnessed by important publications, among which we need mention only the Bible of Jerusalem.

In what follows, I shall first speak of the theory regarding the Bible which is present in the fundamental schema, *De divina revelatione*. Then we shall deal with the actual role of the Bible in the council, and finally, with movements of opposition to the new emphasis on the Bible and with their defeat.

II. The Bible According to the Schema on Revelation

Here we shall deal especially with chapters 2, 5 and 6. First, it must be mentioned that the present schema represents great progress over the one proposed at the first session of the council. It does not "close the doors" to future developments when it says that "Scripture and tradition are interconnected" *(inter se connectuntur)*. More than this, a new door is opened when it says that the magisterium, the teaching authority of the church, "serves" Scripture *(magisterium Scripturae ministrat)*. However, at one point we remain divided. As was said earlier, Scripture is not regarded as standing over against the church, and that is important.

This over-against-ness was not necessary in the apostolic period, but it is necessary in post-apostolic times. The relation of Scripture and tradition must not be defined in the same way in reference to apostolic tradition and post-apostolic tradition.[1] To be sure, as we shall see, I myself admit a certain continuity, but I would like to insist first on the difference. I quite agree with what the schema says about apostolic tradition: "they are interconnected" and "must be held in equal reverence." But this equality does not hold for post-apostolic tradition.

That which authorizes this distinction is *the significance of the event of the formation of the Canon*. The schema says nothing of this.[2] We recall the historical causes of the origin of the Canon. This occurred during a period when apocryphal Gospels were multiplying. At the beginning of the second century some of these played

a greater role in the living tradition of the church than do our
canonical Gospels. I think especially of the proto-Gospel of James
which was so important for the birth of Mariology. It was also the
period when the so-called "apostolic fathers" were writing. With
the exception of those of Ignatius of Antioch, their writings are
theologically poverty-stricken, characterized by a moralism which
distinguishes them both from the books of the New Testament and
from the works of the later fathers of the church who wrote after
the formation of the Canon, such as Saint Irenaeus. Actually these
latter are, once again, much closer to the apostolic sources. On the
one hand, this period was already too far removed from the times
of the apostles, of the eyewitnesses, and, on the other hand, the
Canon did not yet exist. The books of the Canon were all in existence, but they were not yet canonized.

We see from this the historical necessity of the important event
which was the formation of the Canon, and which the schema has
neglected. But there is also a positive theological meaning in this
event which the schema has not taken into consideration. It marks
a decisive step in the history of salvation, and I would even say that
it constitutes a part of that history. It is the climax, for here that
which is the essence of the history of salvation finds its supreme
expression. Throughout the Bible there is a progressive evolution
of events toward the event of Christ and, at the same time, there is
a progressive evolution of the interpretation of these events toward
the culminating interpretation made in the light of Christ (when
the Old and the New Testaments were united).

At the moment when the Canon was born, the generation of the
eye-witnesses of the decisive event of Jesus Christ had disappeared.
What we have, then, is an absolutely decisive step. To be sure, the
history of salvation continues afterwards, but it continues simply as
unfolding; and the same must be said of the interpretation of this
history. In this unfolding, the Holy Spirit himself is at work, and
that is why there is still continuity.

However, the relation between Scripture and tradition is no
longer the same. When the apostolic tradition was being formed,
the eye-witnesses, those who witness in the present and the representatives of the magisterium (i.e., the teachers) were one and the
same. From this follows the interpenetration during this period,

during apostolic times, of tradition, Scripture, and teaching authority. In contrast, since the Canon came into existence, the eye-witnesses and those who witness in the present are no longer the same, but are rather distinct. That is why from then on there is an over-against-ness of Scripture in relation to the church.

During the times of unfolding there are a larger number of sources of error than in the apostolic period. The continuing living tradition is more exposed to errors than it was before. The creation of the Canon was an act of humility in which the church itself recognized this fact: The post-apostolic tradition and the post-apostolic teaching authority are no longer on the same level as Scripture. To be sure, they all depend on one another, and so in this sense can still be said to be "interconnected"; but they no longer have the same status. The post-apostolic tradition and the post-apostolic magisterium were subjected to the norm of the apostolic tradition as this was from that point on fixed in Scripture.

Because of this superior norm, and insofar as it is considered a superior norm, reformation is always possible in the church. The Bible is a dynamic norm. On the one hand, it stirs up renewal and, on the other, it serves as a criterion for distinguishing legitimate developments from deviations. It is the same Holy Spirit who works in the Scripture and in the post-apostolic church and its living traditions; but the Holy Spirit is mingled with other spirits, with sources of error. This is the reason why, in post-apostolic tradition, there are also traditions contrary to the Bible. In order to distinguish the true from the false, the post-apostolic church cannot itself be the judge. The Scripture must be for it a *vis-à-vis*, a superior norm. If this is not the case, if there is no *vis-à-vis*, there is the grave danger that the church will justify and consider authentic all the ecclesiastical traditions which have prevailed and triumphed in the course of the centuries.

Appeal is made, on the Catholic side, to the theory that some truths are contained implicitly in the Bible. The theory, which seems to us dangerous, underlies in latent form a great number of the texts found in the different schemas of this council. To be sure, some truths are contained implicitly in the Bible. The doctrine of the Trinity is an example. However, we can say genuinely that it is implicitly in the Bible because the elements of this doctrine are truly found there. These elements lead in a natural way to the doctrine of the Trinity, they genuinely give birth to this doctrine. However, there are other notions, such as that of the bodily Assumption of Mary, found in the living tradition of post-apostolic times. Because the Bible has not been viewed as over against the church, as a superior judge, the Catholic Church has placed this conception on the same level as that of the Trinity, and has proclaimed that it is a truth contained implicitly in the Bible. In fact, however, it is not the Bible which has in this case given birth to the doctrine, but an attempt has been made to justify a traditional belief by a *post facto, a posteriori* appeal to the theory that some truths are contained "implicitly" in the Bible. If there is no over-against-ness of Scripture and post-apostolic tradition, if the post-apostolic church is itself judge instead of submitting itself to a superior norm, it will not be possible for it to separate authentic from false traditions, and it will always be tempted to justify every tradition which prevails in the course of the centuries as a truth "implicitly" found in the Bible. Without wishing to shock those of Catholic faith, I must say that if the bodily Assumption of Mary really is implicitly in the Bible, then I really don't know what is *not* implicitly in the Bible. I must admit that in this case I prefer the theory of conservative Catholics who flatly affirm that the Assumption is not in the Bible, but only in tradition. Except that I would add that this is a deviant tradition.

What I have said of the necessity of subjecting post-apostolic traditions to the *vis-à-vis* of Scripture holds also for the post-apostolic magisterium. I think that the post-apostolic church needs a teaching authority, but one which is submissive to Scripture. The Bible ought certainly to be interpreted in the church, for the same Holy Spirit who has inspired Scripture is at work in the church. However, once again, if this submission is absent, the magisterium becomes a more dangerous source of error than if there were no magisterium at all. In other words, the post-apostolic tradition is useful, but the proclamation of a dogma by the magisterium apart from submission to the Bible as a superior norm becomes an obstacle to the further development of research into the truth—it becomes a handicap.

Has not the present council implicitly recognized this since it has carefully avoided defining new dogmas, making dogmas a norm equal to the norm of Scripture?

Catholics, on their side, object that the interpretation of Scripture becomes absolutely arbitrary if it is not submitted, in its turn, to an infallible magisterium which is a norm, if not superior, at least equal, to that of Scripture. In reference to this, even while recognizing that there are possible errors in the interpretation of Scripture, I would say that there is less danger of error if we do not place alongside the Bible a norm to which we attribute equal value; there is less danger if, in our submission to the Bible, we limit ourselves to the means of interpretation which God has given us, viz., the Holy Spirit inspiring the exegete and the philological and historical method which we may also consider a gift of God. Certainly this gift is not an infallible criterion, but we may be confident that in this way the sources of error are reduced to a minimum. The grounds of this confidence were well stated in the excellent speech in St. Peter's of Dom Butler during the course of the discussion on the sources of revelation.

There is one other thing that I would like to add. What has just been said regarding the absence of submission by the church to Scripture as a *vis-à-vis*, as a superior norm, applies to Catholic *theory*. Happily, as far as *reality* is concerned, the Catholic Church is very often in practice subject to Scripture and often submits itself to the Bible. It would be possible to show this again and again in church history, and we ought to ask ourselves if the present council, with its desire for renewal, is not, in the last analysis, inspired by practical submission to the Bible.

On the ecumenical level, the dialogue on the problem of tradition is making progress. On the Protestant side, we must recognize the value of the living tradition in the post-apostolic church, and we must recognize the value of a magisterium, while, on the Catholic side, there must be a recognition of the over-against-ness of Scripture as a norm superior to the church. I would replace the formula, "Scripture alone," by the formula, "Scripture, tradition, and magisterium, but the Scripture as sole superior norm."

Before speaking of the actual and effective role which the Bible played in practice at the present council, it will be useful to add a few remarks on chapters five and six of the schema on revelation.

The positive declarations on the legitimate exegetical theses of *Formgeschichte* (though this is not named) are cause for rejoicing. These chapters mention the needs of the early Christian community which determined the retention of certain elements in the Gospel tradition. At the same time it is gratifying that these chapters exclude the mistaken conclusion drawn from this fact especially by scholars of the Bultmann school. These scholars too quickly conclude when some passage applies to the needs of the post-resurrection community, that it cannot be the authentic words of Jesus or that it does not constitute a historical account. In reality, the community could perfectly well have chosen from among authentic, historical elements of the tradition those which did apply to its needs. It is gratifying that these chapters (like the recent biblical "Instruction" of April 21, 1964)[3] implicitly disallow the existentialist exegesis which denies historical events insofar as they are saving events.

However, on the other hand, these chapters fail to mention a point which was quite properly pointed out by one of the bishops speaking in council. In the New Testament, as in the Old, there is, in addition to the events themselves, the interpretation of the events. This interpretation *can* make use of mythical elements. As these elements, like the historical accounts, are in narrative form, they often raise a difficult exegetical problem: that of distinguishing the historical accounts from mythical elements destined to illuminate the meaning of the history. The difficulty of discriminating these elements cannot, however, excuse the biblical scholar from doing this work.

In concluding this section, I would like to underline the ecumenical importance of chapter 6, "The Place of Scripture in the Life of the Church." In this, there are declarations which bring us completely together in our common attitude toward the Bible. Against Protestant views, Catholics have too often objected that the Bible is a "dead letter" while tradition alone is a living element. Now in paragraph 21 of the schema we read this marvelous phrase, "In the Holy Scriptures, the Father who is in heaven constantly meets his children and speaks with them."

Alongside of the lacuna, which I have pointed out from the Protestant viewpoint, there are many specific elements in this schema which bring us closer together. The sentence which I have just cited marks an area in which the agreement is complete. This makes it all the more regrettable that we shall be obliged, at the end of this article, to point out a change which was made at the last moment in regard to this subject and introduced into the *Decree on Ecumenism* and which, in reference to Protestant readers of the Bible, notably weakens what is affirmed here.

III. The Actual Role of the Bible at the Second Vatican Council

At the council itself the Bible occupied a special place even in terms of exterior arrangements. Each morning after mass the deliberations were introduced by an impressive ceremony of the "enthronement" on the altar of a magnificent ancient copy of the Gospels. This recalled the presence of the word of Christ to all the council fathers. Nevertheless, this ceremony led me to ask two questions. First, would not this beautiful book have fulfilled its role more adequately if it had not simply been exposed to view, but if a special text had been read each morning appropriate to the work of the day? Second, why not enthrone the whole Bible rather than simply the Gospels? Is not their special place seen more clearly because of their permanent connection with the other biblical books? This, however, is a question which needs to be looked at in relation to the problem of the liturgical use of the entire Bible in Catholic worship.

The Bible readings in the mass of the Holy Spirit which was celebrated each morning were disappointing because of the monotony with which the same two passages were read throughout the sessions. These were the text from Acts 8 which records how Peter and John were sent to Samaria in order to lay their hands on the new disciples and the verses from John 14 which speak of the Comforter. Surely the riches of New Testament texts on the Holy Spirit (e.g., Romans 8) would have allowed for a much greater variety. It may be asked whether the tendency on the Catholic side to depreciate the "dead letter" of Scripture in favor of "living" tradition does not come from this kind of formalism. It may be hoped that the liturgical renewal envisaged by the constitution on the liturgy will give a new life in the future to the use of biblical texts and will make impossible the liturgical inertness just mentioned.

This leads us to speak of the place of the Bible in the schemas which were discussed by the council. In this connection, as in others, it was the schemas on the liturgy and ecumenism which were the most encouraging from our point of view. Both the wording of the principles and the practical applications which they propose are entirely inspired by the Bible. Biblical references are not simply added as afterthoughts in order to support the various affirmations, but the entire documents come directly from the Bible even where this is not expressly cited. It is not surprising, therefore, to find in the constitution *De sacra liturgia* at the very beginning (No. 7) the statement of principle that Christ is present both in the Sacraments and in his Word *(Praesens adest in verbo suo siquidem ipse loquitur dum Sacrae scripturae in Ecclesia leguntur).* From one end to another, more room is given to the Bible in the different aspects of worship.

Initially, on the basis of a superficial examination of the other schemas, it would be possible to suppose that their biblical foundation is equally solid. If one were simply to count the number of biblical citations, he might even be tempted to think that some of the documents were particularly close to the Bible. However, when one looks more closely, he discovers that very often the numerous biblical references added in parentheses are not really the basis of the document but simply proof texts, *dicta probantia*, added as after thoughts in order to establish a rather exterior relation between a prefabricated schema and the Bible. There is sometimes a heaping up of biblical citations, but there is very often no genuine internal connection between what the schema affirms and the biblical text. Actually, in many cases, the reference applies simply to a word or an expression, and not at all to the idea itself which is developed in the schema. Under these circumstances the reference has nothing to do with the context either of the schema or the biblical passage.

This was especially often noticeable in the original texts laid before the council by the pre-conciliar preparatory commissions. Fortunately, in many instances in the conciliar debates Cardinal Bea criticized this way of citing Scripture, and we shall later note with satisfaction that the final texts have fewer of these external and non-contextual biblical references.

Yet many such references remain. It seems to us that the biblical foundation of the chapter on the Virgin Mary in the *Constitution on the Church* is especially weak and artificial even in the definitively proclaimed document. Here texts are cited whose basic meaning has nothing to do with the statements of the schema and which have been inserted into the document only as afterthoughts.

It is not surprising that the citation from Genesis 3:15—much beloved in Catholic Mariology—is once again repeated (No. 55). But the way and manner in which the Gospel texts are interpreted in this chapter is just as objectionable. They are even used to document statements which flatly contradict their intention. The context of Mark 3:35 makes completely clear that those among Jesus' hearers "who do the will of God" are being contrasted as the true relatives *over against* the blood relatives, mother, brothers, and sisters, who "are outside" (v. 35). The schema tears this verse 35 out of its context and arbitrarily connects it with other texts so that the reader must finally suppose that Jesus in this passage included Mary among those who are designated as true relatives (No. 58). It is exactly the opposite of this which is said by Mark 3:35. This, to be sure, is the worst example of a kind of exegesis which was believed to have been definitively ended also in the Catholic Church.

Exegetically less objectionable, but still scarcely allowable, are the references in the same paragraph to Luke 11:27 f. and John 2:1-11 (including the problematic fourth verse) since these are used without further ado as evidence for that positive attitude of faith on the part of Mary of which the schema speaks.

This way of citing biblical texts without taking in account the meaning of the context becomes even more questionable in view of the fact that there are certain theologically important declarations for which one would like to see the biblical basis. This is true of the principle of apostolic succession which is affirmed in several places in the schema.

Speaking more generally, one would like to see the schema *De Ecclesia* take into consideration the historical situation which prevailed at the time the books of the New Testament were written. Thus the word "bishop" did not then have the same meaning that it has today. A bishop in the New Testament is not the head of a diocese, but of what we would today call a parish. If more consideration were given to this fact, the local church would play a more important role in the schema than is now the case. An analogous criticism could be made of the way in which what one can say of the collegiality of the apostles in the New Testament is applied to that collegiality of the bishops which was the major theme of the second session. Similarly, the relation between Peter and the other disciples ought not to have been so unquestioningly assimilated to the relation between the pope and the bishops.

To be sure, the council dealt less with collegiality than with the relation between the collegiality of the bishops and the primacy of the pope which was proclaimed at the First Vatican Council in 1870. However, because the question of the primacy of the pope has been settled by this previous dogma, those passages which deal with Peter, especially Matt. 16:17 ff., were not again discussed. Those who prepared the schema cannot be criticized for this. However, it must be said that from a purely exegetical point of view, the texts which deal with Peter ought to have been reexamined along with those which deal with all the apostles. This should have been done apart from any concern to find in these Petrine texts a confirmation of papal primacy, and in taking account, rather, of the possibility of interpreting them exclusively in terms of collegiality.

Despite these reservations regarding the use of the Bible in certain schemas, it must, nevertheless, be recognized that there was a constant effort to take account of the Bible. Even though until now, as we have seen, this was done in a way which was often purely formal and rather superficial, still this concern in itself will one day bear fruit when there is a consistent effort to draw inspiration directly from the Bible, as is already the case in many texts.

When speaking of the place of the Bible at the council, it is not enough simply to study the texts which were proposed or voted upon. One must above all consider the speeches of the bishops and here, as an exegete, I must express great satisfaction. The way in which the Bible was not only cited, but studied and interpreted, by the fathers of the council indicates one of the new aspects of this council, an aspect which is full of promise and which, no doubt, would not have emerged if it had not been for the renewal of Catholic exegesis which started before the council and of which we have seen evidence for a good many years.

It would take far too long to deal with the different exegetical contributions of the council fathers during the discussion of the various texts. Significantly, it was not only the council fathers who have come to be called "progressives," but also the conservatives who made use of biblical exegesis in their comments on the schemas. Representatives of both groups pointed out with great accuracy and often with remarkable exegetical pungency the lack of precision and even the errors in the biblical citations. Their own observations were also often inspired entirely by the Bible. Some of the criticisms which we have already formulated above in regard to the schemas were also made by the council fathers. For me it was a special pleasure when the points which I had noted in the margin of my copy of a schema were brought up by the cardinals and the bishops.

Some of the names of those who made exegetical contributions must be mentioned, especially that of Cardinal Bea who, during the sessions, with the authority conferred on him by his exegetical qualifications, pointed out a good many points at which the Bible was cited inexactly or erroneously, and also noted cases in which important texts were omitted in favor of others less appropriate to the subject being treated. In all fairness it must be recognized that on more than one occasion Cardinal Ruffini also emphasized instances of questionable exegesis and, in addition, undertook in reference to a number of passages to show the difference between the situation in apostolic times and that of the later church. His intention, it is true, was the conservative one of opposing episcopal collegiality. This, however, is a dangerous line of argument for a Roman Catholic in view of the Catholic thesis that the pope is the successor of St. Peter despite these differences in situation. The relation between the twelve and St. Peter was dealt with in great detail, independently from the question of succession, by another eminent exegete of the council, Archbishop Weber of Strasbourg. Many other interventions might be cited, for example, that of Bishop Charue of Namur in Belgium, and, above all, that of the Belgian, Cardinal Suenens, on "the work of the Holy Spirit in the laity" which was based on an exact exegetical work which could not have been more in agreement with the spirit of the New Testament texts. It should also be added that, in general, the best and most courageous speeches which we had the privilege of hearing were always those inspired by the Bible, even when they did not contain explicit citations.

IV. The Conservative Opposition and Its Defeat

When dealing with "the conservative opposition," we must first speak of an event which, although it took place immediately before the first session, still cast its shadow over the first half of the council. On the very eve of the council the Biblical Institute of Rome as a whole became the object of attacks and accusations which, as has become well known, had as their goal the separation of the Institute from the Gregorian University and its attachment to the more conservative Lateran University. This basic objective was not attained, but a severe and surprising action was taken against two excellent New Testament professors. Just a few weeks before the opening of the first session they were deprived of permission to teach. The many friends of the Biblical Institute at the council took the opportunity provided by a public defense of a doctoral thesis to show their sympathy for this institution and to encourage the continuation of its work. The result was one of the great days of the first session. The numerous council fathers assembled in the large auditorium of the Gregorian University, and the considerable number of cardinals in the front row, expressed implicitly by their presence that they desired the freedom now possessed by Catholic exegesis to be protected.

It should not be forgotten that the suspension of the professors mentioned above occurred under John XXIII who in this case, probably because his primary interests were not in the exegetical and theological areas, yielded to the opposition. It is to the credit of his successor, Paul VI, whose theological and exegetical interests are much stronger, that he reinstated both professors in the summer of 1964.

Unfortunately, we cannot leave unmentioned in this context a disturbing event, already alluded to, which occurred at the end of the third session. We are referring to one of the last-minute changes which was made in the *Decree on Ecumenism*. The original text of paragraph 21, which had already been given preliminary approval by the council, read, "*Moved* by the Holy Spirit, they [the separated brethren] find in these very Scriptures God speaking to them in Christ . . . " Three changes were made in this sentence. Instead of "moved by the Holy Spirit," the final, corrected text says, "invoking the Holy Spirit"; instead of "find," it says "seek"; and in front of the words "speaking to them" a not altogether clear "quasi"—which can range in meaning between "as" and "as though" —has been inserted ("Invoking the Holy Spirit, they seek in these very Scriptures God as speaking to them in Christ . . . "). The emphasis in the original on God's objective action corresponded completely to the texts which we have already cited from the *Constitution on the Sacred Liturgy* (No. 7) and especially from the schema on revelation: "In the Sacred Scriptures, the Father who is in heaven constantly meets his children and speaks with them" (No. 21). Now, however, this affirmation, insofar as it refers to Protestants, acquires a subjective and even slightly doubtful character. If this sentence had from the beginning been phrased this way, it would—with the exception of the not altogether clear "quasi"—have been accepted without question by every Protestant. Indeed, "seek" would perhaps have corresponded better to Protestant sensibilities, especially when we think of Pascal's saying, "You would not have sought me if you had not already found me." However, the fact of the change and the difference between the texts which speak about Protestants in reference to this matter and those which speak about Catholics is objectionable, especially as the wording places Protestants in questionable proximity to the Athenians in Acts 17:27: "that they should seek God, in the hope that they might feel after him and find him."

Nevertheless, we should not forget that this is a *Catholic* statement on the role of the Bible among Protestants and that, as we emphasized above, this council has made no changes in the doctrine that the interpretation of Scripture is dependent on the magisterium of the Catholic Church as, indeed, is emphasized in the following paragraph of the same section from which we have been quoting. Still, the original statement could have been retained in the context of this doctrine, and the council fathers who formulated and approved it saw nothing in it which contradicted dogma. The *Decree on Ecumenism* contains elements which imply that the Spirit of God and, as a consequence, the presence of God are realities in the reading of the Bible also outside the Catholic Church. Surely this conviction will more and more prevail despite the change in wording.

I would not like to end this essay without recalling both Paul VI's memorable opening address to the second session, with its authentically biblical Christocentric accent on Christ, "the only mediator between men and God," and also the audience which he gave to the observers in which he took up the theme of the biblical history of salvation as the foundation of all ecumenical dialogue, and which he concluded with the invitation that all repeat the Lord's Prayer together. The present pope's feeling for the centrality of the Bible among us is also shown by his presentation in an audience during the third session of copies of Merk's critical edition of the Greek New Testament to all the observers.

To the degree that this council deepens within Catholicism the biblical renewal which started before it, it will contribute to the realization of the distant goal indicated by John XXIII and it will facilitate more than in any other way the dialogue which will be carried on with increased intensity after the council. Both ecumenical and biblical concerns depend upon this. Let me conclude with a sentence from the *Decree on Ecumenism:* "in the dialogue itself, the Sacred Word is a precious instrument in the mighty hand of God for attaining to that unity which the Savior holds out to all men" (No. 21).

Notes

1. The difference itself is pointed out in the *Relatio* or official explanation of the schema which was given in the council. Bishop (now Cardinal) Florit of Florence, who presented this *Relatio,* even mentioned my book in which I base the doctrine of tradition on this distinction. Further, the speech of Cardinal Léger on this subject also took this distinction as its starting point.

2. When I speak here of the formation of the Canon, I am not thinking of its final formulation. We know that this process lasted for several centuries. I am rather thinking of the idea of forming the Canon and of those first steps towards its realization which we can place around 150 A.D.

3. This instruction, dealing with the "historical truth of the gospels," permits and recommends that biblical scholars use the methods of *Formgeschichte,* but it also warns them against introducing "philosophical and theological principles" into their exegesis, and it emphasizes the importance of the historical facts in the Gospels.

Chapter VII

The Church as Mystery and as People of God

I

On November 24, 1964, Pope Paul VI promulgated the great ecclesiastical document, *Constitutio de Ecclesia.* With this action by the pope the most important chapter in the history of the Second Vatican Council had come to an end.

The long way which this document had to travel began on December 2, 1962, and did not end until November 21, 1964, when 2,151 council fathers cast their ballots in favor of it, while 5 voted against it. Within these two years a change had taken place which has been typical for this council. This change was characterized by a struggle that went on between two opposing views. On the one side there were those who were willing to open their minds, to change them, and to think along different lines. On the other side there was stubborn and determined resistance to any ideas that seemed to be irreconcilable with the traditional views as they had been accepted by the Roman Catholic Church. This stormy history is a sign and symbol for the endeavors of this council to formulate the thinking of the church anew in a language that would be acceptable and would not undermine the continuity of the church.

We shall try to trace briefly the way which this theological document traveled.

145

When Cardinal Ottaviani presented the Schema on the Church for the first time, on December 1, 1962, he prophesied with a certain air of resignation that this document could with some justification be called legalistic and unbiblical. As it turned out, his prophecy was fulfilled on the very same day when a number of fathers began to attack the schema in harsh language. They felt that it was indeed too legalistic and scholastic and that it was neither biblical nor patristic. The wording of the document lacked ecumenical farsightedness.

It soon became apparent that the schema had not been written in the spirit which had motivated Pope John XXIII to convoke this council of the church. Neither did it agree with the spirit with which the great majority of bishops had accepted the summons of the pope. The whole document breathed the spirit of the past. Within a few months it became apparent that its language was dated and antiquated. Bishop de Smedt accused the authors of the schema of clericalism, legalism, triumphalism, to which Hans Küng added the words: authoritarianism, centralism, and absolutism. Thus the first draft of this schema had to be revised and was to be presented to the council at its next session.

When the council met for its second session, on September 29, 1963, the schema was again presented, but in a new form. It contained a summary of the several proposals made by German, French, Spanish, and Chilean bishops. The editor of this second draft was said to have worked it over sixteen times. This time the outline contained the following chapters:

1. Of the Mystery of the Church;
2. Of the Hierarchical Order, Especially the Office of Bishop;
3. Of the People of God, Especially the Lay People; and
4. Of the Call to Holiness in the Church.

The differences between this new version and the first draft were striking. The new document did not describe the church as primarily a hierarchical and legal organization, but as the *mysterium*. This was in accordance with the opening address delivered by Pope Paul VI on September 29, 1963. In it he had said: "There can be no doubt whatsoever of the church's desire and need and duty to give a more thorough definition of herself. . . . The church is a mystery; she is a reality imbued with the divine presence and, for that reason, she is ever susceptible of new and deeper investigation."

New also were the expressions dealing with the history of salvation and with eschatology. The character of the church as a pilgrim was emphasized, and non-Roman Catholics were mentioned in an entirely different way than they had been in the first draft. The men who reworked the schema had shied away from expressions that had been peculiar to Roman Catholic scholastic theology at the beginning of the century with its bias against all forms of modernism. They had followed an older tradition of the church based on an ecclesiology derived from the Bible. Yet when this new schema was discussed in St. Peter's Church it became clear on the very first day that even this revised version was not the acceptable final form, but represented merely a way-station on the road to a more satisfactory schema. There was strong criticism of this draft during the meeting of the twenty-fourth general congregation, although it was freely admitted that the new draft meant a long step forward in the right direction.

On October 31, 1963, the discussion of the schema was once more suspended and the whole document was sent back to the Theological Commission which was instructed to sort, evaluate, and add suggestions from the hundreds of proposals that had been made for the improvement of the schema. These proposals had been presented either orally during the discussion of the general congregation or in writing. A long and important stretch of the way had been traversed.

The third session of the council opened on September 14, 1964. The address which the pope delivered at its solemn opening came both as a surprise and as a distinct disappointment to many of his anxious listeners. It seemed to many that now the wind was blowing from a different direction than at the opening of the second session during the previous year. The whole address was an expression of a peculiar type of hierarchical thinking. In it he stated: "We ourselves constitute the church because we are the members of the mystical body. . . . We constitute the church because we are her administrators, her priests, who have received the sign of special consecration. . . . We constitute the church because we, being her teachers, pastors, and administrators of the mysteries of God, represent her in her entirety." Speaking of himself, the pope said: "We who sum up the church in our person and in our sacred office declare that this council is ecumenical." This repeated assertion that "here is the church" is complemented by a threefold assertion that "here is the Spirit."

The bishops and also the observers had been given advance copies of the revised schema. It was at once clear that there had been an important regrouping of the material and the addition of several chapters. The chapter headings read*:

1. Of the Mystery of the Church;

2. Of the People of God;

3. Of the Hierarchical Order, Especially the Office of Bishop;

4. Of the Lay People;

5. Of the Call to Holiness in the Church;

6. Of the Religious Orders;

7. Of the Eschatological Character of Our Calling and of Our Union with the Church in Heaven; and

8. Of the Blessed Virgin Mary, the Mother of God, in the Mystery of Christ and the Church.

From this outline it became clear that in the future Roman Catholic ecclesiology would try to develop a doctrine of the church based on the people of God, and not on mere hierarchical considerations. This aspect of the document will be discussed in greater detail in part three of our presentation.

As far as the overall tenor of the document is concerned, I would like to say that it is—and how could it be different under the circumstances?—merely a faint *echo* of the best thinking in contemporary Roman Catholic theology and of the many excellent addresses

---

*   I.   De Ecclesiae mysterio
      II.   De populo Dei
     III.   De constitutione hierarchica Ecclesiae et in specie de Episcopatu
      IV.   De Laicis
       V.   De universali vocatione ad sanctitatem in Ecclesia
      VI.   De Religiosis
     VII.   De indole eschatologica vocationis nostrae ac de nostra unione cum Ecclesia coelesti
    VIII.   De Beata Maria Virgine Deipara in mysterio Christi et Ecclesiae

given in St. Peter's Church. All documents of the council have been worked over and over again. The schema *Constitutio de Ecclesia* is no exception. In spite of all this work the schema is and remains a compromise and is in more than one sense a disappointment. It is quite possible that the present schema will be outmoded within a few years. Theological developments are taking place at a fast pace. Thus even an ecumenical council is subject to historical changes. It will never be able to make definite pronouncements, but will always be bound to the thinking and the possibilities present in any given era. For the moment the council has not succeeded in going beyond this point.

However, if we compare former official pronouncements concerning the church with the statements made in this schema, then the *Constitutio de Ecclesia* takes a long step forward, both theologically and ecumenically. If we look at the schema in this way, it is an important milestone in a development the end of which cannot yet be seen. It stands at the boundary line between the old and the new theology. In many respects it is a document that leaves us guessing, a puzzling document. As far as we are concerned we must be satisfied with the tension in this document where genuine biblical truths are presented on the one hand while the whole biblical perspective is often bent in a strange way. There is a glaring discrepancy between the church as the people of God and the concept of the hierarchy, or between the Christological emphasis and a Mariology which continues to cast its long shadows over the Christological statements.

But no matter what our misgivings may be, one thing is clear: Something has happened in Roman Catholic theology, and he who cannot see it must indeed be blind. All we can do is to pay attention to the new developments even though they may not always be expressed very clearly. Often these thoughts are expressed indirectly, or they are strangely intertwined with certain old points of view. It is not our task to write an exhaustive critique of the schema *Constitutio de Ecclesia*. Such an undertaking has to await the results of long and detailed studies. But we can try to point out a few important aspects in this document, especially in its first chapter *Of the Mystery of the Church.*

II

Before beginning our investigation let us cast a brief glance at the introduction which has been added to the document.

Although the introduction is rather brief, it indicates quite unobtrusively some of the thinking that made its greatest impact on the council. The church is not seen here as an isolated force, but is seen in her relationship to the world. The council wants to tell the world what the church is and what she wants to be. This is done in a frame of reference which will be understood by contemporary man.

During the meeting of the World Council of Churches at Evanston (1954) all discussions in the plenary sessions were under the motto, "Christ the Light of the World." Similarly this schema of the Second Vatican Council begins with the statement that Christ is *lumen gentium,* the light of the nations. The church is part of this light. The schema expresses this thought in the following way: The church is the symbol, the instrument, and the "sacrament" of the inner unity of man with God and of the unity existing among men. The church must be a part of man's life, especially in our day when people are meeting more and more in social, technological, and cultural areas. She must be an instrument serving the true unity of mankind.

Am I wrong if I interpret these thoughts, which are so lightly indicated but so very far-reaching in their importance, as follows: Mankind is looking for unity. In the midst of the present-day divisions in the world there is still a desire to be united. This desire can be noticed everywhere we look—in our social and cultural yearning for improvement, in technology, and even in the ecumenical movement. Man simply cannot live by himself. He is constantly seeking fellowship. No other period in the history of the world has brought forth such an intense desire for the unity of the human race. This yearning belongs to the signs of our time.

When the document calls Christ the *principium unitatis pacisque,* the author of unity and peace, this wording also includes the unity and the peace for which man is striving and yearning today. Thus the church as the Body of Christ is the guiding light to man on his way to unity, because in the church this unity has found its deepest and most perfect expression. It is the task of the church to illumine the way so that man may realize his yearning for unity and may see that only in Christ and through the church can he find the unity for which he has been striving.

Even when the church is serving the world in its desire to find unity, by illuminating and purifying this yearning, the following statement still stands: Grace presupposes nature. It is not simply the nature of the single man in his individuality which becomes authentically human only by being made a vessel of God's grace, but this is also true of human society in its collective aspects. The strivings of a civilization can, so to speak, be a preparation for the Gospel, for the kingdom of God. Law and order, goodness and fairness, art and literature are related to the kingdom of God as preparatory signs.

Both collectively and individually, the world has become autonomous. This does not at all imply that either individuals or the world is completely independent, but rather that the secular, earthly order with its various functions has its intrinsic value. The world is not a means, but a goal, although not an absolute one. This was expressed by Pope John XXIII, in his encyclical *Pacem in terris,* in terms of the serving function of the church. She does not exist in order to rule the world. Her purpose is not to dominate. Rather, she follows the footsteps of him who came, not to be served, but to serve.

The church is not only the ark which saves us from the world. She also exists to actualize the latent tendency of the world with the help of the supernatural grace of God. This perspective is of decisive importance to the church as the people of God who are in the world. It points the way for the task of the lay people to renew, perfect, and fill with the spirit of Christ the Christian ordering of life. The goal is the *consecratio mundi,* the consecration of the world.

III

In contrast to a theology that looks upon the church as constituting a hierarchical legal entity, the schema *Constitutio de Ecclesia* sees her primarily as the *mysterium,* the mystery of Christ. It indicates that one should not stop with the consideration of the external form of the church as a legal entity or a perfect society. One should look at her from above and from the inside. The church has her roots in the essence of the Triune God himself. She has her being in his action. She is a supernatural, ontological reality, an extension of the inner life of the Trinity into which men are taken up. She is first of all a communion of faith and hope and love. In the last analysis her unity is the same as the unity af Father, Son, and Holy Spirit. It is this which is her *mysterium*. According to Pope Paul VI, the chief concern of the long second session of the council, in the fall of 1963, was "to find out about this *mysterium* and to define it in human speech as far as that is humanly possible so that we may be better instructed about the real and basic *Constitutio de Ecclesia*, the essence of the church."

The mystery of the church is indicated in all New Testament passages dealing with her, especially in the expression *Corpus Christi*, the body of Christ, which is more than a mere picture. In incorporating this expression into the schema and in explaining it in detail, the *Constitutio de Ecclesia* follows, on the one hand, the "Constitution on the Church" of the First Vatican Council and, on the other, the encyclical *Mystici Corporis* of Pius XII. But by using in chapter 2 the expression *Populus Dei*, the people of God, it goes much farther. If the first chapter of the schema saw the church primarily in her Trinitarian aspect, based on the incarnation of Christ, the second chapter places the church in the context of the whole history of salvation.

Even though "People of God" is a traditional name of the church, still it has been relegated until recently to the background. Although in the nineteen-thirties many well-known theologians had taken up this concept in order to counteract the overemphasis on the Body of Christ, it did not play any important part in the great encyclical *Corporis Mystici*, issued by Pius XII in 1943. We could even suspect that this encyclical disavowed this designation. In spite of this, it soon appeared with renewed force. If the expression *Corpus mysticum Christi*, the mystical Body of Christ, gave rise to a static view of the church which may be called the biology of salvation (*heilsbiologisch*) and which disregarded the historical and eschatological aspects, then by the same token the expression "People of God" opened the way for a dynamic concept of the history of salvation according to which the church is not yet perfect, but is on the way.

As soon as the discussions on the schema got under way a number of bishops clamored, probably at the suggestion of their theologians, for the inclusion of the designation "People of God" in the schema. It is important that this happened. We should not forget this, even though the concept of the "People of God" was insufficiently developed in the final draft. But more of this later.

Although the hierarchical moment, especially the importance of the episcopate serving under the pope, is strongly emphasized, we should not forget that the definition of the church as the "People of God," as it is presented in the second chapter, clearly indicates that the hierarchy exists for the people and not vice versa. The Chronicle of the Council issued by the Herder Correspondence wrote (November 1964): "The insertion of this chapter (Of the People of God) before the chapter on the hierarchical order represents an important shift in emphasis, if not a correction, which was desirable and even necessary in view of the overemphasis on the episcopal office."

IV

Of special interest to us is the eighth paragraph of the chapter "Of the Mystery of the Church" entitled: *De Ecclesia visibili ac spirituali* ("On the church which is both visible and spiritual"). Here we are confronted with some important and controversial statements. Certain changes have been made which, as far as I can see, are of basic importance. The spiritual church, the communion of faith, hope and love, exists in an essentially indissoluble communion with the visible church ruled by the hierarchy. Thus communion and institution belong together. The external church on earth and the spiritual church in heaven, i.e., the church as an institution and as the Body of Christ, are not two entities but *one*, in which the human and the divine have been amalgamated. "For this reason, by no weak analogy *(ob non mediocrem analogiam)*, it is compared to the mystery of the Incarnate Word. As the assumed nature inseparably united to Him serves the divine word as a living organ of salvation, so, in a similar way, does the visible social structure of the church serve the spirit of Christ, who vivifies it, in the building up of the body (cf. Eph. 4:15)." This is a strange intermingling of ecclesiology, Christology, and Roman Catholic theology.

At this point I might indicate an extremely important development in the revision of the text of the schema which begins with the first draft and progresses through the second draft to the final form of the schema as it was finally adopted by pope and bishops.

The final text as promulgated states: "This church [i.e., the church founded by Jesus as both a visible and a spiritual church] is the one church of Christ which in the symbol of faith is professed as one, holy, catholic and apostolic, which our Saviour, after His resurrection, commissioned Peter to shepherd (John 21:17), and entrusted to him and to the other apostles to extend and direct with authority (cf. Matt. 28:18, etc.), and which he erected for all ages as 'the pillar and mainstay of the truth' (I Tim. 3:15). This church constituted and organized in the world as a society subsists in the Catholic Church, which is governed by the successor of Peter and by the bishops in his communion, although many elements of sanctification and of truth are found outside of its visible structure. These elements, as gifts belonging to the Church of Christ, are forces impelling towards Catholic unity."

As we look back upon the development of this passage we note that in this first draft presented by the commission on theology the "Mystical Body of Christ" was equated with the "Roman Catholic Church." The unity of faith, hope, and love were considered identical with the Roman Catholic Church. This was clearly and unmistakably expressed in all its exclusiveness: "Only the Roman Catholic Church can rightly be called a church."

It is quite a step from this earlier statement to the second formulation of the *Constitutio*. The identity of the Church of Christ with the Roman Catholic Church was retained, but the sentence which I have just quoted was dropped. Instead the commission added the statement that outside the Roman Catholic communion there can be found some elements of holiness and truth which are constitutive parts of the church of Christ and which lead to Catholic unity.

The third draft of the schema contains another change which, the more one thinks about it, is truly surprising. The absolute identity of the church with Rome is toned down. The document no longer reads: "This church which is both visible and spiritual is the Catholic Church," but "subsists in the Catholic Church."

This change is, as far as I can see, more than a mere linguistic change. It indicates clearly a change in the spiritual climate of the Roman Catholic Church of today. The things that had slowly evolved during the last few years are made clear in the history of this text. In St. Peter's Church some bishops proposed that this expression, subsists in, should be further explained. However, the text was left as it had been written and thus will probably cause many and different interpretations in years to come.

But not only the unrestricted identification of the church with Rome was given up in the final text of the *Constitutio*. The fathers also changed the statement of the second draft that elements of holiness and truth "can be found" *(invenire possint)* to "are found" *(inveniantur)* in churches not in communion with Rome. In this form it is incorporated into the final text. We have heard many fine speeches in St. Peter's Church in which speaker after speaker declared that the reality of the Body of Christ transcends the narrow boundaries of the visible church. Thus the mystery of the church bursts through the boundaries erected by canon law.

Even so, it might be possible for the Roman Catholic theologian to interpret this section of the document in the traditional way. But this should not keep us from saying that there are signs of new directions in the Roman Catholic Church which have clearly found expression in these linguistic changes. This change in Roman Catholic theology manifests itself also in a certain lack of clarity and even embarrassment. Many theologians experience a sense of helplessness because the clear and firm statements of traditional ecclesiology which could be so easily applied are no longer absolutely valid. Other Roman Catholics rejoice that after a century of "traditionalism" which had seen a shrinkage of the catholicity of the church, the true image of the *Catholic* church is being re-emphasized. What is happening today, although opposed to the so-called "tradition" of the last one hundred years, is a continuation of a great and true Catholic tradition of former times.

Both the embarrassment and the rejoicing are symptomatic of the Second Vatican Council and can be found also in this document. The difficulties of this council are at the same time its hope. What is happening in the *Constitutio* to the doctrine of the church cannot be overlooked and will have consequences in spite of the emphasis on the hierarchical viewpoint which we have indicated. Even today the forces of resistance against change are still strong, but there are also signs that a new era is beginning in which the truth that had been veiled for so long will be seen clearly. Other truths, although they may remain veiled for the time being, will certainly see the light of day. As yet they have not been fully understood both in theology and practice, and perhaps they *cannot* be understood fully at this moment.

V

Another important aspect of the *Constitutio de Ecclesia* is its emphasis on eschatology.

In this area too there has been a notable development from the first draft of the schema to its final form. It has often been stated, and rightly so, that the Roman Catholic Church has neglected the eschatological dimensions of the church. There is always the temptation to identify the church with the kingdom of God. In his book *The Mystery of the Church,* Abbot Ansgar Vonier even goes so far as to say that the church is the final reality, as perfect as the glorified Christ in the state of perfection and of his final victory. Here, of course, the eschatological perspective has completely disappeared.

The *Constitutio de Ecclesia* takes a different point of departure. When the second draft of the schema was submitted it was clear that the critique of the bishops had been largely accepted. Eschatology was strongly emphasized in this document. The authors spoke of the church as a wanderer, a pilgrim, who has not yet reached the state of perfection. But even this second draft did not satisfy the fathers, as became clear during the discussions in St. Peter's. They felt that the tension between the *in via* and the *in patria,* the "already" and the "not yet," had not been brought out strongly enough. They stated again and again that the schema "had not clearly defined the difference between the church in her final state in the kingdom of God and her present existence as a pilgrim. Thus the thinking of the church has lacked a turning towards the coming One, towards the future of God." In this way Karl Rahner, in a speech at the German press office on the council, expressed his apprehension and added that at the coming of God the church herself will be consummated and become what one might call "the church

in eternity, unless one prefers to say that she ceases to exist—thank
God!—because she belongs to God's *time* and not to his eternity."

This critique became quite strong during the discussion of the
last chapter of the second draft of the schema, entitled "Of the
Call to Holiness in the Church." Cardinal Bea thought that there
should be a much stronger distinction between the church at the
end of time and the church in its pilgrimage. To be sure, the church
with all her members is striving for sanctification. But at the same
time she is still a church of sinners. If this were not the case, there
would have been no Reformation. Therefore the holiness of the
church is a living and dynamic force. It is not something static that
has been secured for her.

A chapter on the eschatological character of the call to holiness
was added in the third draft of the *Constitutio,* but this also was
strongly criticized. Bishop Elchinger of Strasbourg said in a council speech that this chapter "treated only the purely personal and
spiritual aspects of the final consummation. In our day it is absolutely necessary to say something about the social, cosmic and *heilsgeschichtliche* (history of salvation) aspects of eschatology, but this
is not done here. According to revelation, salvation is not first of all
a matter of isolated individuals, but rather of a people called out
for the sake of all mankind, and thus for the sake of the calling of
all the children of God to ultimate unity. The world itself is also included in this."

This and other objections are to some extent taken account of in
the final version, but even here the peculiar character of the eschatology of the constitution still remains evident. Eschatology and hope
for the beyond, for heaven as this has been traditionally conceived,
are made to correspond to each other. The aspects of the cosmic
renewal of the world, of the end as the fulfillment of history, and
of the kingdom of God as involving a new earth recede into the
background. What is emphasized is the communion between the
church on pilgrimage and the heavenly church at rest, the unity of
the faithful on earth and the saints in heaven. The chapter culmi-
nates in a hymn of praise to the universal church on earth and in
heaven, and to him who is sitting on the throne, the Lamb of God.

But we shall return to the question of eschatology later when we discuss the problem of the relationship between the kingdom of God and the church.

VI

During a press conference held in Rome during the third session Hans Küng said the following: "I am completely in favor of criticism. I often criticize myself. But let us try always to speak from the point of view of our own church in reference to our own church. . . . Let *the* church that can say that she has made the same progress in the course of three years as we have come and lecture us on what we should do next. . . . We expect a fair evaluation of this council from Protestant and Orthodox theology. But this evaluation must not avoid self-criticism." Apart from the fact that *at no time* is there the possibility of lecturing to the other "from above," I subscribe to the statement of Hans Küng. But I would like to expand somewhat what he said: There *must* be criticism because in the last analysis such criticism is not of our own choosing, if it is *genuine,* but it is something that comes to us from above, and all of us are bound to listen to it obediently.

In the following I shall try to formulate a few questions that concern all of us, Lutherans and Roman Catholics alike. This does not mean that there are no other important factors in the *Constitutio* which force us to think about them because they challenge us with dimensions which had been forgotten for a long time. But my questions are directed only to the Catholic understanding of the church as it is developed in the *Constitutio de Ecclesia.* These are the dimensions which had been forgotten in the past.

1. The Roman Catholic interpretation of the church as we find it in this document lacks the *ultimate dimension of history.*

Before I continue to talk about this point of view I would like to stress that historical thinking is not foreign to the Catholic concept of the church. On the contrary, it is one of the significant factors in modern Roman Catholic theology that history plays an important part in it. History was a decisive factor in the organismic thinking of Johann Adam Moehler (d. 1838) and later of Karl Alam, and in the evolutionary thinking of John Henry Newman (d. 1890). What do we understand by organismic thinking?

It means that history is an organic development. For church history this means that the history of Christianity must be interpreted as growth developing from the revelation of God. Only as we think organically can we comprehend the reality of this growth. The principle of organic growth was first clearly formulated by Schelling. Ever since that time it has made a deep impression on both Protestant and Catholic interpretations of history. One can say that almost by force of necessity, church history is seen from an idealistic, even positivistic, point of view where everything that happens is seen as part of the whole. This led to an almost unavoidable attempt to describe the history of the church as sacred history. I would like to ask: Is the organic principle really suited for the understanding of church history? Does it not lead to a basic misunderstanding of the essence of history?

Although this organic way of thinking still dominates areas of Catholic understanding, it has been challenged by an entirely different thought process. According to this philosophy of history we are not dealing with an organism, but with a progressive *cursus vitae (Lebenslauf)*. History becomes something personal. It is actual life history. The history of the church is not a neutral development of formation and change, but a "living history" with all its decisions and responsibilities. On the one hand, the history of the church is completely the work of men; on the other hand, it is completely the work of God. The great problem is how to relate these two factors to each other. Not every form is a *true* form. Every epoch has had its temptation and perversion. The often beautifully retouched presentation of church history by the apologists for the church cannot be taken seriously. Church history is human history, i.e., sinful history. We are not implying that we should only be concerned about the phenomenology of a church history which has to be presented and analyzed, but we are able to present a theological judgment and a serious *critique* of the church in her former and present forms. There has been all too often a temptation for the church to identify herself with things "as they are now" and to claim that "this is *the* church." Thus the essence of the church has been obscured by human sinfulness to which she has often yielded. This is felt by many Catholic theologians today. For example, Yves Congar writes in *Pour une église servante et pauvre (For a Serving and Poor Church,* Paris 1963) that the periods when the church was authoritarian and oppressive were also periods of increasing secularization. The church has often succumbed to this temptation. How often was she not interpreted as an organization of the priests in which the people played only a passive role. "This frightful view left its mark on many structures and customs so that they were conceived as self-evident and unchangeable. This is a betrayal of truth" (p. 135).

Here we find a concept of history which, if it is carried to its logical conclusion, may lead to a radical revision of the concept of history from which its last dimension could be comprehended. Just think of the concept of history as we find it among the prophets of the Old Testament. How much is there to be found in this history of the Chosen People of darkness and veiled understanding, of abysses and heights, of guilt, of the judgment and the grace of God! How often did he not permit the nation to be led into judgment to the point of near-extinction. Yet again and again his unfathomable grace was effective in his judgment. The mercy of God awakened the people again and again to a new life. In the Old Testament, history was not seen as the development of a seed which grows slowly, almost automatically, and ends in perfection. To be sure, this history too had a *telos,* an end. But the final consummation of history was completely in God's hands. The way toward this *telos* was no gradual development, but was prescribed by the leading of God's hand. The way of history which God prescribes for his people, his Son, and his church leads through death to life. This is a far cry from any evolutionary interpretation of history.

The people of Israel tried again and again to gain their ends by their own power. This attitude was contrary to the covenant that God had made with them. Therefore God's wrath descended upon his people. How often did it not happen that the people perverted the fact of their election into a special privilege! This was their special sin, and for it they were punished. God's election of his people did not mean a special degree of security. On the contrary, "You only have I known of all the families of the earth; therefore I will punish you for all your iniquities" (Amos 3:2). And yet, Israel was God's beloved son to whom he showed mercy and whom he took back into his arms again and again.

But this discussion has led us to a dimension of history which can be reconciled only with difficulty, if at all, with what we find in the *Constitutio* concerning Roman Catholic ecclesiology. In the *Constitutio de Ecclesia* the people of God in the New Testament are compared with the people of Israel. However, significantly the point which we have just made is missing completely. It is stated that Israel has been chosen by God as his own people, that he made his covenant with it, that he educated it progressively by revealing himself and his counsels in the history of this people, and that he sanctified it to be his own. Thus the history of the people of the Old Covenant is seen as a preparation or type for the New Covenant which is complete and perfect. This is God's covenant with the church. Is this by any chance an attempt to make history look like something that is harmless and far removed from the stern and passionate concepts which the prophets proclaimed? This attempt has very serious ecclesiological consequences.

In an essay, written for the book series *Concilium* (Vol. I, 1965, pp. 19 ff.), Congar writes that the concept of the People of God is appropriate to express the continuity between the church and the people of Israel. He then describes this continuity in some detail. But never a word is said about the breaking of the covenant, of judgment, and of the wrath of God. Why not? Perhaps Congar is thinking that to emphasize these things he might give in to Protestant bias to lead the church of the Incarnate Word back into a relationship which existed for the People of God under the old order of salvation (p. 29). This is exactly the crossroads where our ways must part. We must ask whether silence on this important thought does not lead inevitably to an ecclesiology of glory. And this is one of the weaknesses that permeates the *Constitutio de Ecclesia*.

Fortunately there were a few voices at the council who spoke differently. The Italian archbishop Andrea Pangrazio of Gorizia, who was only a member of the Press Commission and not of the Theological Commission, made a speech in St. Peter's Church which unfortunately finds no echo at all in this document. He spoke of the mystery in the history of the church. He stated that the Roman Catholic Church had been described throughout the document in a very static and abstract way. She had not been seen in the light of the people of Israel. "In the history of the people of God in the Old Testament the Church can and should contemplate the mystery of her own history mirrored in a type, as Paul says to the Corinthians. 'All these things that happened to them were symbolic, and were recorded for our benefit as a warning. For upon us the fulfillment of the ages has come' (I Cor. 10:11). Just as God in his unsearchable justice punished his people of the Old Covenant in their history for their infidelity, and raised them up again in his almighty power, as he saved them and exalted them when they repented and begged for divine mercy, so he does the same thing now for his people gathered together in the Church of the New Covenant." (*Council Speeches.* Edited by Yves Congar, Hans Küng and Daniel O'Hanlon, 1964, pp. 188 f.).

This may suffice to show that the dimension of history, which penetrates to the lowest depths of human existence and from which both Christology and church history receive their final mystery, was not unknown to at least one conciliar father. But in the document *Constitutio de Ecclesia* it is a dimension that is forgotten and unnoticed.

2. The question concerning the meaning of history leads us to a second question concerning the sin of the People of God. I do not believe that we can understand the mystery of the church without taking into account the tension of judgment and grace which permeated the history of God in his dealings with the people of Israel, even though the history of the new people of God may be somewhat different. Nevertheless, the history of the church, too, has its hidden history, dark and incomprehensible. In the church, too, there is a dimension of guilt, apostasy, and of the wrath of God which strikes down his people. With this background of church history, the unspeakable depth of the love and mercy of God is seen as the final, all-embracing mystery of the church. For there is no greater mystery on earth than the forgiveness of sins. This is true especially in reference to the church as the people of God.

The document furthermore speaks in a surprisingly reticent manner about the relationship between God and his people. The people of God are called the Bride of Christ whose desire it is to be united with the heavenly Bridegroom. The church is described as a wanderer who lives in exile and is yearning to go home. It is acknowledged that in her ranks there are sinners. Therefore she is in need of constant purification although in herself she is holy. The power of the risen Lord constantly strengthens her in times of persecution and other difficulties. She is given humility and love that she may overcome all temptations. Although she herself is still living in the shadows, she is able to reveal the mystery of the Lord until that day when it is manifested in a clear light. While the church is growing she is at the same time homesick for the kingdom of God. She hopes and waits with all her strength to be united with her king. The church on earth is seen primarily as a church that is growing.

To be sure, there is some talk about her weaknesses and shadows. But why are the fathers afraid to make clear and honest statements about the sins of the church? If only the Roman Catholic Church would dare to call these things by their proper names she would be able to say something meaningful not only to herself but also to the other churches.

I would like to quote one of the council fathers, Bishop Stefan Laszlo of Austria. During the sessions of the council he often spoke concerning the eschatological emphasis within the church. He said that "the eschatological pilgrimage should not be understood in the abstract sense. There has been talk of the needs and the lack of illumination on the way of the church in this world. But when we talk about the pilgrimage of the church in the biblical sense we mean a great deal more. The church is called a church on its pilgrimage because the people with all their needs and their miseries are not without guilt or sin.

"Thus the New Testament people of God form a continuity with the people of the Old Testament. Often this people wants to follow the way of the Lord, but unfortunately just as often it strays away from him. It wants to be faithful, but again and again is found unfaithful. It wants to be a holy people, righteous under the grace of God, but again and again becomes a people of sinners who are under the wrath of God. The people of this world see clearly that the actual church is very different from the one that has been extolled by theologians and preachers. Theology always seems to be concerned with the church of the *saints,* while life itself shows us the

church of *sinners.* What can we say about this question which seems
to puzzle many contemporary Christians?

"If we want to find a convincing answer, it should not be expressed in terms of triumph or even hypocrisy, but should be completely realistic and honest. That means in plain words that it is
not our job to proclaim here on earth an ecclesiology of glory which
will not be attained until the end of time. When we speak of the
church on the pilgrimage we must always ask ourselves: what does
the Cross mean for ecclesiology?" (cf. *op. cit.,* pp. 44-45).

Why did this address by Bishop Laszlo, which was a critique of
the second draft of the schema, not find an echo in the *Constitutio
de Ecclesia?* The council fathers should have known that their
schema would have been much more convincing if the voices of
the critics had been reflected in its final form.

I would also like to quote Karl Rahner as a third witness whose
words have great bearing on our topic. Rahner said: "If we would
only say: 'We know that in the church there are sinners, but this
fact does not have anything to do with the true church' then we
would lay ourselves open to the charge that we are harboring an
idealistic concept of the church which is theologically questionable.
. . . But this is not the meaning of the theological concept of the
church. In this concept the only church that really exists is the visible
church that embraces the sum total of her baptized members, has
the same confession of faith and is obedient to the pope in Rome.
Of this church no one can say that she has nothing to do with the
sins of her members. Of course, she does not condone these sins.
Of course, there are always people in her midst (and perhaps a
great number) who may rightfully be called 'saints.' We shall not
further elaborate this point. But if she is real and if her members
are real sinners, then she too is sinful. The sins of her children is a
spot and defect on the mysterious body of Christ. The church is a
sinful church—that is a true statement of faith, not a mere primi-
tive fact of experience. It is the terrifying truth!" (*Kirche der Sünde,*
1948).

Let me tell you a story which sheds light on this concept and
which impressed me very much. During the discussions on Friday,
November 8, 1963, Cardinal Ottaviani spoke on the topic of the
college of bishops as a continuation of the college of New Testa-

ment apostles. He asked the question: "When did the apostles really act collegially?" The cardinal had inquired about this problem before and had asked a famous New Testament scholar for his opinion. This scholar had admitted that he did not know of any instance where the apostles acted collegially. Afterwards I spoke to a Roman Catholic priest about this question. He was silent and we went our separate ways. But some time later he returned to me and gave me a small picture of the crucified Christ. On the back he had written: "The apostles acted collegially when they forsook their Lord in the Garden of Gethsemane." We might smile at this explanation because it was certainly not the intent of the question of Cardinal Ottaviani. But suddenly I did not smile any more. I was silent. The story of the failure of the apostles at the cross, Christ's resurrection and the testimony of his mercy, his fathomless love, and the tremendous power of God suddenly dawned upon me. Without this dimension of love and power we cannot understand the mystery of the church. And this is exactly the dimension which the *Constitutio de Ecclesia* did not grasp.

How different, how much more truthful, would the *Constitutio de Ecclesia* have been if these voices had been heard and found an echo in it. Nevertheless, we cannot deny that this schema constitutes real progress when compared with earlier ecclesiological documents.

3. Of the call to holiness in the church.

Surprisingly enough and somewhat perplexingly the schema ends with a lengthy exposition on the holiness of the church, culminating in the last chapter on the Virgin Mary. Immediately after the chapter on the lay people there is one on the holiness of the church. Then the document continues with a chapter on the religious order and with a chapter on the eschatological character of holiness. This brings us to the decisive crossroads in the relationship between Protestantism and Catholicism. We can only briefly allude to it.

Rarely has it become more clear to me than in this document that for the Roman Catholic Church sanctification is the first and the last concern. Is this not a great challenge to us? Who would dare to deny that here we are confronted by something that is central and should never be underestimated? We Lutherans should not be the last ones to listen to this exposition carefully. Are there not many references in both the Old and the New Testaments to holiness, to sanctification? But why do the words that are used to describe holiness in the *Constitutio de Ecclesia* not ring entirely true? I think the reason is that the good news of the kingdom of God has not been clearly enunciated. Therefore the council fathers are unable to proclaim with confidence and joy that there is life and blessedness where there is forgiveness of sins. But the importance of the doctrine of sanctification remains undiminished. It must be placed in a different context, however. Otherwise the poor, the real sinners (i.e. all of us) are deprived of ultimate comfort, and the church is in danger of becoming "the church of the rich." This, of course, the Roman Catholic Church does not want to happen.

According to the wishes of Pope John XXIII the council was to help lead the church out of herself in order that she might be in and with the world. How can the church come closer to the world? The most important gift the church has to bestow is "to preach the good news to the poor . . . to proclaim release to the captives and recovering of sight to the blind, and to set at liberty those who are oppressed, to proclaim the acceptable year of the Lord" (Luke 4:18, 19).

I would like to ask: Is not something lacking in this chapter of the *Constitutio de Ecclesia* of the sovereign freedom which is so powerful in the proclamation of the New Testament concerning the kingdom of God and which brings to nothing all the righteousness of the scribes and of the Pharisees? Is there not here a great and fateful danger that holiness and sanctification are perverted into "supernatural morality"?

Let us listen to a few words from a *Pentecost Prayer in Times of Necessity* which the Roman Catholic priest and theologian Dr. Joseph Dillersberger wrote in 1931:

"O Holy Spirit, where art thou here on earth? They say that thy church is full of thee, and yet there it is so quiet, so still—almost deathly still! Must we believe that thou art only in the Catholic Church where it is so still and quiet? . . . Spirit of the Lord, thou who dost love the new, when wilt thou renew the face of thy church? When wilt thou show us how much must disappear so that her face may again become new, beautiful and young? In the time thou hast ordained the old will vanish with the blast of thy tempest and all will become new. When thou wilt—yes, already I hear thousands of distant voices of unbelievers who cry out, astounded and with re-awakened faith, 'old things are passed away; behold all things are become new' (2 Cor. 5:17). Yet it is often hard, O Holy Spirit, to believe on thee, and it is agonizing to add a 'Hallelujah' to the prayer which says that thou dost renew the face of the earth. . . . O Holy Spirit, the men of today are so deeply enslaved. They have become the bondsmen of money, the bondsmen of mammon. They are compelled to labor for the rich even while they themselves are as hungry as slaves, hungry for bread, hungry for righteousness, hungry for freedom. What a marvel for them if once again in thy church freedom were proclaimed loudly and clearly! Show us how we may become free from bondage to the letter. Free us to love oppressed humanity. Unleash the tempest of thy love! Yes, let the storms again rage through thy church. Renew her face. Let the banner of freedom fly high above the children of God. Then they will once again believe in thee, O Holy Tempest of the Lord, Renewer of mankind, Spirit of Love and of Freedom. Amen."

Don't we anticipate in this prayer already the concern of John XXIII? Yet the question remains: Do the chapters on the holiness of the church even approximate the greatness of this prayer? The Bible calls us to holiness. The call to holiness issued by the church, however, leads us astray if it is not clearly based at all times on the doctrine of justification by faith which has been given to us and is daily renewed to us. It is a question of *semper a novo incipere,* "always to begin anew." That means that justification must *actually* precede any sanctification. If this thesis is not firmly believed, then all our talk about holiness is lacking the most important element, Christ's authority.

VII

Finally let us turn to the difficult question of the relationship between *the church and the kingdom of God.*

In the first two drafts of the schema the idea of the kingdom of God was mentioned only in passing. It was said that the church rightfully represented Christ here on earth and that she possessed his dynamic power because Christ had become her Lord and she had become the Body of Christ. She was described as the seed and the beginning of the heavenly kingdom toward which she is moving in hope.

In accordance with the repeated wishes of the fathers the third draft, when it was finally accepted, discussed the concept of the kingdom of God in a separate subdivision. The commission had realized that it was necessary to deal with the church and the kingdom of God in their mutual relationship.

Therefore the Constitution of the Church describes very clearly how the kingdom of God has broken through in the proclamation and the miracles of Jesus. The kingdom is present now in the person of Jesus himself who "came not to be served, but to serve and to give his life as a ransom for many" (Mark 10:45).

As stated in the earlier drafts the church here on earth is the seed and the beginning of the kingdom of Christ and of God. That means that both the visible and the spiritual aspects of the church as well as her historical and eschatological character are underlined. This is stated in a note to the third draft.

But here again we must ask the serious question whether the relationship between the church and the kingdom of God is understood in all its depth, and whether the words "historical" and "eschatological" are understood in their basic meaning. Here too the whole complex of relationships is being discussed in a strangely "harmonious" and "soft" light. We may ask the question whether there should not be a clear outline that will define both the correct concept of the kingdom of God and the concept of the church. This is admittedly a difficult theological undertaking. The task of distinguishing between the reality of the church and the reality of the kingdom of God has been tackled again and again. We are not called to separate these two concepts, but to differentiate between them sharply. The *Constitutio de Ecclesia* did not succeed in this art of differentiating. Failure to do so is due primarily to the total structure of the document.

The *Constitutio* does not express clearly enough the sovereignty and the basic meaning of the kingdom of God. The ears that should hear and the eyes that should see are strangely closed by preconceived concepts of the church. In this document the church always takes precedence over the kingdom of God. The words of Jesus: "The time is fulfilled and the kingdom of God is at hand; repent, and believe in the gospel" (Mark 1:15) which had been quoted in the first part of the document are not explored in all their tremendous depth. Conzelmann *(Die Religion in Geschichte und Gegenwart,* Vol. 5, cols. 915 f.) had defined the consummation of the kingdom of God in the person of Jesus very clearly when he stated: "Time as *our* time has come to an end. What remains is the time to repent." Even though this statement is not complete, it goes without saying that under no circumstances should this kind of emphasis have been omitted in this document. In the proclamation of Jesus the kingdom of God is *the* end, the *eschaton*. It is eschatological while existing in "the midst of time."

But the lack of dialectics and precision which we have missed here is clearly in evidence at the end of the chapter where the fathers state that after Christ had risen and had poured out the promised gift of the Spirit, the Church, endowed with the gifts of her divine Founder and true to his command of love, humility, and renunciation, has been entrusted with the mission to proclaim the kingdom of Christ and of God among all nations. She is the seed and the beginning of this kingdom here on earth. Through gradual growth her inward desire to bring about the kingdom and to be united with her King in glory is being strengthened. As far as this statement goes, it is quite correct. But the truth concerning the relationship between the kingdom of God and the church can be expressed only in *two* statements, and the second statement is missing here completely. An organic point of view dominates the whole reasoning of the document and thus prevents it from arriving at a clear distinction. To state that the church is not the kingdom of God in all its perfection but the beginning of it still cradles the idea of her unbroken continuity.

I would like to illustrate this point by placing side by side and opposite each other two approaches which I shall call, for brevity's sake, the "perspective of religion" and the "perspective of the kingdom."

In the "perspective of religion" God and the world are conceived as two powers which stand in the relationship of the here-and-now to the beyond. This world and the world beyond confront each other as metaphysically distinct modes of being, as far removed from each other as the profane is removed from the sacred.

In the "perspective of religion" piety takes on a mystical and psychological character because the goal is to redeem the individual soul from the clutches of this world. To accomplish this purpose, acts of consecration and certain ceremonies have been established through which we participate in the world beyond and through which the supernatural and sacred is communicated to us. In this perspective there are occult traditions and mystic symbols. The perspective of religion points the way to an inner piety of the soul, to a cleansing from profanation and perhaps also to the permeating power of the sacred in the profane. But in the final analysis the perspective of religion is anthropocentric and not theocentric. On this plane there can be no real meeting between the true God and the true man. In its place there is the functioning of a system of piety.

We must admit that Christianity in its historical development has often dangerously followed this religious perspective. This is true of the Roman Catholic Church as well as all other churches. But when this path is followed the biblical perspective of the kingdom of God is always lost sight of.

What are the essential ingredients of this biblical "perspective of the kingdom of God"? In contrast to the static perspective of religion, the biblical perspective is simultaneously dynamic, historical, and eschatological. The Bible is not a mystical "book on religion" showing us the way out of this world and its history to a "higher religious" world. On the contrary, the Bible is the witness of the kingdom of God in the history of God's people. Thus it gives us a new dimension of history. Our God active in battle enters the history of his chosen people and at the same time the history of all mankind. He fights against Satan to save his creation from the distortion and alienation to which it has been condemned through the Fall. The perspective of the kingdom of God is a prophetic and eschatological outlook upon history. It is concerned with God's plan of salvation for the concrete world and not only with the salvation of individual souls. The contrast between "this world" and "the other world" is expressed in terms of the "here and now" and the "future." In the perspective of the kingdom of God hope is directed toward the final victory of God. In this perspective the true God meets real man in the God-man Jesus Christ who was delivered unto death and raised again and glorified. He is the kingdom of God, *auto basileia,* as Origen has said. In him alone the kingdom of God becomes operative. In him the prince of this world has been overcome. In him the new world is already here in the midst of the old.

It is clear that the church must always see her existence from the perspective of the kingdom of God, and not from the perspective of religion. Her ecclesiology must change from the static perspective of religion to the dynamic perspective of the kingdom of God, or ecclesiology will suffer. The divine worship with its proclamation of the Gospel and the celebration of the Sacrament does not have its basis in a semi-Platonic and somewhat mysterious "sacred perspective of religion" with its system of piety which incorporates, and makes a prisoner of, the Word of God, but in the biblical, historical, and eschatological perspective of the kingdom of God which permits the Word and the Sacrament to shine in their full light here and now.

In other words: The church is not the kingdom of God, but she exists for the sake of the kingdom of God. The kingdom itself must always be the final *raison d'être.* When the church passes from the scene of history the kingdom of God will be here. The church must never be an end to herself, but she must direct the hearts of men to look toward the end. The tension which is part of the church's essence cannot be removed here on earth. On the one hand she is a part of the new *aion* of the kingdom of God, on the other she is in the old *aion* here on earth. The church is the communion of those who have accepted the kingdom of the Son and yet remain children of this world. They remain under the law and are exposed to the temptations of this world. This is the ecclesiological center which Luther defined with the words *"simul justus et peccator."* And this tension will continue in the church as long as the church is on the way.

We can formulate a definition of this tension in the following sentence: "The kingdom of God is judge of the church's existence and at the same time gives all her divine content."

1. The church is always being challenged by her adversary, the Antichrist "who opposes and exalts himself against every so-called

god or object of worship, so that he takes his seat in the temple of
God, proclaiming himself to be God" (2 Thess. 2:4). Satan always
tempts the church to declare herself autonomous. This chapter of
the history of the church is missing in the *Constitutio de Ecclesia*.
But it should not be missing in an ecclesiology. True, it is a chapter
that no one likes to write. But if it is not written, there is no truth
and no reliability in ecclesiology. The whole doctrine of the church
thus loses its meaning. If we are honest, we will readily admit that
the church has often succumbed to this temptation. It does not make
sense to present the relationship between the church and the kingdom of God as a "relationship of extension." We must break once and
for all such traditional organic concepts.

If we look at the kingdom of God as the limiting factor sur-
rounding the existence of the church, we will not claim that the
church is sufficient unto herself and that she can save herself. The
church must always be living with the cleansing fire of the kingdom
of God. This is the point at which the word "reformation" becomes
truly meaningful.

2. The power of the kingdom of God is effective in the church
because God's kingdom is the reality of the crucified and risen Lord
Jesus Christ. The breakthrough of the new *aion* in the church occurs
through the Holy Spirit. The new world of God's truth, of his
fathomless mercy, of his great joy, and of the new life found in
him comes to us in the church. The church is thus both an eschatological and a sacramental force. Eschatology and sacrament belong
together. Without the eschatological dimension the basic function of
the sacraments cannot be understood.

The church is an eschatological force, not only because her allot-
ted time will come to an end, but also because in her the "Sacrament of the Kingdom of God" is present here on earth. The kingdom
of God is a continuous reality in the church. Through her the kingdom comes to us who are living in this old *aion*. This is the church's
sacramental character. It is in her visible signs; that is, in her proclamation of the Word, in her administration of Baptism and Eucharist
the new world in Christ is truly present. Both Word and Sacraments
are the realities of the Christ who is present here and now.

It is a fatal mistake if the kingdom of God is interpreted on the
basis of the self-understanding of the church, and not vice versa.

If this is done, the kingdom of God as represented in the proclamation and in the person of Jesus Christ appears before our eyes without depth of meaning and does not help us to understand the church. This is the case in the *Schema de Ecclesia*. The addition of a chapter on "The Kingdom of God" adds nothing to the ecclesiology contained in this document. The whole concept of the kingdom of God is incorporated harmoniously into a preconceived idea of the church. I believe that here we are at the decisive point where our entire theological thinking must part company.

Only if the idea of the kingdom of God is taken seriously can new light be shed upon the understanding of Word and Sacraments. Only then can the two dimensions, the dimension of the Word and the dimension of the Sacraments, be seen in their unity. Both dimensions are equally necessary. When this is understood then the whole question of the episcopal office as a sacramental office upon which the church has been built can be seen in a new and critical perspective. Not everything that has been defined will then be taken for granted, and the meaning of the strong statement by Luther that the church is a *"Creatura Verbi,"* a creature of the Word, will be understood much better. This statement of Luther should be taken under consideration very seriously.

The more we place the kingdom of God in the center of our whole theological thinking, the more we shall be led to the portal of the mystery which will change our old concepts and will reform the language of theology and councils. The parable of the new wine in the old skins is given to us both as a warning and as a promise. It applies to contemporary theology in general and to the *Constitutio de Ecclesia* in particular.

I realize that I have emphasized in this essay only one point of view. This may be considered its point of weakness and at the same time also its strong point. With it I have not said everything that could be said about the *Constitutio de Ecclesia*. In many ways this document presents a challenge that should be met by Lutheran theology with sincere openness and should be thought through carefully. In a book entitled *Dialogue on the Way* the rubric entitled "critique" must not be missing. It may not be an absolutely essential part of a book, but in this case, I think, it is necessary. I purposely did not enter into a discussion of the chapter on the hierarchical structure of the church. But what I have said here cannot be without consequence for a discussion and evaluation of that chapter too. Finally, I would like to emphasize that criticism—and in the final analysis this has been very insistent criticism—must also always be self-criticism.

Even if the critique of the *Constitutio* that I have offered here were merely a "Protestant criticism" it still would not be a bad criticism. As I understand it, it is based on an authority to which all of us are subject, the Bible itself.

Chapter VIII

Problems of Mariology

One of the most sensitive topics in theological discussion between Roman Catholics and Protestants is that concerning the place of Mary. Roman Catholics hold doctrinal positions and maintain devotional attitudes which are quite incomprehensible to a Protestant. If discussion is possible at all, its first result is to show both parties that here they seem to inhabit different worlds, or at least move about in quite different atmospheres. Here the common tradition of the past does not seem effective, and both parties to the discussion must walk warily to avoid offending the other unnecessarily. The Roman Catholic suspects that the Protestant lacks realism and depth in his theology; the Protestant fears that the Roman Catholic has confused Christological, ecclesiological, and Marian theological themes and as a result is in real danger of drifting into idolatry.

When the Protestant examines the history of Marian theology and devotion he is not reassured. He notes that the biblical material drawn into the Marian discussion is rather limited, especially if it is compared to the amount of material relating to Christ, the Spirit, the church, or the Sacraments. He sees few references to Mary in the theologians of the second or third centuries. He observes dubiously that the first flowering of Marian thought and devotion occurs in the period following the Council of Ephesus in 431 which reinforced Christological dogma by the declaration that Mary is Mother of God. Since this coincides with the period of imperial establishment of the church with its tremendous problems of instructing throngs in the Christian faith, he suspects the worst: that the growth of the Marian cultus represents an accommodation to pagan religions such as the cult of the Great Mother.

The examination of medieval scholastic thought concerning Mary does not still his skepticism. The speculative thought of this period does not commend itself to one brought up in the empirical traditions of modern science. The scholastic escalator, "it is possible, it is fitting, therefore it happened," seems an invitation to a jungle of unpruned growths. He notes how St. Thomas argues against the doctrine of the Immaculate Conception and finds him far more persuasive than is Duns Scotus in his attempts to support it.

He notes with interest that Roman Catholic theologians explain the remarkable growth of Marian theology and piety in the seventeenth century as opposition to Protestantism and to the excesses of an abstract theology cut off from the spiritual life. He reads an article by a Roman Catholic layman suggesting a psychological connection between the celibacy of the priesthood and the encouragement of devotion to Mary. If the people who understand and practice Marian piety can talk this way, he thinks, perhaps explanations based on comparative religions and psychology may very well be true after all.

He reads the legends of the Marian shrine at Loretto and the stories of the appearances of Mary at Lourdes and Fatima. He hears the Hail Mary mechanically recited in a radio broadcast, passes a gaudily painted billboard extolling the promise of world peace through devotion to Our Lady of Fatima, and is repelled by the garish and sentimental representations of Mary on prayer-cards, in grottoes, or in churches. He wonders what connection there is between these manifestations and faith in Jesus Christ, what essential relation between the dogmas of the Immaculate Conception or the Assumption and the Ecumenical Creeds.

When these reflections flood in upon him, he begins to wonder if the new atmosphere opening up to dialogue between the churches can really lead to anything. The differences seem so vast, the common elements so few, that it seems a waste of time to even contemplate discussion. What common ground is there to provide a base for dialogue? There are at least three elements which must be scrutinized carefully by the Protestant side before entering upon conversation.

The first is the New Testament presentation of Mary. The reaction of the churches of the Reformation to what they consider the excesses of Roman Catholic theology and piety has caused distortion at this point. Luke records Mary's assertion that "all generations shall call me blessed" with every indication that he believes and approves it. But even Fundamentalist Protestants seem tempted to use source criticism and its techniques to tone down or explain away if not to eliminate this passage. But a theology of reaction is seldom a balanced one, and in this area Protestants have blinded themselves to much that the Scriptures have to say for their edification.

Mary does have a unique role in the history of salvation. She was chosen by God to bear the Savior, and her response to the angel's announcement, "Be it done unto me according to thy will," made her "God's partner here," who "furnished thus half of that Sacrifice, which ransomed us" (John Donne). Her assent to the incomprehensible message is one of the high moments in human history. She does not calculate or question; she responds in simple faith and becomes thus an example and inspiration to troubled and perplexed believers of all times. She endures the misunderstanding of her fiancé, the gossip of neighbors, the ungracious hospitality of Bethlehem, the strain of not comprehending the ways of her Son, the anguish of seeing him killed like a criminal. She shares the life of the poor, undergoes the darkness of temptation, but emerges from the obscurity of her experience still believing. The perceptive reading of the Scriptures produces a brief but rich picture of a simple, troubled but triumphant faith in the person of Mary. From annunciation and nativity, through the childhood and manhood of Jesus, through the crucifixion and resurrection and into the early Christian community, Mary is an example of and stimulus to faith in Jesus the Christ.

Secondly, there is a true and proper commemoration of the saints in the Christian church. A horrified withdrawal from the excesses of the medieval cult of the saints is no guarantee of an evangelical response at this point. God is not praised when the story of his wondrous works among men is suppressed and forgotten. What he has done in Israel, in the incarnation, and in the early church has been remembered and traditioned on to us, not only for our edification in faith, but also as the raw material for our worship, for our confession of the greatness of God who uses the lives of ordinary men in extraordinary ways. We remember the apostle and the saint, not for their glory and fame but for the praise of God who gave them to his church. It is notable that Protestants feel no reluctance to dwell on the greatness of Paul or John, Martin Luther, John Wesley, or Roger Williams, but somehow stutter off into silence when the names of Peter or Mary enter the discussion. Mary's role in the work of redemption should not be overlooked or understated, not because her feelings are sensitive, but for the praise of God who did such wonderful things through her.

A cult of saints done to excess is a chamber of horrors for church history. But the neglect of saying thanks for the gifts of God avenges itself also on the church. Where no word can be said about what God has done through his redeemed people, there are no examples to inspire and to evoke faith and sacrifice. But testimonial banquets and dedication of buildings in honor of rich donors testify to a perverted and secularized form of commemoration which forgets that men are justified by the grace of God. The elimination of the sanctoral cycle from the calendars of some churches has not had uniformly evangelical consequences. It has sometimes resulted in an inane succession of "special emphases" where the Festival of the Annunciation has given way to Mother's Day, and sentimentality can go to seed again under ecclesiastical auspices. The neglect of Mary's true role in the history of salvation may well contribute to the loss of realism in Christology, an understatement of the humanity of Jesus Christ, with resultant abstraction and aridity, or by way of reaction, a false mysticism and shoddy emotionalism.

Thirdly, it is necessary that the church confess that Mary is *Theotokos*, the Mother of God. Some Protestants recoil in horror from this assertion as the root of all Mariological aberrations. But the churches that remember their theology continue to affirm it as a touchstone of Christological orthodoxy. For it is not primarily a statement about Mary but about her Son, who did not receive sonship with God as a reward for good behavior, but is Son of God from all eternity, and the God-man from the very moment of his conception in the womb. Jesus Christ is the only Mediator; he is the Word of God, the Reconciler, the Redeemer. He brings God to us, and he is sufficient. Emphasis upon Mary the Mother of God is not a move to displace him, but to ensure his solidarity with us as the Word became flesh. Mary stands in the Christian tradition as the assurance of the humanity of Jesus, the reality of his life on earth, the genuineness of his entry into the experiences of doubt and temptation. We approach no Olympian ideal, austere and abstract, but one tempted in all respects as we are. For Christian faith and the possibility of prayer it is important that Jesus the Christ toiled, sweat, knew weariness, disappointment, and defeat. Four centuries of history of Protestantism should make us wary of rejecting too quickly the importance of Mary in the work of salvation. We may find the Roman Catholic development strange and unacceptable, but our own history of rationalism and legalism should at least humble us enough to prepare to discuss the role of Mary in the mission of Jesus Christ.

In the preparatory work done before the Second Vatican Council, a separate schema or document on the Blessed Virgin Mary was projected. Its teaching was highly "conservative"—which, in this context, really means that it attempted to carry official Catholic teaching about Mary farther than ever before. To be sure, it was much milder than some had feared. It did not propose new dogmas even though 800 bishops had petitioned for this before the council opened. Everything which it said could be supported from statements of recent popes. Yet it proposed to raise these sometimes rather devotional remarks to the level of official teaching. It ignored the contemporary trend back to older, particularly patristic, traditions which view the Virgin Mary, not in isolation, but as the most perfect member and type of the church. Many felt that it laid the foundation for possible future dogmatic definitions of the Virgin as "Co-Redemptrix" and "Mediatrix of all grace."

This extremist tendency was disguised, however, by the schema's insistence on its own moderation. It was emphasized, for example, that it tried to avoid giving offense to non-Roman Catholics by not using the actual term "Co-redemptrix." But the idea was there.

Interestingly enough, the most vigorous warnings against the dangers of this approach came from South Americans. Cardinal Silva

Henriquez of Chile, speaking in the name of 44 Latin American bishops, said that nothing should be done to encourage the "exaggerated and sentimental devotion" to Mary which often existed in his part of the world. Bishop Mendez Arceo of Mexico went so far as to say that Protestants are "rightly shocked" at the deviations which sometimes exist in Marian piety.

During the discussion of the schema on the church, it was proposed that the theological statement on Mary be included in it. It was urged that this would put the Marian problem in its proper perspective, in relation to Christ and his church. This reflected what H. M. Koester has called the ecclesiotypical tendency in Marian theology. This kind of thinking sees Mary as a creature, a member of the church facing God alongside other members of the church. Opposed to this view is the Christotypical tendency which sees Mary beside Christ and over against the Christians in the church. This tendency sees parallels between Christology and Mariology: Christ is King, Mary Queen; Christ is Mediator, Mary Mediatrix; Christ is Redeemer, Mary Co-Redemptrix; Christ ascended into heaven by the Ascension, Mary by the Assumption.

The Christotypical approach, which stresses Mary's superiority to the church, has developed mainly among the Latin nations. The ecclesiotypical approach was pioneered among German theologians and is followed by many northern European theologians. It is a comparatively recent development and is regarded with suspicion in some quarters as depriving Mary of the honor due her. Its defenders maintain that the best way to honor Mary is to expound properly her relation to her Son within the Christian church. This is so exalted that she needs no borrowed finery.

The discussion on the place of the Marian chapter in the second session quickly developed into one of the most heated and tense debates of the council. Those who wanted a separate schema were especially agitated, suggesting that their opponents bring dishonor upon Mary. They distributed tracts and handbills to bishops in their hotels and even in the aula of St. Peter's. Someone even went so far as to publish an article in the format and typography of the conciliar documents, complete to the *sub secreto* on the cover. To keep the debate within manageable bounds it was decided to have the arguments on both sides summarized, by Cardinal Santos of

Manila for those advocating a separate schema, and by Cardinal Koenig of Vienna for those asking for inclusion of a Marian chapter in the schema on the church. The vote turned out to be vary close: a margin of only 40 votes in favor of including the Marian chapter in the schema on the church.

The treatment of the Blessed Virgin was submitted to the bishops before the opening of the third session as chapter eight of the schema on the church. The chapter is comparatively brief, consisting of four sections: (1) The objective of the council. (2) The witness of the Bible. (3) The relationship of Mary to the church. (4) The cult of the Blessed Virgin in the church. It is a restrained and cautious statement, seeking to find a middle way between strongly contending viewpoints. Its style is uneven, with biblical language set alongside scholastic language, biblical materials side by side with traditional Marian themes. The chapter was the second item on the agenda at the session and evoked sharp debate. Progressives criticized its use of Scripture, thought some of its language not sufficiently cautious, and warned against the use of the term Mediatrix because it would cause misunderstandings. Others insisted that the title "Mother of the Church" should be employed, accused the schema of "doctrinal minimalism," found it too cautious in praising Mary, and warned that the omission of the title "Mediatrix" would be a scandal to the faithful. The bishops of Belgium, Brazil, and Poland presented requests to the pope asking that the church be solemnly dedicated to Mary for the protection of morality, furthering the mission of the church, promoting the unity of the human race, and working for the cause of peace. The progressive bishops expressed themselves quite strongly, urging that the schema be modestly stated for ecumenical reasons, so that no additional barriers be laid before Orthodox and Protestant Christians. Others urged as strongly, even indignantly, that Mary's privileges be adequately stated and that Marian devotion be encouraged. In view of the strong feelings on both sides, leaders of the council urged that the chapter be accepted with only minor modification. In the event the only significant change was that the term Mediatrix remained in the text, but accompanied by other titles, Advocate, Auxiliatrix, and Adjutrix. The logic of the change seems to be to make a concession to the progressives by making the term Mediatrix less conspicuous than it would be if standing alone, and at the same time add more flowers to Mary's crown, thus pleasing those who found the chapter too cautious.

A Protestant evaluation of the chapter should recognize certain obvious merits in its treatment of a sensitive and controversial question. It is a sober and cautious treatment, a fact which became clearly apparent in the course of the debate. Some bishops from Latin countries, who have traditionally encouraged Marian devotion, found it offensively cautious and said so with vehemence. But a greater number of bishops, including many from Latin America, spoke out against abuses and deviations in Marian devotion and desired a chapter which would help them curb excesses.

The chapter is impressive also for its use of Scripture. An attempt is made to bring to focus the biblical teaching on Mary, and to do so in terms of sound critical exegesis. It stresses throughout the unique mediatorship of Christ and insists that the role of Mary neither adds to nor takes anything away from his redemptive work. It stresses that Mary's function must be understood in relation to Christ and the church, an emphasis which can serve as a useful corrective to overheated Marian devotion. But when the chapter has been scanned for its praiseworthy features it must be said that it is not the best document produced by the council, nor even very good. Let us note some of its weaknesses.

1. *Its exegesis.* Some passages of Scripture are used to illuminate the role of Mary which do not bear the theological freight which has been imposed on them. For example, the application of the nuptial imagery of the prophets to Mary is at least debatable. Sound historical and contextual interpretation would seem to point to an analogy between Israel and Christ and Israel and the church, rather than Israel and Mary. Here, of course, one must also avoid a polemical thrust which pushes Mary entirely out of the picture and thus threatens the reality of Christ's humanity. Strangely enough, many New Testament passages are omitted which show Mary as one who was tempted and who through temptation became an example of faith and submission. Some passages (John 2:1-11, 19:26-27) are subjected to a psychologizing exegesis which reads the devotional tradition into the texts and causes them to say things which the evangelist neither states nor implies. The hymn *"Stabat Mater"*

most likely provides the notions which are ostensibly drawn from John 19:26-27. This is not to repudiate homiletical or devotional reflection upon a text of Scripture; it is simply to caution against treating such reflections as the ideas of the Evangelist.

Another questionable exegetical technique used in the chapter is to draw dogmatic conclusions from traditional spiritual interpretations. The parallel between Eve and Mary first encountered in the writings of Irenaeus and Tertullian is certainly not objectionable as an illustration. But what may be permissible in preaching or in meditation should not be extended to become the foundation for dogmatic statements. The more cautious exegetes among the doctors of the church long ago warned against using any but the literal sense of Scripture for establishment of doctrine. To move from devotional language to dogmatic assertions is dubious theological method. By it Mary is transformed from a most eminent member of the church, having indeed a unique role in the history of salvation and chosen to be called blessed by all generations, to a heavenly figure who at times absorbs the role of her Son, the church, or the Holy Spirit. In a similar way the expression "Mother of God," which is essentially a Christological affirmation, is detached from its Christological function and made the starting point for dogmatic speculations about Mary.

2. *Theological method.* The chapter insists that Mary's role in the work of redemption in no way adds to or detracts from the work of Christ. It also insists that the cult of Mary must be clearly distinguished from the worship offered to God. It is notable, however, that there is no definition of the role of Mary in redemption, nor of the meaning of devotion offered to her. The chapter rather gives the impression that it would prefer to avoid definitions and rest content with the negative delimitation of Mary's role in relation to Christ. But given the dogmas of the Immaculate Conception and the Assumption, given the approved Marian devotions, the numerous Marian shrines, and congresses of Marian theologians, the Protestant reader is left with the disquieting sense that neither the dogmatic nor the liturgical caveats are sufficient. For Mary is ascribed a role which goes far beyond that attributed to any other saint and which at times shades into that of her Son. And the very

promotion of the cult of Mary maintains a pressure toward a more extensive and more precise definition of her soteriological role.

As noted above, the Christological affirmation that "Mary is Mother of God" provides another kind of impetus for the exaltation of Mary. The traditional scholastic procedure has been: (1) Mary's unique role as Mother of God is deserving of pre-eminent distinction. (2) It is entirely within God's power to accomplish this honor. (3) Since it is both fitting and possible, we may assume that it has been done. The Eve-Mary parallelism of the ancient fathers has also been productive. The Adam-Christ typology of Paul provides the pattern for the Old and New Eve scheme of thought and suggests some contrasts between man's loss in the fall and his recovery in redemption. With the seed of these two lines of thought, the atmosphere of the Mediterranean world provides the heat and humidity to force these theological plants. A highly developed emotional attitude toward mother and the family, the sensuous beauty of Baroque architecture, painting, and music—these are elements which contribute to the exuberant growth of the Marian cult. Amid the sunbursts over the altar, the ornate decorations, and the glowing music one hardly notices that the focus has shifted from Christ to Mary. The theologians doggedly insist on their footnotes—that Mary's mediatorial function is not in the *cause* but only in the *application* of redemption, that the devotion offered to Mary is qualitatively different from the worship accorded to God. But in the atmosphere of the Counter Reformation the footnotes are easily overlooked, inasmuch as Protestants, too, make much of Christ, while Mary is the object of a special Roman Catholic cultus.

In comparison to what is sometimes done, the titles for Mary employed in the chapter are restrained but suggestive. In addition to those enumerated above, she is called "Mother of Christ and the Faithful," "Mother of God and Mother of Men," and "New Eve," and "Queen of the Universe." Reference is made to her maternal role in the church, her maternal charity, her maternity in the economy of grace, as well as her exaltation above all angels and men, her faithfulness, power, prudence, and mercy. The title of Mediatrix is surrounded by other titles, and hemmed in by the warning that Mary's mediation is entirely different from the mediation of Christ. No specification is offered, however, as to what the differences are or what precise meaning attaches to this Marian function. More than one speaker in the debate at the council called attention to the dangers of using the expression, inasmuch as no guarantee can be offered that the cautious context of the chapter will always accompany it.

A remark should also be made about the theological language of the chapter. The council hopefully looks forward to the renewal of the church and to theological dialogue with other churches. As a part of this program it has been suggested that biblical language and patristic language are to be preferred to the language of scholasticism, inasmuch as they are more easily understood by those outside the Roman Catholic Church and also offer certain advantages for expounding the riches and variety of the church's heritage. The opening chapters of the schema on the church carry out this methodological program. The chapter on Mary is unfortunately a blend of two theological styles, one striving for biblical language and biblical content, the other using the argot of the schools. The result is an interesting text on which to practice form-and-tendency-criticism, but unsatisfactory as a literary and theological work. It probably has greater value as an indication of the tensions in contemporary Roman Catholic Marian thinking than as a document to promote ecumenical discussion. In this area it serves rather to dramatize the painful consequences of centuries of separation and to demonstrate how much discussion is needed before various church groups even understand each other, to say nothing of making common progress in theological studies. It is a late and not altogether satisfactory beginning of an effort to do this, but in our ecumenical poverty even a beginning is an occasion for thanks to God.

Chapter IX

The Decree on Ecumenism

The great importance of the Decree on Ecumenism which was adopted by an overwhelming majority of 2,129 votes (against 64 negative and 11 invalid votes cast) and was proclaimed by Pope Paul VI during the final public meeting of the third session of the Second Vatican Council can be seen if one compares the instructions given in it with the attitude formerly shown by the Roman Catholic Church toward the ecumenical movement. Until a few years ago the attitude of the Roman Church toward that movement was completely negative. When a deputation of Anglican bishops, from the Protestant Episcopal Church of the United States, visited Pope Benedict XV on May 16, 1919, to present him with an invitation, issued to the Roman Catholic Church, to participate in the contemplated first World Conference on Faith and Order, they were received by the pope in a friendly way, but their invitation was most emphatically declined. Said the pope: "Doctrine and practice of the Roman Catholic Church concerning the unity of the visible church are known to everyone. Therefore it is impossible for the Roman Catholic Church to participate in the planned congress." When the World Conference met in 1927 and when all major non-Roman communions including the Orthodox Church were represented, Pope Pius XI reiterated the negative answer to the ecumenical movement given by his predecessor. In his encyclical *"Mortalium animos"* he wrote: "There may be many non-Catholics who

186

highly praise brotherly communion in Jesus Christ, but at the same time none of them is willing to submit himself to the *magisterium* and the pastoral office of the Vicar of Christ. They constantly emphasize that they would gladly discuss these matters with the Roman Catholic Church. But they want to carry on these discussions as equals having the same rights. If such discussions should take place they would undoubtedly try to protect themselves through contractual understanding against the necessity of giving up those opinions which have forced them to this day to remain outside of the only sheepfold of Jesus Christ. Since this is the way things are, it is quite clear that the Apostolic See can under no circumstances take part in these meetings and that Roman Catholics are not permitted to favor such undertakings or to promote them. By participation they would merely increase the renown and the influence of the erring religions who are separated from the one Church established by Jesus Christ."

When, two decades later, a number of Catholic theologians whose hearts had been touched by the earnest desire for encounters with non-Roman Catholics wanted to participate as guests and observers in the meeting of the World Council of Churches, held at Amsterdam in 1948—i.e. the constituting convention of the World Council—they were forbidden by Rome to do so. Shortly afterward, by issuing an Instruction concerning the ecumenical movement, the Holy Office warned Roman Catholics expressly against the dangers of irenicism and indifference and permitted mixed conferences only if there was a well-founded hope for success which would lead to a return of the separated brethren to the Roman Catholic Church. The Holy Office ordered Catholics to withdraw from such conferences if there was no hope for success.

Again, in 1954, several Roman Catholic theologians traveled to Evanston, Illinois, to attend the meeting of the World Council of Churches as observers. Rome forbade them to enter the city limits of Evanston. In addition, severe restrictions were imposed on some important Catholic theologians who had embraced ecumenical ideas. This negative reaction by the Roman Church was based on her self-interpretation that she alone was the One Holy Catholic and Apostolic Church. This is also the reason why she insisted on calling her own "General Synods" by the time-honored name of

"Ecumenical Councils," although neither the Orthodox churches nor the churches of the Reformation had any voice in these synods. Moreover, this self-appraisal of the Roman synods is completely divorced from the question whether a particular synod even discusses the reunion of the churches. There is a deep-seated difference between the self-appointed concept of the Roman "Ecumenical Councils" and the concepts held by the other Christian churches who since the schism have carefully avoided the term "Ecumenical Council" as designation for their general synods.

But there was a tremendous change in the relationship of the Roman Church to the other churches when Pope John XXIII, whose name will rightly be remembered by many non-Roman Christians with great love and esteem, created the Secretariat for Christian Unity. He sent official Roman Catholic observers to the World Council of Churches meeting at New Delhi (1961) who in turn invited the non-Roman churches to send their observers to the planned Second Vatican Council. He rehabilitated Roman Catholic theologians who had been accused of ecumenism by calling upon them to serve as theologians of the council. He decreed that ecumenism should be one of the themes of the council. While the council was meeting in its first session, Pope John created an atmosphere of fraternal openness in which a cordial and fruitful exchange of ideas could take place between observers and Roman Catholic theologians who had gathered for the council. Observers were even asked to offer suggestions and to make contributions. During the meetings of the council we were witnesses of the ecumenical dynamism which had arisen in the Roman Church and now has found its expression in the Decree on Ecumenism.

This decree which has now become the law of the church is without a doubt a significant change and correction of the traditional positions of the Roman Catholic Church. Until its promulgation members of non-Roman churches were usually treated as people who by their own guilt had separated themselves from the one church of Christ. But the decree now speaks plainly about guilt on both sides (3). It mentions the "sins against unity" for which this council "begs pardon of God and of our separated brethren just as we forgive them that trespass against us" (7). Instead of the critical reserve which the Roman Church had shown toward the ecumenical movement it now gladly notes the fact that "among our separated brethren, with the help of the Holy Spirit, a movement has come into being which is spreading more and more from day to day and is aiming at the restoration of unity among all Christians. . . . Taking part in this movement are those who call upon the Triune God and confess Jesus as their Lord and Savior" (1). These are the words which the council uses to refer to the ecumenical movement represented in the World Council of Churches without, however, mentioning it by name. In contrast to the former refusal by the church to sanction participation in the ecumenical movement, the document proclaims that "this Holy Council exhorts all Catholic believers to recognize the signs of the times and to take an active and intelligent part in the work of ecumenism" (4). It further recommends that bishops throughout the world should seek to advance the work of ecumenism and give prudent guidance to it (End of 4). Thus the Roman Church in this decree has accepted the concept of ecumenicity which had become part of the non-Roman Christian world during the present century and reflected the yearnings of Christians everywhere for unity. To be sure, with the decision of the council to approve of ecumenism the church did not become a member of the World Council of Churches which has been the official expression of ecumenism since 1948 and which embraces all non-Roman confessions. But she became at least a partner in the ecumenical dialogue which has occupied the other churches since the beginning of this century.

This fact alone is reason enough for non-Roman Christendom to pay close attention to the *Decretum de Oecumenismo*. Christians should study and examine the text of the decree carefully. They should find ways to respond to it. Although the decree is primarily directed to the members of the Roman Church, it is also addressed indirectly to members of other churches, because it discusses the attitude of the Roman Church toward the others.

It is not our task to write a commentary on this decree. Such a scholarly commentary can be written only after the various drafts of this decree *(schemata)*, the introductory reports *(relationes)* with which these drafts were presented at the council, and the various opinions *(vota)* expressed at the council have been made available to the public. For our purposes we shall look only at the basic concepts involved in this important decree, such as the relationship between the canonical and dogmatic exclusiveness expressed in the self-understanding of the Roman general synods and the new understanding of ecumenicity as it is represented in the thought and life of the ecumenical movement outside of Rome and as it has been adopted by the Second Vatican Council. First, however, permit me to make a few hermeneutical remarks.

I. Problems Connected with the Interpretation of the Decree

The impressive struggle of the Second Vatican Council to come to terms with ecumenism was carried on both within the council hall and in public discussions. Expectations and evaluations differed considerably. On the one hand, there were the extreme optimists who stated that now all important obstacles to reunion have been removed and that reunion was close at hand. On the other hand, there were the extreme pessimists who evaluated the decree and found that basically nothing had changed and that the relationship between the churches had become even more difficult because it was confronted by the new ecumenical program of the Roman Church. Between these two extremes a variety of more or less confident or reserved judgments made their appearance. Therefore it is advisable, first of all, to clarify the most important ways of interpreting this decree, for without a doubt the great differences in the evaluations with which this decree has been greeted are in part due to a lack of clarity on this point.

1. We find that quite often this decree is being interpreted in isolation as if it were the single theme given to the council. But ecumenism was only *one* of the themes of the council. There are many others. Remember that the Decree on Ecumenism is surrounded by a number of constitutions, decrees, declarations, and opinions which are just as important as the Decree on Ecumenism as far as the council fathers are concerned. Often the subject of these other constitutions, decrees, etc., is so closely tied to the text of the Decree on Ecumenism that the latter cannot be interpreted correctly apart from the former. This is especially true of the important dogmatic *Constitutio de Ecclesia,* of the Constitution on Revelation, and

of the Decree on the Catholic Oriental Churches, i.e. the Uniates in communion with the pope. But even the Decree on the Lay Apostolate, the Proposals on Missionary Activity of the Church, the Declaration on the Freedom of Religion, and all the statements concerning the attitude toward the Jews and toward non-Christian religions, the *Votum* on Marriage and—last but not least—the schema on the Presence of the Church in the Contemporary World, make their impact upon the Decree on Ecumenism. We should not overlook the relationship between the Decree on Ecumenism and all those other documents. For whatever answers the council gives to the questions concerning religious freedom, mixed marriage, and cooperation of Christians on the mission fields must be accepted as authentic interpretations of the total ecumenical program of the Roman Church. In this connection it should also be remembered that of the numerous schemata submitted to the council for action, only the Decree on Ecumenism, the Constitutions on the Church and on the Liturgy, and the Decrees on Mass Media and on the Oriental Churches have been accepted by the council and propagated by the pope and are thus the law of the church. The other schemata have been discussed by the council fathers but have not yet been accepted.

2. A greater importance has often been attributed to the Decree on Ecumenism than to other decisions of the council. The dogmatic Constitution on the Church is thereby minimized, for this has been more strongly influenced by the conservative theologians and presents a narrower concept of the church than the Decree on Ecumenism. The high evaluation that has been made of the Decree on Ecumenism has been defended by the opinion, advanced during the second session of the council, that there is no clarity concerning the question whether a decree or a constitution has more binding force. Some fathers were interested in the possibility that the statements of the decree which are much more open toward other churches might prevail in the future against the *Constitutio de Ecclesia* which presents a narrower concept of the church. There is a great lack of clarity at this council on the question of the importance of the various constitutions, decrees, propositions, declarations, and opinions of the fathers and their relationship to each other. Future theologians will not have an easy task.

The question of the degree of importance of the various pronouncements of the council will be discussed in commentaries long after the council has been adjourned. But it would seem that much can be said for the opinion that a dogmatic constitution has more binding force than a decree. Moreover, during the third session the relationship of the Decree on Ecumenism to the Constitution on the Church has been decided definitely in favor of the constitution. The explanation with which the *Schema de Oecumenismo* was presented in its revised version declared that the Constitution on the Church is normative for the Decree on Ecumenism. In this way the text of the decree itself refers to the Constitution on the Church (End of 1). Therefore we must conclude that the Decree on Ecumenism must be interpreted on the basis of the statements found in the Constitution on the Church, and not vice versa.

3. Differences in the interpretation of the decree have also arisen because some people understand the decree less on the basis of its written text from the ecumenical dynamism which it represents. They are impressed by the ecumenical spirit that has taken hold of the Roman Church and that has developed progressively during the three sessions of the council. They see the meaning of the decree in the fact that closed doors are being opened by it and that ecumenism has been recognized as legitimate for the first time in the history of the Roman Catholic Church. They feel that the actual wording of the decree is of lesser importance since this remains both in goals and outlook far behind the impulses which have been loosened in the Roman Catholic Church by the advance guard of ecumenism. Thus the cautious phraseology and the great reserve of the decree are to be explained by the fact that the fathers of the council were concerned to win over the whole Roman Church to the new ecumenical ideas. In this way the decree is interpreted less as a text than as a historical phenomenon, namely the breakthrough and unfolding of ecumenism within the Roman Catholic Church. True, the decree must be interpreted against this backdrop as a part of the total dramatic happenings at the council. But even when doing this we recognize that only an interpretation of the decree which takes its text seriously can claim any reliability.

It is quite clear that strongly forward-pressing ecumenical forces have taken hold of the thinking of the fathers during the first three sessions of the council. This has become quite clear from the many opinions which were submitted during the sessions and the various corrections and improvements which have been made in the text of the decree. The council considered a total of four drafts of the schema. The second and third drafts incorporated the opinions which had been offered in the previous sessions. In the work of trying to assimilate and incorporate these thousands of *vota* the Secretariat for Christian Unity did a piece of outstanding work. Both the second and the third drafts showed important improvements in ecumenical openness. On the other hand, it must also be mentioned that beginning with the second draft some of the statements in the schema were substantially weakened, in order to make the originally indeterminate and therefore open understanding of the church fit more closely the narrower concept of the church found in the *Constitutio de Ecclesia*. Thus the decree was clearly subordinated to the constitution.

The council fathers and the observers were greatly surprised when the third draft, which had already been accepted by the council and whose three chapters had passed by an overwhelming vote, was changed at the last minute by direct intervention in the name of the "highest authority" of the pope. The changes made before the final acceptance of the decree disappointed the ecumenical expectations of many fathers. To be sure, most of the changes were of a stylistic nature, but some of them very definitely narrowed the ecumenical openings which had been established during the previous discussions. For example, the statement on the Lord's Supper as celebrated in the churches of the Reformation was altered in such a way as was also the statement concerning biblical scholarship in the non-Roman churches. Of course, we must not overemphasize the import of these changes, for on the whole they were not essential. Other statements which might be interpreted as being much more favorable toward the non-Roman churches were left unchanged. But it became clear that the ecumenical dynamics did not overcome the slowing-down tactics of the Roman conservatives. This was made clear especially during the last few days of the third session when there occurred a number of surprising interferences. The forces of conservatism were stronger than many had expected. The centralized structure of the Roman Church was not changed in favor of the definition of collegiality of pope and bishops.

After what has happened, it is impossible to prophesy what will happen. It is not clear which opportunities will be given to the ecumenical movement within the Roman Catholic Church and whether in the future anything will be permitted that goes beyond the Decree on Ecumenism. Under these conditions the only interpretation of the decree which can claim reliability is one which refuses either optimistic or pessimistic prognoses and hews close to the line laid down in the text of the decree. In this type of evaluation all preceding *relationes, vota,* and revisions of the drafts will have to be taken into account. But one should not expect that the directives for the execution of the decree which are now in preparation, i.e. the scheduled *Directio* for Ecumenical Action, will go beyond the framework that has been established in the decree itself. Those who have followed the discussions of the council have gained the impression that the council has gone as far in giving definitions of ecumenism as can be done at the present time without endangering the consensus of the bishops. The statements of the decree have been formulated with great care.

4. Differences in the interpretation of the decree will finally arise on the basis of the evaluation of the council as a whole. In part the council is called bold and progressive. In part it is called timid and reactionary. Some discern in it an understanding of the principle of ecumenism, some merely a resigned acceptance of changed realities. It may mark the beginning of a new relationship to other churches, or it may mean only the change in Rome's methods of operation. Aside from the fact that such evaluations should be the result of a careful interpretation of all conciliar decrees and not merely preconceived prejudices, none of these generalizations, whether positive or negative, will do justice to the complexity of the council. It is useful to differentiate measuring sticks and different points of view which are the basis for such an evaluation.

If, for example, one compares the decisions of the council with the conditions prevalent in Roman Catholicism before the Second Vatican Council, one is impelled to state with great respect and even with admiration that almost all the problems which the Roman Church had to face were attacked and tackled by the fathers. Furthermore, this work was done with readiness to be reoriented. The general congregations of the council worked with great seriousness and tremendous care in their various commissions and conferences. Bishops and theologians wrestled with these questions and carefully worked out the various arguments and without a doubt have made great progress if one compares the work of the council with the general conditions in the Roman Church until recently. Just think for a moment about the impact of the Constitution on the Sacred Liturgy which has introduced the use of the vernacular into the mass and even opened up the possibility of celebrating Holy Communion under two kinds and reduced the abuses inherent in the simultaneous celebration of several masses by several priests officiating in one church. Or think about the statements concerning religious freedom—not yet officially promulgated—or the directives which are being planned for the distribution and general use of the Bible.

But our evaluation will be different if we compare the actions and decisions of the council with the order of service in the other churches. Both the Eastern churches and the churches of the Reformation have been conducting their services in the vernacular from the very beginning and have been celebrating Holy Communion under two kinds. They also have rejected the celebration of masses without Communion. The basic ideas concerning freedom of religion, the instructions concerning the distribution and use of the Bible, are nothing new to these churches. New is merely the fact that the *Roman* Church has finally decided to accept these ideas. The other churches may ask the question why the Roman Church has waited until now to take these necessary steps. They may ask why Rome has rejected freedom of religion and the work of non-Roman Bible Societies until now.

Again our evaluation will be different if we ask ourselves of what importance the event of the council is for the non-Christian world. Will the event of the council be interpreted as a merely sensational demonstration by an ancient, but foreign, Western institution? Or will the council be able to give a clear witness to Jesus Christ and break through the wall that surrounds the Christian Church by touching the hearts of unbelievers?

Any fair evaluation of the council must distinguish between these various ways of evaluating the *Decretum de Oecumenismo*. In spite of this the viewpoints just outlined cannot be separated and isolated from each other. All of us Christians find ourselves in one boat. What is happening in one church concerns also the other churches. If anything positive is accomplished in the council of the Roman Church, this accomplishment also means joy and encouragement to other churches. On the other hand, it would be a loss for all churches if the witness which has been given at the council for Christ were not able to break through the walls into the world. For we are concerned about one and the same Christ whose lordship all of us have to proclaim in our relationship to the world.

II. The Practice of Ecumenism

The second chapter of the Decree on Ecumenism bears the title "De Exercitio Oecumenismi." In an impressive simplicity it gives instructions for the implementation of the decree which may lead, ecumenically speaking, farther than anything else in the council's documents. These instructions have been improved constantly since the first draft was submitted. For example, later drafts added the thought that the church on her pilgrimage is called "to a continuing reformation" (6). Later drafts also make reference to 1 John 1:10: "If we say we have not sinned, we make him a liar, and his word is not in us" and apply it to the sin against the unity of the church. The fathers state: "In great humility we ask God and the separated brethren for forgiveness as we also forgive those who have sinned against us" (7). Although the instructions given in this chapter are addressed to members of the Roman Catholic Church, they apply in their essential parts also to members of other churches and should be taken to heart by them. They spell out matters which are most important in the relationship between separated Christians. Unfortunately the things which are most important in our mutual relationships are not always present in reality. But when we practice the basic directives for the ecumenical stance we may expect that on both sides of the fence new fields that have not borne fruit in the past will be plowed anew. Thus this chapter shows in an especially impressive way the seriousness of the ecumenical yearning which influenced both the Secretariat for

Christian Unity and many of the council fathers. Every member of the Roman Church is told to take to heart the following:

1. The spiritual renewal of the heart (6). Without conversion, sanctification, self-denial, humility, readiness to serve and dialogue with the separated brethren, a growing in love, and a search for unity, ecumenism is impossible. True ecumenism is always an acceptance of repentance. Ecumenism must not begin with a demand made upon the separated brethren to repent of their sins, but with repentance in one's own church. It does not issue an order to others to change, but shows readiness to change one's own heart.

2. Prayer for unity (7) and, if possible, common prayer with the separated brethren. Although it was brought out during the discussions in the council that common prayer is deceptive because everyone would be praying according to his own preconceived intentions—the Romans would certainly pray for the return of the separated brethren to the fold—Cardinal Bea answered, paraphrasing Couturier, that it is sufficient to know that everyone who prays leaves it to God to decide when and in which way a more complete unity can be established. He knows better than those who are praying. It was made clear that this common prayer, which is recommended, is distinct from the holding of union services for which bishops may give permission only in exceptional cases.

3. Careful attention must be given to the doctrine, worship, piety, and the historical and cultural bases of the faith of the separated brethren. In this connection the council called for a broadening in the education of priests (10).

4. The dialogue with the separated brethren must be carried on on the basis of equality (9, 11). In this dialogue the Roman doctrine should be presented clearly and in a way that can be readily understood by the separated brethren. Irenics and polemics must be eliminated from such dialogue. The dialogue would first be carried on primarily on a scholarly level by theologians and not the church as such. In this statement concerning the dialogue as it appeared in the first draft of the schema it was not in this way merely a matter of presenting Catholic truth to the dialogue partner, or whether one could engage in a common attempt to find the truth. But it is quite clear that in any dialogue there will be a

search for truth, there will be common questions and common investigations. For it is not we ourselves who hold the truth, but the truth takes hold of us. There were some voices heard in the council which demanded that Roman scholars should engage in a common search for truth with the separated brethren. Auxiliary Bishop Elchinger of Strasbourg offered an impressive array of criteria that should apply to such an ecumenical conversation. Thus in the final draft of the decree there is mention of a common search with the separated brethren. This search must deal with "the divine mysteries" with the goal that "all involved in this fraternal rivalry may be incited to a deeper realization and a clearer presentation of the unsearchable riches of Christ." The following instruction will be especially helpful: "In comparing the various doctrines with each other we must not forget that according to Roman Catholic doctrine there exists a 'hierarchy' of various truths, depending on how closely these truths are related to the foundation of the Christian faith." But this understanding of a "hierarchy" of truths can be applied only to a systematic evaluation of the contents of the dogmas, and not to their validity because there is no distinction in binding force between central and peripheral dogmas. All are equally binding in Roman theology.

Let us stop here for a minute. As we look back at the extreme reluctance of the Roman Catholic Church to enter into dialogue with other churches, these instructions of the Second Vatican Council mean more than may appear to the casual observer. Their special importance for our time lies in the fact that they are no mere words which hover somewhere in space, but must be understood in the light of the concrete happenings at the council. They are not just "pious wishes," but an expression of the real accomplishment of this council and of something that we as observers at the council have experienced again and again in our meetings with the fathers and the theologians of the Roman Church. A new dialogue has begun which is based on mutual esteem, love, and frankness and is wrestling with the problem of "what is truth."

5. Further emphasis is given to the demand that Roman Catholics cooperate with the separated brethren (12). This cooperation extends especially to social questions, to problems connected with

the technological evolution and the overcoming of the conditions and shortcomings of the present age, e.g. the fight against illiteracy. The examples given in these directives were at first kept within the limits of natural law. But during the discussions the council went a step farther, including the service work of the church in the under-developed countries as one of the places where cooperation between Protestants and Roman Catholics might help to solve the problems facing Christians, e.g., in Africa. An ecumenical offering, similar to the one suggested by Oscar Cullmann, was recommended where Catholics would have an opportunity to help Protestants, and vice versa.

The final draft of the decree also mentioned the duty of Christians to give a common confession of faith. "All Christians should confess before the world their faith in the Triune God, and in the incarnate Son of God, our Redeemer and Lord. United in their efforts . . . let them give common witness of the hope which will not disappoint us." This willingness of the council to advocate a common witness for Christ in union with non-Roman Christians is very important for the future of ecumenism.

6. If we ask further what the Decree on Ecumenism says concerning the many tensions which make the living-together of Roman Catholics and non-Roman Christians at times difficult and which often give the lie to the talk about Christian unity, we should consider carefully the controversial proposal *"De Libertate Religiosa."* There may be a great number of reasons for this belated interest of the Roman Church in religious freedom. Nowadays the Roman Church needs this freedom as much as do the non-Roman communions. Her freedom is threatened not only behind the Iron Curtain, but also by the nationalist movements of the younger nations which have just recently cast off their colonial yoke. Yet it should be admitted that the call for freedom of religion has also been raised in those parts of the world where the Roman Catholic Church predominates. In some cases, as in the case of Protestant Christians in Spain, there has already been an improvement in the conditions of the non-Roman minority. This is to a large extent due to the impact of the council. It was made clear in various opinions presented to the council that an understanding of, and an esteem

for, believers who are not Roman Catholic is a necessary presupposition for ecumenism. This includes freedom of religion. There was a great deal of resistance to this chapter, but the majority of the council fathers were for it. They were tremendously disturbed in the council hall when near the end of the third session the vote on this schema was suddenly postponed.

There are no directives in the Decree on Ecumenism for the removal of certain difficulties between separated brethren. For example, the Roman Catholic practice concerning mixed marriages has not been touched upon. Changes were proposed, but a schema on matrimony was referred, after a brief discussion in the council, to the discretion of the pope. Many council fathers sincerely hope for a change in the present practices as tangible evidence that ecumenism is at work even in this area. Indeed they admit that it is irreconcilable with the ecumenical stance when a marriage between two pagans is recognized as marriage, while a marriage between two baptized Christians belonging to two Christian communions is declared to be a concubinage unless it is contracted before a Catholic priest according to the Roman rite.

Also not mentioned in the *schema* is the necessity of eliminating the competition among the various churches in the mission fields. There is no attempt to eliminate the duplication of missionary work in any country or even to decrease such competitive efforts. It is to be hoped that this question will be aired in a schema on missions which is scheduled to be submitted in the final session of the council.

Furthermore, there is not a word about restricting conditional Baptism which the Roman Catholic Church practices in many parts of the world even when she is reasonably sure that the newly converted Catholic has been baptized in the name of the Triune God. Thus, for example, the rebaptism of the Dutch Princess Irene, administered by Cardinal Alfrink of Utrecht during the council session, troubled those who would like to believe in the assurances of Roman ecumenism that true ecumenism, including Roman ecumenism, begins with Baptism. It is based on a Baptism that is recognized by Rome and the separated churches.

Thus the instructions of the Decree on Ecumenism concerning

the ecumenical stance of Roman Catholicism represent the very first steps. Without a doubt these instructions are of great importance. They may even be considered revolutionary by many Catholic theologians and lay people. But between these very first steps and the desired unity there is a stretch of the way. Unity cannot be expected unless there is a rapprochement, a conscious elimination of the most difficult stumbling-blocks to peaceful life together among brethren. Only then will a common witness to Christ become a reality. Such a witness all Christians who have been baptized owe to God and the world. However, other proposals which are now before the council waiting for adoption offer a possibility for such a progress in the ecumenical stance of the Roman Church.

III. The Goal of Unity

The avowed goal of Roman ecumenism is the unity of the separated churches, or more precisely, the reunion of the non-Roman churches with Rome. To be sure, reunion was not the *immediate* goal of the Second Vatican Council. Its primary concern was the renewal of the Roman Catholic Church. But the goal of reunion was always present during the first three council sessions and it was expected as one of the *results* of Roman renewal. One major purpose for the renewal of the church was to present a better image of the Roman Church to the separated brethren and to open the doors of the church wide so that they may return home to the Catholic household. Thus the aim of Roman ecumenism is a sequence of coordinated goals. It is quite in keeping with this aim that the renewal of their own church was the chief goal of the Roman Catholic bishops. This renewal emphasis corresponds to what is said in the unity dialogue among the other churches. We can look upon the seriousness and the humility with which the council fathers undertook their task only with the highest esteem and admiration.

1. The Renewal of the Roman Catholic Church

The insistence on renewal as we find it spelled out in the Decree on Ecumenism is not addressed to individual members of the Roman Church but to the Roman Catholic Church as a whole (4, 6). The decree states that "Christ summons the Church, as she goes her pilgrim way, to that continual reformation of which she always has need, in so far as she is an institution of men here on earth. Consequently, if, in various times and circumstances, there have been deficiencies in moral conduct or in church discipline, or even in the way that church teaching has been formulated—to be carefully distinguished from the deposit of faith itself—these should be set right at the opportune moment and in the proper way." As a matter of fact, the demand for the renewal of the church was presented in so many opinions during the discussions of the council and was accepted so willingly by the fathers (demand for an up-to-date theological language, a streamlined ecclesiastical structure, elimination of pomp and circumstance in the church, etc.) that the topic of renewal has long since passed the stage of mere discussion and has widely become a fact. There were moving expressions of this new attitude when, for example, the father spoke freely, without any attempt to whitewash history, of the times when the church had failed the world and the separated brethren. In several of the opinions there was express reference to the words from the opening address of Pope Paul VI in which the need for mutual forgiveness was stressed. The objection raised by some conservatives that all this talk about the share which the Roman Catholic Church bears in the guilt of the schism caused uncertainty within the church and that those who cannot get rid of their guilt complex should see their father-confessor—this was said by Bishop Muldoon of Sydney, Australia—was definitely not shared by the majority of the fathers. Presiding Abbot Butler of England stated that a public and sincere admission of guilt was the first step before one can begin to talk about reunion. In spite of all the discouraging aspects of slow progress, a movement of renewal has undoubtedly broken through at many points.

A renewal in the thinking of the church was also evident during the struggle concerning the order of the church. The council tried its best to move away from the centralized structure of the church by emphasizing the collegiality of the bishops. It wanted to make clear to the world that in place of strict uniformity there is room for diversity within the church. I was impressed by the way in which the morning masses during the council sessions presented various types of the liturgy, most of them in the vernacular languages. Add to this the long discussions concerning the collegial administration of the church together with her liturgical and canonical renewal, then there is room for the expectation that a renewal of the church in the right direction will take place.

However, the scope of this renewal is limited by the dogmas of the church. Thus the liturgical reforms do not in any way repeal the doctrine of the sacrifice of the Mass as it was codified at Trent. Likewise, a discussion of Mariology both within the framework of the Constitution on the Church and outside of it, cannot change the doctrinal definitions of 1854 and 1950. At the beginning of the council the fathers re-affirmed the conciliar oath, and during the celebrations marking the four-hundredth anniversary of the Council of Trent they expressly reiterated their acceptance of the dogmatic decisions of that council together with all its anathemas against the doctrines of the non-Roman communions. The statements of faith promulgated at Trent and the corresponding anathemas are the greatest stumbling-block against reunion. The most that can be expected of this council is that it will not formulate new dogmas and thus deepen the chasm between the churches. But we cannot hope for an abrogation of the anathemas in order to make possible the reunion with the non-Roman churches. To be sure, we see today in both Protestant and Roman Catholic theology our task in a re-interpretation of these old dogmatic statements and in explaining them in their historical setting. We are trying to translate the thinking of former times into the problematic of our times. There is a possibility for such a new interpretation of dogmatic expressions and for a better understanding of them, which may lead us to a consensus with the separated brethren of the Roman Church. But this insight into the historical background of Roman Catholic dogmas and this possibility of a modern interpretation of them has not been attempted by this council, as far as I can see. For example, no attempt was made at any time to differentiate between more important and less important dogmas and to determine their binding force upon the church. Such a distinction is, however, possible on the basis of our confession in Jesus Christ. But the council was silent on this point.

2. The Development of the Catholicity of the Roman Church

The catholicity of the Roman Church, too, is superimposed upon the goal of reunion. It is closely tied up with the Roman renewal.

An unfolding of this catholicity would mean first of all a readiness to give greater freedom to various expressions of Roman Catholic spiritual life, to the theological output of the Church, etc. But it also would force the church to recognize the "riches of Christ and the virtuous works" in the life of the separated brethren (4). As long as the Roman Church interprets her existence as being exclusively *the one* Catholic Church she will be able to recognize in the separated churches only the means and the effects of grace which she recognizes as elements of her own dogmatic and canonical structure. There are, however, indications that in the Roman Church an understanding for the spiritual realities in other churches is opening up. Many Roman Catholics do not only recognize those expressions of the spiritual life in other churches which are present in the Roman Church, but also those elements which are part of catholicity in the widest sense of the word. More and more people recognize that true "catholicity" is wrought by God and is greater than anything that has been actualized in any one church, including the Roman Catholic Church. The schisms have made it "difficult" for the Roman Catholic Church "to express the fulness of her catholicity in the various aspects of the reality of her life" (4).

The obligation of the church to open her windows and doors and to accept as true expressions of Catholic life those spiritual values which are found in other churches is seen more and more clearly. These include biblical interpretation, concern and experience in the field of social obligations, etc. Even before the theme of ecumenism was accepted some of the Reformation hymns had found their entrance into Roman Catholic hymnals, and methods and results of Protestant biblical research, including problems connected with systematic and ecumenical theology, had been accepted by Roman scholars. One striking example was the acceptance of the theme of the role of lay people in the church. Included in this rapprochement was also a re-evaluation of the liturgy, of the theology of the fathers, and of mysticism in the Eastern churches. This opening of the windows is now being carried out systematically at the council. Thus it is hoped that the catholicity of the Roman Catholic

Church will be unfolded as much as it is possible under the existing conditions. In this connection it might be mentioned that there have been some sharp words of criticism in the council hall in regard to the practice of forcing uniformity and Latinization upon the Eastern Uniate churches.

But these attempts to "broaden the view" of the Roman Church are, of course, limited by the dogmatical definitions and by canon law. It may, however, be possible that a widening of the boundaries of catholicity will take place which will lead farther than can be deduced logically on the basis of the existing dogmatic and canonical positions of the Roman Church.

3. The Concept of the Union of the Separated Churches

In the presence of all the differences in their statements concerning the mystery of the church and concerning the evaluation of the churches which are separated from Rome, the council fathers are agreed on one point: That the unity of the church exists in the Roman Church and that therefore true and genuine union can be only a reunion within the boundaries of the Roman Catholic Church. It is the goal of *Roman* ecumenism that "all Christians will be gathered, in a common celebration of the Eucharist, into the unity of the one and only Church, which Christ bestowed on His Church from the beginning. This unity, we believe, subsists in the Catholic Church as something she can never lose" (4). To accomplish a complete union of the Christian Church it is necessary to confess the one faith and to participate in the celebration of the one Christian worship, to accept the communion of the sacramental life and unity in the direction of this church. This means acceptance of the primacy of the Roman bishop in matters of faith and discipline according to the decrees of the First Vatican Council.

This is not a new goal. Yet we do not do justice to the Decree on Ecumenism if we see in it only an invitation to return to the Roman Catholic Church, repeated here with other methods and under a different name. We must not overlook the fact that ecumenism means very different things to different people. Also the return to a unity which is found in the Roman Church is not always the same. There is a difference whether it takes place under present conditions or at some time in the future when that church has been truly "renewed" through a far-reaching renewal. For example, if the primacy of the pope is understood in the sense in which it was promulgated at the First Vatican Council, it will be impossible to accept the invitation to return. But it is a different matter if the pope is *primus inter pares*. It is also a different matter whether the return to Rome is understood as a mere return to Roman jurisdiction, or as a mutual reconciliation between the Roman Church and the others. We must also ask the question whether according to Roman understanding the others become "churches" only by return. The idea of a "return" to the Roman fold has not wholly vanished from the various opinions presented to the council and in the various papal pronouncements. On the other hand, the offensive word "return" has been avoided in the discussions of many important members of the council and especially of the theologians. We should not look upon this courtesy as a mere tactical maneuver, but accept it as an indication of a better understanding of the fact that both historically and ecclesiologically "return" is not an adequate designation of Christian unity.

The goal of Christian unity depends very much upon the depth of the renewal of the Roman Church and how inclusive her understanding of catholicity will be in the future. We must ask the question whether this renewal and this "opening up" of the Roman Church has been accomplished by this council, or whether the full solution of these problems has to await a future day.

a) Those who are convinced that the Roman Church in her present form is a renewed and fully Catholic church will interpret the call to reunion to mean a return to the Roman Church. The Roman Church stands ready to give of her riches to those who are lacking in them. Many of the fathers of the council probably voted for the decree because they interpreted it in this way. This attitude leads to the danger that the Roman Church may feel that she has done all that could be done. She has issued a general invitation to return. If this invitation is not accepted, there is bound, on the basis of this attitude, to be a new sense of disappointment which will heighten the consciousness of separation among the Christian churches.

b) But suppose the Roman Church looks upon this Decree on Ecumenism as a mere beginning. The renewal of the church is still to come. Thus the call to reunion is not the result of the Roman renewal, but a call to all Christians to have a change of heart, to engage in dialogue, to talk with the separated brethren. It is not a call to "return," but to "reconciliation." It is not a call to become subject to Rome, but to receive mutual benefits from each other. It is a call for the restoration of Christian communion, not a one-sided giving by the Roman Church, but a mutual giving and receiving. If we understand the call to reunion in this way, then there is room for a discovery of each other's spiritual heritage, for a rapprochement, for cooperation whose end cannot be determined now and whose road cannot be chartered in advance. It will be a way toward reunion which will be charted by the Holy Spirit. It is true that also in this interpretation of the Decree on Ecumenism it is assumed that the dogma of the Roman Church and the claim of papal primacy remain unchanged. But this fact does not exclude the possibility of a new interpretation or a different expression of the dogmas of the church and of their relation to reunion.

c) But there are also theologians and lay people within the Roman Catholic Church who are less definite in their understanding of future Christian unity than are the Decree on Ecumenism and the Constitution on the Church. They are completely open on the question of the way this goal may be reached and even concerning the goal itself. They are open to the Holy Spirit who cannot be put into the straitjacket of canon law. In their view it seems possible that changes will take place within the dogmatic structure of the church which factually are not merely the result of reinterpretations, but of corrections of existing dogmas. This avoidance of a dogmatically and canonically fixed conception of unity opens up, in the widest and most immediate sense, a way for mutual giving and taking. It establishes a communion which essentially is a yearning for the realization of unity in confession, in the sacraments, and in the understanding of the ministerial office in the church. It is a communion between separated Christians that prays for a God-pleasing order by which this yearning for unity might be satisfied.

The Decree on Ecumenism leaves open the door for very different understandings of Christian unity and its desired goal. On the whole, the text of the document seems to point toward the second understanding (b) without, however, completely excluding the first (a). The weakest link in the decree, and especially in the Constitution on the Church, is the fact that it disregards the third possibility (c). Those who advocate the third possibility may be tolerated in the Roman Church at least for part of the way, because the presuppositions of the Decree on Ecumenism allow this. This is related to the fact that the council lacks clarity concerning the question where ecumenism ends and where the work of conversion begins (4).

The hope that in the future there will be an expansion of the possibilities for dialogue will always be with us. But in the meantime the non-Roman churches can take for granted only the present realities of the Roman Catholic Church. They must recognize soberly that the recognition of *all* Roman dogmas including the *primacy of the pope* and the *full* implications of the definition of papal infallibility proclaimed by the First Vatican Council is the Roman *conditio sine qua non* for reunion.

IV. Possibilities and Limitations of Ecumenism

The goal of Roman ecumenism was determined by decisions, both dogmatic and canonical, which had been made before the convocation of the Second Vatican Council. These dogmas are not subject to correction. Neither are the stipulations of the canon law insofar as they are considered divine law. To be sure, the Roman Catholic Church differentiates between the historical background and the lasting validity of the contents of these documents of an earlier era. But while proclaiming that dogmas as such cannot be changed, the church also admits that it is possible to meet with the other churches and to discuss their dogmas and orders. Undoubtedly there are many and great opportunities here that have not been utilized by the Roman Church until now. Even so, the limitations of dogma and canon law impose upon her a narrowness from which she cannot escape. This is not because she is bound to her dogmas with special stringency—other churches are bound also— but because she has evaluated herself in such a limited way and has established such a comprehensive system of canon law and dogma with all the numerous anathemas that she has separated herself from all the other churches more radically than any other church has ever done. This hampers now her ability to assume the ecumenical stance. She is hamstrung more than other churches.

There is much to indicate that this ecumenical dilemma of the Roman Church was clear to Pope John XXIII when he instructed the council—called by him in part to begin the ecumenical dialogue—that it should employ pastoral language in its discussions and should not attempt to define a new dogma. The non-Roman churches must recognize this desire of Pope John and accept it as a sign of his ecumenical concern. Also the successor of John XXIII has refrained, until now, from defining a new dogma and has thus avoided the temptation to deepen the abyss existing between the Roman Church and the non-Roman churches. This fact should be recognized by the other churches in gratitude, especially since there had been within Roman Catholicism, including also in the council hall, considerable agitation in favor of defining a new Marian dogma. The council, however, has steadfastly resisted this agitation. It is true that in the last chapter of the *Constitutio de Ecclesia* Mary is called the *Mediatrix*, and that in the final meeting of the Third Session Pope Paul VI went out of his way to proclaim Mary the "Mother of the Church." But these developments do not represent a solemn definition of dogma, although we must realize that they may well prepare the way for such a definition at a later date and thus may lay the groundwork for an even wider separation between the churches. Furthermore, there is no clarity about the question whether the Constitution on the Church does or does not contain any definitions of dogma. In the third chapter of this constitution, dealing with the hierarchical structure of the church and especially the office of bishop, we find the words: "This Holy Synod teaches and solemnly declares." Thus there is room for the assumption that this part of the constitution has the same force as a solemn dogmatic definition. But even if this unlikely interpretation of the constitution should prevail, there is nothing in the introductory sentences of the *Constitutio de Ecclesia* that would go beyond the dogmatic definitions of the First Vatican Council and increase difficulties in relationship to the other churches.

In spite of these factors we cannot overlook the fact that the Constitution on the Church which has been accepted by the council and has been promulgated by the pope, even if it should not be considered dogma in the traditional sense of the word—i.e., binding without a chance for correction—still has great binding power for the doctrinal development of the church and her actions. Without a doubt it is more binding than a papal encyclical. To this we must add that for most non-Roman Christians the fine distinctions in the authority of the whole "hierarchy" of Roman Catholic teachings are far less important than the contents of such teaching. They look at these documents as expressions of opinions that are dear to the hearts of those who draw them up. Therefore the *Constitutio de Ecclesia* is indeed very important for the future development of ecumenism. This is true all the more because the Roman Church, as well as all other churches, has never defined a clear doctrine of the church. We could ask the question: "What possibilities does this constitution offer for an understanding and for the application of the ecumenical program? Does it indicate a step forward or a step back for the ecumenical movement which has now finally begun to take hold of the Roman Church and has been recognized by her?"

It is not our task here to evaluate the Constitution on the Church in its entirety. Our interest is centered on its bases for ecumenism. We are looking for statements concerning the doctrine of the church and the collegiality of the bishops. Even in this brief discussion we must not overlook the fact that this constitution marks a considerable progress over against the *Schema de Ecclesia* which had been prepared for the First Vatican Council but was not acted on by it, except for its doctrine on the primacy of the pope. This progress can be seen especially in the statements concerning the history of salvation and the Trinity which are the basis for the statements concerning the church, and in the purposeful introduction of a number of concepts and images under which the church is here described, concepts taken from the New Testament, such as "the Body of Christ," the "People of God," the "Sheepfold of God," the "Vineyard of God," the "Temple of the Holy Spirit," the "Bride of Christ," etc. In this connection it is important that in the final version of the *Constitutio de Ecclesia* the church is described—in the second chapter—as the People of God, i.e. she is discussed under this concept *before* the hierarchy of the church which dominates the last chapters of the document. Also in the statements concerning the collegiality of the bishops there is a clear indication that the essence of the church has been understood more clearly in the frame of reference of the New Testament and of the ancient church. We must also emphasize the fact that an attempt was made to bring out the eschatological aspect of the church as a people on the pilgrimage, although in the seventh chapter dealing with eschatology there is greater interest for the present unity of the church on pilgrimage with the church in heaven, for the communion of saints on earth with saints above, than for the perfection which she will not possess until the day of judgment. Yet other facets can be accepted with joy by non-Roman theologians.

But at the same time it is only fair to point out that the limitations of this document are manifold. The concept of the church is decidedly a narrow one. To be sure, many a church believes that she is the Holy, Catholic, and Apostolic Church which we confess. But among non-Roman Christians this statement is understood in a quite different way. The identification of an existing church body with the one and holy church does not have to be interpreted in an exclusive way as is done in Roman Catholicism. It is possible that a certain church should confess her identity with the one holy church and at the same time accept other churches as parts of this same one holy church. But the Constitution on the Church, promulgated by the Second Vatican Council, understands this identity with the one holy church quite exclusively as being vested in the Roman Church, although the final draft of the schema substitutes for the former exclusive statement that the one holy church "*is* the Catholic Church which is directed by the Roman Pontiff and the bishops who are in communion with him (*est ecclesia catholica*)" the more general statement that the church "*subsists* in the Catholic Church which is directed by the successor of St. Peter and by the bishops who are in communion with him (*subsistit in ecclesia catholica*)." But the very next sentence makes it clear that "outside of this communion" of the Roman Church there are found merely "elements of holiness and truth" which "as a gift given to the church by Christ press toward catholic unity." There is no statement that the One Holy Catholic and Apostolic *Church* exists outside of the Church of Rome. This point is also brought out in the statements concerning the mystery of the church, found in the first chapter of the constitution, which reiterate with a certain onesided emphasis the traditional concepts of the Body of Christ, concepts which more than any other New Testament passages on the church express the unity of the Body of Christ with the visible church. In addition, chapters three to six of the constitution, in spite of the earlier emphasis on the people of God, place great stress on the hierarchical order of the church. The self-interpretation of the church, according to the *Constitutio de Ecclesia,* is extremely legalistic at the expense of pneumatology. The attempt to justify dogmatically the legalistic emphasis in Roman Catholicism as it has existed to the present time is quite clear. The council has changed canon law very little. The church remains exclusively the *one* holy church. Also the hope of the council fathers to change substantially the extremely centralized concept of the Roman Church in favor of a more biblical understanding based on the New Testament and on practices of the ancient church was dampened by a *Nota Praevia* which gave an authorized interpretation of the third chapter of the constitution prompted by the personal intervention of Pope Paul VI during the last few days of the third session.

In comparison with the draft of the Constitution on the Church the first draft of the schema on ecumenism was much more open. The first chapter of the schema dealt with the principles of ecumenism and discussed the question of the essence of the church. Statements were made here about the church in which the *Roman* Church was not even mentioned. Nowhere was she interpreted in an exclusive way. From the beginning there was great openness for the reality of the church outside of the narrow boundaries of Rome, and thereby greater respect was shown for the mysteries that pass all human understanding. The pope was not expressly mentioned, but only Peter whom the Lord had chosen from among the Twelve. He was chosen to preside over the College of Apostles and to strengthen each one in his faith. He was chosen to tend the sheep. Certainly this statement was not only historical. But the emphasis was on the historical basis as it had been present in the apostolic age and not on the Roman primacy as it developed in the West. This treatment of ecumenism opened up important avenues for a dialogue concerning a theme which has always been a controversial one in the church.

But the council criticized the ecclesiological basis of the schema on ecumenism quite harshly. Cardinal Frings of Cologne, Germany, stated that the document should express clearly the fact that the church does not have to await the one church in the future, since the church is adequately represented in the Roman Church as she is now constituted. She had been founded by Christ and built upon Peter, the rock. Frings stated that this was the church that would be perfected at the end of time. Other fathers too demanded that the schema should state more clearly that the unity of the church lies in her faith and her direction so that the separated brethren would not misunderstand the position of the Roman Church. The fathers criticized the fact that the schema did not proclaim the complete identity of the Mystical Body of Christ with the Roman Church as it had been taught in the encyclical *Mystici Corporis Christi*. They said that love for the separated brethren demanded a complete confession of the truth and should avoid the type of irenical statements contained in the schema. By not mentioning the primacy of the successors of Peter in the schema its authors had adopted a false ecumenical stance. Basic truths concerning the church had been omitted. The use of quotes from the Bible should not give rise to incorrect statements concerning controversial questions.

It is clear that these strong objections by the fathers are responsible for the fact that the final draft of the Decree on Ecumenism emphasizes again and again that the unity, the fullness and all the riches of the One Holy Catholic and Apostolic Church are found only in the Roman Church, of which the successor of Peter is the head. "Only through the Catholic Church of Christ which is the all-embracing means of salvation can one obtain the fulness of the means of salvation" (3). But even taking into account these statements, the Decree on Ecumenism is still more open toward the outside world than the Constitution on the Church. It has, however, been adjusted to resemble more the constitution than did its first draft.

What are the results of the acceptance of these ecclesiological presuppositions for the ecumenical dialogue of the Roman Church with the other churches?

1. The Basic Evaluation of Non-Roman Churches

Every dogmatic statement defining the self-understanding of a church contains, *implicite* and *explicite,* also a judgment concerning the ecclesiological status of other churches. For future ecumenical discussions these statements are of the greatest importance, for in them is expressed the degree of mutual understanding and trust which may be presupposed in any endeavor toward a rapprochement and elimination of existing controversies.

The *Schema de Ecclesia,* in the version presented to the second session of the council, spoke merely of non-Roman *Christians,* i.e. individuals outside of the Roman Church who through Baptism and the *votum ecclesiae* are united in spirit with the Roman Church. There was no talk of any non-Roman *Church* where they had received their baptism and through whose witness they had come to faith. The schema spoke, however, of the effect of the grace which those who had been baptized outside of the Roman Church had also received, and the language of the schema on this point was more encouraging than St. Augustine's who had given to such persons only the *sign* of Baptism, but not the *grace* of Baptism. In addition, the old Cyprian thesis *Extra ecclesiam nulla salus* had been in effect discarded. Yet this did not remove the stigma which recognized only non-Roman *Christians,* and not non-Roman *churches.* The churches were perhaps understood as the phenomena which they represent, but were not interpreted theologically. The so-called separated brethren are aware that they are members of those churches and that they have also become members of the Body of Christ through the ministry of their respective churches. They know that their membership in the Church of Christ is not based on their yearning to be reunited with Rome as had been imputed to them by the so-called "*Votum*-Theory."

The *Schema de Oecumenismo* went much farther from the very start. It spoke clearly of *churches* and *communions* outside of the Roman Church and emphasized in a positive way the effectiveness of the grace of God, not only in the individual non-Roman Christians, but also in those communions which are not united with Rome. It did not limit itself to the Sacrament of Baptism—which was rightly stressed as basic for the Christian life—but it pointed much farther toward many concrete means and applications by which the grace of God has become powerful in these non-Roman communities.

The question of how these non-Roman churches should be evaluated was hardly discussed during the consideration of the *Schema de Ecclesia*. It simply did not play an important enough part in it. Only occasionally did some father criticize the fact that it had limited its references to non-Roman individuals. Consequently we do not find any statement concerning non-Roman churches in the completed Constitution on the Church. The constitution is not interested in non-Roman churches as such, only in persons who are not in communion with Rome. Yet it mentions at one point that non-Roman Christians receive baptism and the other sacraments "in their own churches and ecclesial communities" (15).

In contrast, the discussion on the *Schema de Oecumenismo* took up the question of the ecclesiology of the non-Roman churches in full force. We noted especially those voices that declared that the designation of the churches of the Reformation as "communions" was not sufficient. Cardinal Koenig of Vienna, Austria, and others demanded that they should be called at least "ecclesial communities." A group of thirty Indonesian bishops requested that the churches of the Reformation should be designated as *churches,* a title given in the schema only to the Orthodox churches. This demand was supported by others, among them Bishop Helmsing of Kansas City. On the other hand, there were also voices that deplored the fact that the schema spoke too positively about the separated communions and attributed to them too many spiritual treasures. These conservatives warned against the danger of indifferentism among Roman Catholics.

When the final draft of the Decree on Ecumenism was submitted, it did not merely mention non-Roman Christians, but the churches and communions to which they belong and in which the spirit of Christ is working "as a means of grace." "These separated churches and communities are in spite of the shortcomings we have mentioned not without importance and significance in the Mystery of Salvation" (3). The suggestion by Cardinal Koenig had been accepted and in most places these non-Roman churches were referred to as "churches and *ecclesial* communities." It is not quite clear why some are called "churches" and others are called "ecclesial communities." This distinction is not based on their self-evaluation, but on the ecclesiological presuppositions of Roman theology. They are not on the same level with Rome, but receive the title *honoris causa* or by way of analogy. The failure to define these concepts more clearly is not necessarily a shortcoming of the decree. The designation "churches and ecclesial communities" has opened up new dimensions for the entire ecumenical dialogue for which definite concepts are lacking in all churches, not only in the Roman Church. As a result of the discussions in the council hall it should be clear to everyone that Rome has finally recognized that the non-Roman churches have a greater ecclesiological importance than was attributed to them in traditional Roman theology. This intention of Rome should be recognized by the other churches. Therefore we may say that the Decree on Ecumenism opens the doors wider toward the non-Roman churches than the Constitution on the Church.

2. The Concrete Evaluation of the Non-Roman Churches

After the basic discussion of non-Roman churches in the first chapter of the decree (3) the third chapter takes up the historical development of these churches under the heading "Churches and Ecclesial Communities Which Are Separated from the Roman Apostolic See." In its first part it discusses "The Oriental Churches," and in its second, "The Separated Churches and Ecclesial Communities in the West."

A very important and new development is the desire to seek and emphasize the positive aspects in the separated churches. This is definitely a new note when compared with past Roman Catholic declarations in regard to non-Roman churches. Here for the first time the things which the Roman Church and the other churches have in common are emphasized. There is a clear intention to avoid statements which might hurt the other side. There is no mention of schismatics and heretics. There is no discussion of the age-old question whether the Orthodox Church should be designated as schismatic or whether she should now also be called heretical since she has rejected the definition of the primacy of the pope promulgated at the First Vatican Council. This does not mean that the distinction between schismatics and heretics is completely forgotten. It continues to exist in the more gentle appellation "churches" and "ecclesial communities." But the schema never bothers to mention which churches outside of the Orthodox churches are designated as "churches" and which are relegated to the minor role of "ecclesial communities." Thus the obvious intention of the decree is to emphasize the positive aspects in the non-Roman churches. The response of the non-Roman churches in their relationship to Rome should be equally charitable.

But there are not only positive statements concerning the separated churches. Each paragraph also contains indications of where the differences between Rome and the other churches are found. Speaking about the Eastern churches, the schema states that the differences between Rome and the Orthodox are complementary in their various aspects, while in the case of the churches of the Reformation the document rather points to the oppositions between Rome and these churches. On the basis of the acceptance of these distinctions, certain themes are deduced which might serve in developing a future ecumenical dialogue. This way of dealing with the differences between the churches should receive our enthusiastic support, for a fruitful ecumenical dialogue can begin only when the participating churches do not only see their agreements but also their differences more precisely. Then they may be able to recognize "their agreements in their differences" and "their differences in their agreements" (K. Barth). With these considerations in mind they will be able to formulate questions which must be explored, taking into account the views of each side and dealing with them thoroughly. This method has been effective in ecumenical work elsewhere.

In spite of all these good points the first chapter of the Decree on Ecumenism has been found lacking by the observers from the separated churches and also by many of the council fathers themselves. It is of little help in starting an ecumenical dialogue, and that for two reasons.

In the first place, many of the representatives of the separated churches felt that their communions were not understood correctly. This became evident from the way in which these churches were grouped and characterized. Here are a few examples: In the preamble (13) brief mention is made of the origin of the non-Chalcedonian churches, the Copts, the Nestorians, etc. But in the first part of the same outline only the Orthodox Church had been mentioned, which was surprising since the heterodox representatives were more numerous at the council than the orthodox. But the orthodox also were irritated because they were not affected by the document on the "Catholic Oriental Churches Which Are United With Rome." This made clear in a very tangible way the difference between the Roman self-interpretation of the church and the Orthodox understanding of ecclesiology. Moreover, the second chief part glosses over the many medieval schisms in the West, of which of course only the Waldensians have escaped complete annihilation. The characterization of the churches of the Reformation is quite inadequate and seems to be motivated by a general concept of Protestantism which does not correspond to reality. In discussing the churches of the Reformation, no mention is made of the various church bodies as legal entities and the order of offices existing within them. How would Rome feel if she were characterized by us on the basis of a general concept of Catholicism in which all the marks of Catholicism as they exist in the Roman, Old-Catholic, Orthodox, Monophysite, Nestorian, and Apostolic churches were thrown together into one heap? Of course, the evaluation of these defective characterizations should take into account that the brevity of the third chapter made a detailed account of the characteristics of the various churches impossible.

Secondly, it disturbed many non-Roman Christians that the characterization of the non-Roman churches was tied up, even before the opening of conversations with them, with judgments concerning the divine work done in them which could not be reconciled with the ecumenical spirit and the opening of windows toward other churches which had been officially proclaimed. Such judgments are not in the province of man, but should be left to God alone. Thus, for example, how should the Orthodox Church react when she is praised on the one hand, while it is stated clearly in the document that the fullness of the church is found only in Rome? Or what should the church of the Reformation think about all the kind words and the considerate treatment meted out to her in the document, when this same document denies that the Body and the Blood are received in her during Holy Communion? By what right does the council pass the judgment that in the church of the Reformation "the proper reality *(substantia)* of the eucharistic mystery in its fullness has not been preserved" (23)? Does not the Evangelical Lutheran Church confess that the Body and Blood of Jesus Christ are present in essence and in truth in the Lord's Supper? By what right did the pope eliminate a statement which had been accepted by the council and which stated that by the movement of the Holy Spirit they (the Lutheran and other Reformation churches) *find* God in Holy Scripture and reduced it to a weak phrase that they call upon the Holy Spirit and *seek* God in Holy Scripture? Would it not be more fitting to open up the ecumenical dialogue to God's action instead of judging all the other churches *a priori?* It is quite evident that the non-Roman churches who are affected by these statements will reject these generalizations of the document. The only excuse they may find is that the brevity of the document, and especially of the third chapter, made such statements possible. But is there not also a deplorable lack of knowledge concerning the reality of the other churches on the part of Rome? The third chapter of the Decree on Ecumenism certainly does not express clearly the spiritual realities of these churches.

In addition, there is no mention made of the World Council of Churches in this document which deals with the ecumenical movement. Strangely enough, this officially constituted organization, organized in Amsterdam in 1948 and embracing over two hundred non-Roman churches, is not even referred to. There are only references to the ecumenical *movement* and its confession of the Triune God. But who can speak today of the Oriental and non-Roman Western churches as isolated groups and forget that they are also members of the World Council of Churches, which has established a communion of giving and receiving among them that leads to new openings in the ecumenical dialogue?

3. The Criteria for the Evaluation of Non-Roman Churches

The measuring stick that is applied to the separated churches in order to determine their ecclesiological status is of the greatest importance for the ecumenical dialogue. What is the measuring stick that is applied to the other churches of Christendom in the two schemata *(De Ecclesia* and *De Oecumenismo)?*

In keeping with the self-interpretation of the Roman Church as the One Holy Catholic and Apostolic Church, the measuring stick is first of all the Roman Church herself, as she has developed in her history and has defined herself in dogma and canon law. This measuring stick is not the ancient Christian church, the church of the apostles, or the church of the first centuries. These earlier forms of Catholicism are taken into account only to the degree in which they are identical with the present Roman Catholic Church or find their fulfillment in her. This measuring stick is another indication that as far as Rome is concerned, not the Holy Scriptures but the Roman Church, her teaching office (*magisterium*), is normative. If the ecclesiological reality of the non-Roman churches is measured on the basis of the present reality of the Roman Church, the judgment concerning these churches must of necessity be quantitative. They are judged according to the numbers of typically Roman elements which they have retained in their faith and life, the quantity of Roman dogmas, offices, sacraments, etc. On the basis of this quantitative thinking, a hierarchy is established among the churches, in which the existence of the hierarchical order and the *successio apostolica* play an especially important part. This strange way of evaluating other churches became clear when during the discussion of this schema some council fathers mentioned only the Orthodox Church. They did not include the Anglican communion because Leo XIII years ago had made a negative decision in regard to the validity of the Anglican orders. Naturally, such a quantitative thinking makes it extremely difficult to evaluate the non-Roman churches from the center of their existence which is Jesus Christ. Even the special spiritual qualities of the Eastern churches is hidden from this thinking.

But we also find that there are in the Decree on Ecumenism and also in the opinions offered during the discussions certain indications of a breakthrough in this purely quantitative thinking. Statements were made that gave testimony of the immediate impression made by faith in Jesus Christ, by prayer, by the liturgical life, by the sacramental piety, by the service to the world and by the martyrdom experienced in the separated churches. This measuring stick is Christological, pneumatological, and biblical. Here we have a criterion common to all churches. There was talk of an experience of the mystery found in the unity of Christ that cannot be defined by traditional concepts of the church. Hearts are meeting in the certainty of faith, even though the forms in which this faith is defined and carried out in the life of the church may be different. There was also a breakthrough in the quantitative thinking of the Roman Church when the fathers discovered and recognized the results of the grace of Christ in the various churches, results which have not yet found expression in the *Roman* Church but which were declared to be necessary for the realization of the fullness of Christ in the church and thus for the realization of complete catholicity. In a number of opinions the traditional quantitative thinking of the Roman Church was harshly criticized. It was stated that Christ Jesus himself is the center of all church life. The American Cardinal Ritter of St. Louis demanded that all thinking concerning unity should start with the person of Christ.

It is difficult to state which of the basic tendencies prevailed in the lively discussions of the council. Considering the majority of the opinions offered at the meetings, it may be safe to state that the concept which does not consider the churches according to their apostolic foundation and according to the ever-present power of Jesus Christ and of the Holy Spirit, but look upon them as splits and schisms from Rome, was more in evidence at the council. The chief point in evaluating these churches was the question as to what had remained in these churches after their separation from Rome. The historical consideration that also Rome had changed since the medieval schisms was completely disregarded. But according to all past ecumenical experience a deeper understanding between the churches can develop only if we go back to the common apostolic roots of all churches and when the separated churches meet with a willingness to hear the witness of Holy Scriptures, from which all churches must take their directions. Only in this way can they open up toward each other. Such a dialogue is possible even if the relationship between Scriptures and Tradition has not been fully clarified. Holy Scripture still remains the common basis on which all separated churches stand. But unfortunately the measuring stick of the Roman Catholic Church is not primarily the Bible, but the church herself.

4. The Role of the Holy Scriptures at the Council

Before the beginning of the meetings of the general congregations the Gospel was carried down the nave of St. Peter's Church and deposited on a golden throne on the altar on which Mass was celebrated. During this solemn procession the council fathers sang the ancient hymn *"Christus vincit, Christus regnat!"* This hymn taken together with the symbolic recognition of the Gospel as the lord and judge in the deliberations and decisions of the council corresponded to the understanding of the ancient churches and of the churches of the Reformation that Christ himself is the center of Holy Scriptures and that he is present in his Word.

Therefore it is surprising that the Holy Scriptures played only a minor part in the discussions of the council. During the first three sessions there was no sermon on a biblical text. Almost no biblical scholars served as theological experts to the council. The proposals submitted to the council for action contained more footnotes from the encyclicals of the last few popes than from Holy Scripture. It is true that Holy Scripture played a part in some of the opinions presented to the council. But the important discussion concerning the collegiality of the bishops and their relationship to the pope did not take into account present-day New Testament scholarship and its findings concerning the apostolic form of the church, the historical position of Peter, or the relationship of the office of bishop to that of presbyter. One outstanding speech during the discussions dealt with the New Testament statements concerning the *charisma*. But it was not incorporated into the texts nor really applied to the church of the present day. As a whole, the Bible was used for apologetics and for illustrations. It was not the norm for the decisions of the council. In spite of the solemn enthronement of the Bible on the altar, it was not effectively used in confrontation with the church nor was the authoritative position of the apostles in comparison with the church as she exists at all later times really clear.

This relationship between Holy Scripture and Tradition and the present-day *Magisterium* of the church is of the greatest importance for any desired ecumenical dialogue. In contrast to the traditions and orders of any one church, the Bible is the common foundation for all churches. The more we are ready to subordinate our ecclesiastical traditions and the teaching office of the church to the authentic original proclamation of the apostolic message and its resonances in the early church as it is presented to us in the Bible, the more we may expect our ecumenical dialogue to bear fruit. These questions will be decided in the dogmatic *Constitutio de Revelatione*. During the discussion on this schema several excellent improvements were made and suggestions for the use of the Bible. The Word of God remains, however, surrounded by the tradition of the church and by her *magisterium* so that the historical witness of the apostles and the primacy of the Bible in their confrontation with the dogma of the Roman Church and the present position of the pope cannot come clearly into view. As long as the primacy of the Bible and of the apostles remains obscured by Roman dogma the basis for a fruitful dialogue between Rome and the other churches remains small. It is hemmed in and hindered, in spite of the fact that both Rome and the other churches have the Bible.

5. The Challenge Addressed to the Church by Christ

In the discussions of the council and in its decisions Jesus Christ, like the Bible, has not been permitted fully to confront the church critically. He was seen as having his existence within the church herself. He is in her and she is his Body. That he is also the Lord who is the *Judge* not only of the world but also of the church has not really been taken into account during the council discussions. That he will proclaim on the last day to some of those who have eaten with him and have prophesied in his Name, "I never knew you, depart from me, you evildoers" (Matt. 7:23, cf. Luke 11:27 f.) and that he warns the whole church, "I will come to you and remove your lampstand from its place, unless you repent" (Rev. 2:5) and, "I will spew you out of my mouth" (Rev. 3:15) has been disregarded in the dogmatic definition of the church. That the Old Testament prophets proclaimed the judgment of God to the people of God in the Old Testament seems to be unimportant to the people of God in the New Testament.

As long as a Christian Church does not permit herself to be shaken to her very foundations by the challenge addressed to her by her Lord, as long as she does not permit her self-interpretation and her history to be questioned by him, she will not be able to arrive at the full meaning of herself and her mystery. The mystery is that Christ in confronting us sinners does not cease to judge us. But in his judgment there is forgiveness for our sins. The unity of the church has been distorted by the various schisms and controversies which have beset her in history, but her unity has not been destroyed.

Thus the ecumenical openness of the Roman Church toward the other churches is limited not only by the many dogmas which were adopted by her long before this council was convoked, but also by the pronouncements of the Second Vatican Council. Was it really necessary that at this time the essence of the church had to be defined and proclaimed? For Rome also have not many problems and dimensions of ecclesiology become visible because of the ecumenical movement? Could she not have applied the definitions of modern ecumenism to her problems? Would it not have been better to have an ecumenical dialogue first so that some of the problems of Roman ecclesiology and of the ecclesiology of the other churches could have been jointly removed? Ecclesiology before the council, after all, was much more open than such areas as justification and the sacraments. Could Rome not have waited to find out whether there are not *common* answers to some of these problems which might be found through the process of theological cooperation by the various churches? Should the council not have limited itself to dogmatic pronouncements concerning the office of the bishops and concerning the diaconate, problems which had become burning questions within the church? Historically speaking, did not all councils until the present take up only questions that dealt with acute problems, such as heresies within the church? Why did Rome have to deal with the whole of ecclesiology? It is quite clear that the Second Vatican Council, coming so soon after the pre-ecumenical and narrow encyclical of Pius XII *"Mystici Corporis,"* could not define the ecclesiology of the Roman Church in a much different way than it did in the Constitution on the Church. But did it have to limit the ecumenical dialogue by passing the *Constitutio de Ecclesia* at the very moment when it made it a possibility on the basis of the *Decretum de Oecumenismo?*

V. Comparison Between the Ecumenism of the Roman Church and the Ecumenism of the World Council of Churches

If we look at what has been said earlier in this chapter and keep in mind all the many developments of the Vatican Council, we may doubtless discern certain views on ecumenism common to Rome and the non-Roman ecumenical movement as it has found its official expression in the World Council of Churches, organized at Amsterdam in 1948.

1. In both groups ecumenism had its beginnings in certain basic spiritual impulses. These impulses opened the eyes so that they could see the separated brethren. They awakened a yearning for unity. We cannot derive the existence of ecumenism from the external tribulations of the churches, from the march of secularism in our time, or from a reaction against totalitarianism with its persecutions of Christians everywhere. Neither is it due to the reawakening and missionary thrust of non-Christian religions, etc. Ecumenism is not the expression of a "common strategy" against these dangers. Rather it is an awakening of the separated churches to the reality of their unity in Christ and to a feeling of sin and guilt. Thus the ecumenical movement is a movement of repentance, shaking us and yet blessed. It tears down the dividing walls and edifies the hearts. There is no doubt in my mind that also Pope John XXIII was driven by these spiritual impulses to instruct the Second Vatican Council to place the discussion of ecumenism on its agenda and that these same impulses were effective during the deliberations of the council.

2. Furthermore, there seems to be a general agreement concerning the way that must be followed. There is agreement that ecumenism is helped by genuine repentance, by prayer, and by mutual understanding. The churches must be renewed. There must be open dialogue on a basis of equality and cooperation in many fields, including a common witness to Jesus Christ. The directives given in the second chapter of the Decree on Ecumenism correspond to a large degree to the methods that have been tried and proved effective in the ecumenical movement of the non-Roman churches.

This agreement in ecumenical methods is especially important because Rome did not adopt these methods from the World Council of Churches, but developed them on the basis of her own desire for a fruitful dialogue with the separated brethren.

3. But the goal of ecumenism is different. Rome and the non-Roman churches are agreed that the goal is visible unity of the churches and thus also unity of faith, sacramental unity through the receiving of the Body and Blood of Christ and mutual recognition of ministries. But while the World Council of Churches leaves wide open the question under which form this unity will be realized, Rome must insist on the form of unity which is already attained within the Roman Catholic Church. This means a recognition by all non-Roman churches of Roman dogma and of the papal primacy. The World Council of Churches makes it possible to establish a unity based on the communitarian patterns of the New Testament and of the ancient church. It invites churches to grow together in mutual conversion to each other. The differences between the Roman and the non-Roman understanding of unity are due to the differences existing in the dogmatical and canonical presuppositions of the Roman Church as she confronts the separated churches. This is a point that cannot be discussed in detail within the scope of this chapter.

4. These differences in the understanding of the goal of unity cannot be without effect on ecumenism in spite of the areas of agreement that have been indicated above.

We know that the ecumenical movement among the non-Roman churches also began with a comparison of the various liturgical, dogmatic and juridical aspects of these churches. As a result of these comparisons these churches tried to determine how much they had in common. But they soon began to realize that this method was not sufficient to ecumenism. It did not really lead towards unity. Rather one had to go back to the times of the apostles and to the ancient Christian church, and to the Bible itself as the authentic basis for the understanding of the church. From this basis the separation of the churches and their divergent traditions are to be evaluated. In this area Roman Catholic ecumenism is hemmed in by the boundaries of Roman dogma and canon law.

Likewise, ecumenical dialogue and proselytizing went side by side for a while in the non-Roman ecumenical movement. There was at first no clarification of the goal of ecumenism. But it soon became clear that true ecumenism could not be reconciled with proselytizing. True ecumenism is based on respect for the convictions of others. It protects the freedom of the other churches and is willing to help them to preserve and to strengthen their particular historical heritage. One of the fruits of this attitude was the establishment of the unique Inter-Church Aid of the World Council of Churches where helping love goes beyond the boundaries set by particular dogmas and church law and where nothing is asked in return. Here too the Roman Church is handicapped in that she finds it harder to divorce ecumenism from proselytizing.

Finally, ecumenism is walled in when the future form of church government is determined *a priori* as is the case in the Roman Church. In that case the Holy Spirit does not have free rein to bestow his gifts upon the church.

5. But in spite of these differences in the ecumenical approach we must not overlook the fact that the ecumenical stance of the Second Vatican Council and of the World Council of Churches does not only have one and the same origin, but have also many methods in common. They are moving toward each other from opposite directions, since in the case of Roman ecumenism the movement is from a highly centralized church characterized by its extreme uniformity to a unity of churches of many shapes and forms, while in the case of the non-Roman ecumenism the exact opposite is true. Here we find a movement from a weakly connected aggregate of churches to an ordered community.

Summarizing these analyses of agreements and contrasts it becomes clear that the decree of the Second Vatican Council expresses an ecumenism which is specifically Roman Catholic. It is an attempt to find a synthesis between the exclusive concept of the church as it is found in the self-interpretation of the general synods of the Roman Church as ecumenical councils of Christendom and the wider concept as it is present in the World Council of Churches. Both sides are agreed in their desire for unity. Both work for communion among the separated brethren. But the whole

concept of Catholic ecumenism, both as related to the narrower
canonical understanding and to the wider non-Roman understanding, needs further clarification. This need has been expressed at
various times by the council fathers. Roman ecumenism as expressed
in the decree is a compromise in which there are possibilities for a
further narrowing as well as a further expansion of the ecumenical
stance.

In view of these ambiguities of the Decree on Ecumenism it should
not surprise us that the reactions to the council's handling of this
matter has given rise both to joyful hope and—for example in the
case of the Greek Church—to considerable worry. All churches are
looking for closer communion. However, the suspicion that Roman
ecumenism is not interested in unity as such, but wants submission to the Church of Rome, has not been allayed by the promulgation of the decree. The methods and the proximate goals may be
truly ecumenical. But what about the ultimate aim of Rome? Are
not the presuppositions of Roman ecumenism typically "Roman"?
Is it not too early to predict what will be the effects on Christendom
of this type of ecumenism?

Although these and many other questions still go unanswered,
I think it would be wrong to give a negative evaluation of the Decree on Ecumenism. As clearly as the limitations of Roman ecumenism seem to be drawn, as limited as the ecumenical opening
in the Decree on Ecumenism as it was discussed in the council and
promulgated by the pope may be, I think it would be unfair to
make this into a reproach. Every church can open the door to other
churches only so far as her dogmatic presuppositions will permit.
Each claims in some sense that she is the One Holy Catholic and
Apostolic Church. Even the Toronto declaration of the World Council of Churches assured to every member church the right to hold
fast to her ecclesiology and to judge other churches on the basis of
this ecclesiology. Even within the World Council of Churches there
are different types of ecumenism. Most non-Roman churches do not
teach their identity with the One Holy Catholic and Apostolic
Church with the same exclusiveness as Rome does, but our concern
is not so much to find out to what degree various churches dif-
fer in their exclusiveness, but with what degree of intensity they
are working toward unity with other churches. When we look at

the Second Vatican Council in this way, we will notice a remarkable breakthrough of the ecumenical impulse in the Roman Catholic Church. This breakthrough is even more impressive if we take into account the dogmatic and canonical restrictions which this church had imposed upon herself. She is ecumenical *in spite* of her dogma and canon law. No matter what our final judgment may be, the Decree on Ecumenism of the Second Vatican Council is so important that no church can pass it by. It has brought about a new relationship between the Roman Church and the other churches. Every church will have to study it carefully and will gratefully acknowledge the possibilities which this decree opens up for the future.

A skeptical attitude which assumes that after the adjournment of the council everything will be as it was before would certainly be out of place. Likewise we should not rejoice over the fact that there have been setbacks at this council. We should not try to find confirmation for our skepticism. All of us are addressed by this council. We can no longer retire to the safe haven of our apologetics and polemics.

It would also be wrong to wax enthusiastic to the extent of assuming that this decree has removed all hindrances to ecumenism and that unity is just around the corner. We should not expect that any of the Western or Eastern churches will interpret the Decree on Ecumenism and the discussions of the council as sufficient basis for reunion with the Roman Church.

Finally, it would be wrong to stop with mere analyses of the decree in its relationship to the other decisions made by the Second Vatican Council and to sit back and wait for further developments. For in this decree the Roman Church with whom we have tried for a long time to enter into dialogue has finally decided to reach out to us and to give us her hand. She is asking us to do our share in this dialogue and cooperation. Let us take the will of the Lord seriously. It is his wish that all should be one. We must not refuse to accept this invitation. Success of this ecumenical dialogue does not depend only upon Rome, but also upon the other churches. We can work together so that this specifically Roman ecumenism which has been born at the Second Vatican Council will develop into a truly catholic ecumenism. Although union between the churches cannot be established on the basis of this decree, yet there is the possibility of rapprochement, of increasing cooperation, and of a common witness to Jesus Christ in this world. These are the first important steps toward union among the separated churches. When, how, and in what form this union will be accomplished we do not know. This is left to God's own pleasure. But we can certainly pray for it.

Chapter X

Church and World:
Schema 13

A new attitude towards the world and the church's relation to it is becoming dominant in Roman Catholicism and is finding expression through Vatican II. In part this simply means, from the Protestant point of view, that the Roman Catholic Church is finally catching up with most of the rest of Christendom. For example, it is finally coming to recognize the principle of religious liberty. However, this is not all. New questions are being raised for which Protestants, like Catholics, have no definite answers. What is the meaning of modern developments for Christians, for the church? What are we to make of the ever-accelerating rush of scientific and technological progress, of the increasing unification of the world and the socialization and urbanization of mankind, of the new status of women and the disappearance of old social structures? What should the churches say and do about the problems raised by these developments: problems of atomic war, the population explosion, developing nations, competing ideologies, social, economic, and racial justice, crises in marriage and the family?

The effort to deal with these questions constitutes one of the two main aspects of Vatican II. This was not part of the original plans for the council, but this omission seemed intolerable in the face of the *aggiornamento*, the "bringing-up-to-date," of the church which Pope John proposed as its main objectives. Cardinals Lercaro, Suenens, and Montini made this point towards the end of the first session. Suenens put it this way: The council must describe the church *ad intra*, from within, but also *ad extra*, from without, in relation to the world. Montini, when he became pope, officially confirmed this view in his opening speech of the second session. Since then, both the general public and many bishops have been more interested in schema 13, "The Church in the Modern World," which is to concentrate on this topic, than in any other council document.

However, there are great difficulties in writing about this phase of Vatican II. First, what we shall say must be highly tentative. Work in this area is only beginning, in contrast to work on the church *ad intra* (including its ecumenical dimensions) where the council has now completed its formulations of theological principles, even though the speed and the extent of the implementation of those principles still remain in doubt. In reference to the church *ad extra*, there are, to be sure, some hints in the documents already promulgated or given preliminary approval. However, the main document, schema 13, is still undergoing drastic revisions; the declaration on religious liberty may be considerably changed, even though it is not likely to be weakened; and we as yet know practically nothing regarding the final shape of other documents which may prove relevant, such as those on the lay apostolate and on missions. (For brief descriptions of the first drafts of these documents, the reader is referred to Chapter IV.) We cannot rely on these drafts, but must instead try to discern the thinking of the council chiefly on the basis of the recommendations made in the bishops' speeches or in the statements of the theologians who are involved in preparing the new drafts.

Secondly, what we have to say cannot be a "Protestant" evaluation of "Catholic" thought to the same extent as in other chapters of this book. As we have already mentioned, the problems raised by the modern world are new for all of us. Our various traditions do not provide us with any clearcut answers. The lines of division cut through confessional boundaries, as is clear when we consider that there are both Catholic and Protestant existentialists and anti-existentialists, evolutionists and anti-evolutionists. The author of the present chapter cannot claim to offer a "typically" Protestant point of view, but can only speak as one theologian among many.

It must be emphasized that the very newness of this area presents great opportunities as well as difficulties. It perhaps represents one of the most promising growing edges of ecumenism. Here, as in the area of biblical research, Protestants and Catholics can cooperatively seek common answers to common problems, rather than simply struggle with differences inherited from the past. Yet, even in such an area, the burden of our divisions is with us. While the demarcation lines are not rigid, still there are characteristic differences between the usual Catholic and the usual Protestant approaches to the modern world. These differences can lead to misunderstanding and opposition, so one of the purposes of this essay will be to point out such points of tension and suggest ways in which both Catholics and Protestants need to learn from each other.

Before doing this, however, we must outline some of the things which are being said in the conciliar documents and debates, as well as indicate their background.

I. The Historical Background

It is impossible to understand the changes now taking place in Roman Catholic attitudes to the world unless we keep in mind certain familiar historical facts regarding the *de facto* transformation of the church's place in the world. In the Middle Ages the church was the major agent in shaping a new social and cultural order. In part because medieval civilization was so largely born in the bosom of the church, the church itself became a great worldly power and, as even Catholic scholars now admit, was deeply corrupted thereby. The history of the last centuries is largely that of the struggle of modern man to escape from a traditional society and culture of which the church was an inseparable part. Perhaps inevitably the established churches resisted this process. They sought to preserve the old order in which they had a privileged position, not only in matters of theology and piety, but also in the social and political areas. As they lost influence, they often gave up this struggle in the public domain, only to retire into defensive ghettos in which they sought to protect those who were still faithful from the acids of modernity.

While this nostalgia for the past has been characteristic of many Protestant bodies, it has been particularly true of the Roman Catholic Church. Because of its size and authoritarian structure it was able to resist modern developments much more massively and rigidly. Further, the past for which the Roman Catholics longed was not that of Reformation or New Testament times, but that of the medieval period when the church lorded it over even secular rulers and when the state obediently suppressed heresy on its behalf.

Looked at from this perspective, what the Roman Catholic Church is now doing is simply recognizing the realities of the new situation after a surprisingly long delay. The losses which it has suffered, especially in areas where it has been dominant, such as the Mediterranean countries and Latin America, are convincing it that it must get rid of its medieval and feudal forms in theology, organization, and liturgy. Instead of hankering after the past, it must once again, as in the early Middle Ages, enter the mainstream of historical development and seek to help mold the future, to contribute to the building up of the new world society which is now emerging. Thoughts such as these were expressed time and again by the bishops, and they are also reflected to a certain extent in the first draft of schema 13.

This outlook, of course, is not altogether new. Already in the nineteenth century, Leo XIII sought in some respects to change Roman Catholicism from being a socially and politically reactionary force. John XXIII carried this process farther than anyone before, as is illustrated by his encyclicals, *Mater et Magistra* (1961) and *Pacem in terris* (1963). He liberated reforming movements in the Roman Catholic Church and tended to discourage a certain kind of conservatism. As a result, for example, the Christian Democrats were able to win a totally unexpected victory in Chile in the fall of 1964. Many observers, including non-Catholics, think that the possibilities in Latin America of finding genuinely reformatory alternatives between sterile reaction and Communist revolution have been greatly enhanced. Further, in some places behind the iron curtain, the relations between Catholics and Communists are changing. Less spectacular but nevertheless real results are to be seen in places such as the United States, where the path of the first Catholic President, Kennedy, was no doubt eased by the new liberalism of his church, and where the Catholic participation in the struggle for racial justice has probably been more active than it would otherwise have been.

It is important to remember these facts. Especially in the case of the Catholic Church with its unified organization and five hundred million adherents (even though many of them are nominal), theologically determined attitudes towards the world and its problems can still, even in our day, exercise a perceptible influence on the course of history. This happens whether the church counsels reaction, as in the past, or passivity, as on most important issues in recent times, or active affirmation and molding of the forces shaping the future, as it now seems inclined to recommend. It is important to everyone, therefore, and not only to Christians, to know how the Roman Catholic Church is proposing to exercise its influence in the world.

II. The Form of the Church's Action in the World

On the practical level, the fundamental feature of the new attitude towards the world is the conviction that the era of church-state relations which began fifteen centuries ago with Constantine, when Christianity became the official religion of the Roman Empire, is now definitively ended. The church, says the first draft of schema 13, "places no hope in the privileges offered by civil authorities" and will gladly renounce the exercise of rights when, through them, "the sincerity of her witness is being called in doubt."

Many express this point more strongly. Not only will the church never again have the kind of dominating role in society which she has had at various times in the past, but it is good that this is so. Phrases familiar in some Protestant circles became equally common at the council. "The world has come of age." It has attained a certain maturity and autonomy which make it both impossible and undesirable for ecclesiastical authorities to try to direct or control it from above.

In this new situation the only way to exert an effective Christian influence is for the church to serve human needs as humbly and self-forgetfully as did Christ himself. It must not use coercive measures by trying, for instance, to legislate Christian morals for

society at large. Rather, it must encourage Christians to promote all
worthwhile causes, from the artistic to the economic, whether these
bear a specifically Christian label or not. It must seek to humanize,
rather than insist on overtly Christianizing, the new orders which
are emerging, and it must be willing to cooperate, when possible,
even with atheistic Communists in doing this. (This point was made
explicitly in John XXIII's *Pacem in terris*, but not in the first draft of
schema 13, for which it was criticized in the council.)

In order to build up this "fraternal community" between Christians and non-Christians it is necessary to be permeated with "the
spirit of poverty . . . to suffer with those who suffer, to weep with
those who weep, to become poor with the poor for the sake of
Christ. . . . Christians who recognize Christ in their brethren cannot
be at ease in the midst of plenty and riches, while so many men are
in distress from want and hunger" (schema 13).

Perhaps one might say that in contemporary Catholicism a Fran-
ciscan *theologia paupertatis* is beginning to replace the old triumphalist *theologia gloriae*. This is by no means identical with the *theologia crucis*, but it must be recognized as giving authentic expression
to a central element in the Gospel.

More than this must be said, however, for not only should the
church serve the world in the spirit of poverty, but it must also learn
from the world. "The progress of sciences . . . the experience of history . . . the riches of different cultures . . . increase our own awe
of God. The Church is greatly aided by the growth of human experience and of human knowledge and by them she is stimulated in in-
vestigating revealed truth ever more deeply, and in understanding,
propounding, and clarifying it" (schema 13). Indeed, the whole of
schema 13, as of *Pacem in terris* before it, is presented as an exercise
in discerning "the signs of the times," in listening to the world, to
the events of history. "In the voice of time, therefore, we must listen
to the voice of God." Further, the declaration of religious liberty
develops the same line of thought. It acknowledges that it is in part
through the development of a new kind of society and ideal of the
human person that the church has come to see the need and the
rightness of a positive and sweeping affirmation of religious liberty.
Cardinal Alfrink (Holland) and Archbishop Rada (Ecuador) even
went so far as to assert that Christians must take seriously the par-

tial truths in certain atheistic views in order to deepen their own understanding of human freedom.

Lastly, in this new perspective, the action of the church in the world becomes, so to speak, lay rather than clerical. When the laity is passive, when it is simply a flock at the beck and call of the hierarchy, it can perhaps be mobilized to defend the *status quo,* but it cannot function as a force in the positive shaping of the future. In order to do this the church must act through its laity, for it is they who are directly involved in the life of the earthly city. Further, laymen and laywomen must take responsibility and initiative, for only with their help can the church discern the signs of the times, and only they are in a position to calculate what concrete actions and decisions have a chance of attaining truly humane ends in our increasingly complex society. The role of priests and bishops, therefore, is not that of directing the details of lay action, but rather that of equipping the laity to make their own decisions with a truly enlightened and sensitive Christian conscience. The clergy must be the ministers of the ministers, the servants of the servants of Christ in the world.

These ideas, which are thoroughly familiar in contemporary Protestant discussions, were clearly stated in many speeches, but they have so far been only partially expressed in the conciliar documents, most notably, perhaps, in the fourth chapter, "The Laity," of the *Constitution on the Church.* The initial draft of schema 13, however, does make the point that "The faithful must not think that their Pastors are either competent or called to give them an answer to all questions, even serious ones . . . in such a situation, let them be bold enough on their own responsibility to take matters into their own hands . . . "

It would not be fruitful for us to go on and explore the specific recommendations in schema 13 for dealing with specific problems, from war and peace to sex and marriage. Once again the reader is referred to the brief summary in Chapter IV. With the exception of very moderately expressed reticences about birth control, the substance of these recommendations would be approved by most Christian churches, as well as by vast numbers of the "men of good will" of which the draft speaks. Further, these recommendations will be reformulated in the final draft; and, finally, as in the case of most

church pronouncements, it is not so much the content of the statements which counts as the degree and the way in which they later
come to mold and inspire concrete attitudes and actions. In short,
what is of fundamental importance for its action in the world is that
the Roman Catholic Church is trying to become a servant, rather
than a ruler; a listener, rather than simply one who instructs others;
and a community of active lay participation rather than of exclusively
hierarchical control.

These changes are clearly required by the present historical situation. Unless they occur, the influence of the Catholic Church both
in the world and on its own laity will continue to diminish. It is not
surprising, therefore, that these viewpoints have been vigorously
represented by many of the leaders of the majority at the council,
and that they are finding at least partial expression in the conciliar
documents. We may, it seems to me, confidently expect them to
triumph even more completely in the future.

In saying this, I do not mean to minimize the importance of theological motives. After all, it is the return to the sources, especially
the Bible, which is providing the categories for the reinterpretation
of the church as fundamentally *laos*, people of God, rather than hierarchy, and as fashioned after Christ in his humility and service,
rather than in his final triumphant glory. Nevertheless, I have chosen
to stress historical developments because these, as so often before
from Old Testament times onward, seem once again to be God's
way of calling his people to reconsider its nature and task in the
light of his Word.

We must now turn, however, to a more explicit consideration of
the theological background for the more positive evaluation in this
council of earthly realities and, especially, of modern developments.

III. The Theology of "Earthly Realities"

Why should the Christian, why should the church, be concerned
with the promotion of culture, with human progress, with the building of the earthly city? Why should the church be open to truths
and values found outside the explicitly Christian orbit? Are not such
ideas in contradiction to convictions deeply embedded in both
Protestantism and Catholicism, that this world is a wilderness, a vale

of tears, through which we must pass with our eyes fixed on the future glory, and that, far from learning from the world, we must strive to keep ourselves in every respect unspotted from it?

The first draft of schema 13 tells us little about how contemporary Catholics are trying to answer these questions. Other council documents supplement this, but it is chiefly to the council speeches that we shall have to turn. Let us take these sources of information in order.

The major answer in schema 13 is completely traditional (and, to be sure, in itself correct and necessary): "love for one's neighbor and our own salvation urge us all to lend our cooperation to the building of a more just and fraternal society . . . that the order of charity and justice may daily be more apparent . . . and that men may be delivered from want and servitude, by which so often they are impeded from observing good morals and from opening their minds to the things that are above." However, both reactionaries and revolutionaries can agree with this. It could be used as an argument for returning to an idealized version of the medieval pattern just as much as for trying to build a new type of society.

A new element does enter in, however, in the affirmation of freedom, "excluding any kind of force that may be offensive to the dignity of the human person. . . . For the Gospel wishes to call forth a free response from men." Once again, however, this scarcely explains the schema's positive attitude towards modern developments, including the scientific and technological ones, many of which run counter to traditional ideas of freedom, such as those of Jefferson or of nineteenth century liberalism.

At one point "the progress of science and art" is represented as being "in keeping with the plan of God, who handed over the earth to men to be replenished by them and to be brought under their control (Gen. 1:28)," but this by itself does not get us very far simply because such progress, in many of its aspects, far too often represents simply another tower of Babel (Gen. 11).

In only one place does the schema speak directly to our problem: "there is no lack of Christians who wonder whether the effort spent on the progress of the earthly city ought not more fittingly be devoted to supernatural realities, not adverting to the fact that . . . Christ came to raise the whole man to a higher dignity. . . . By assuming human nature in His incarnation, he raised the whole man, body and soul, and the totality of creation, even matter itself, to a higher dignity, and inserted all things, including earthly duties, into a more sublime relationship with God that surpasses man's nature." This seems to suggest that somehow the "building up of the earthly city" is a participation in the cosmic redemptive activity of Christ. This same idea is given an eschatological expression when it is said that "Although the complete deliverance of the creature from its slavery to corruption (Rom. 8:18-21) will be made manifest only in the second coming of the Lord, nevertheless the redeemed must communicate the beginnings of their hope in the best way possible, even by earthly agencies and conditions."

In other council documents also, there are hints that the "building up of the earthly city" is somehow a preparation for the coming of the kingdom, but before noting these, we must once again point out certain traditional themes.

The classic Catholic doctrine that "grace presupposes nature" is expressed when dealing with non-biblical religions. Thus, in the *Constitution on the Church,* it is said of all religions (and not simply of Judaism which, it must always be remembered, belongs within the sphere of revelation) that "Whatever good or truth is found among them is looked upon by the church as a preparation for the Gospel" (No. 16). To this is related an equally ancient Catholic view that salvation is possible even apart from explicit faith in Christ, but this is now being expressed much more sweepingly than before. It is being applied even to atheists: "Nor does divine providence deny the helps necessary for salvation to those who, without blame on their part, have not yet arrived at an explicit knowledge of God and, with his grace, strive to live a good life" *(ibid.).*

As a consequence of these emphases, the task of the church is looked upon as being, in part, the *consecratio mundi,* the sanctification and perfecting of the values and truths already present in the world. This is a principle which has at the very least, from the Protestant point of view, been dangerously misused. It has been employed, for example, as a justification for the pagan elements to be found in the cult of the saints and of the Virgin. However, it also has its good uses, as is illustrated by the present emphasis on de-

Westernizing Catholicism and adapting it to different cultures and mentalities, as well as to modern outlooks. In the *Constitution on the Church* it is expressed in such terms as these: "Through her [the church's] work, whatever good is in the minds and hearts of men, whatever good lies latent in the religious practices and cultures of diverse peoples, is not only saved from destruction but also cleansed, raised up, and perfected" (No. 17).

This idea receives a new and startling development, which may be of great importance for the future of Catholic missions, in the statement on non-Christian religions (which, though not promulgated, has been given preliminary approval): The church "exhorts its children that they, by means of conversations and collaboration with the faithful of other religions, while maintaining the integrity of the Catholic faith, serve and promote the spiritual goods and socio-cultural values which are found among them" (No. 2). In other words, the church's task of "elevating" nature is not accomplished exclusively by overtly "baptizing" men and their values, but should also be carried on outside the explicitly Christian sphere. Activities are being recommended which have as their effect the making, not of Christians, but of better Buddhists, Hindus, and Moslems (who to be sure, from the Catholic point of view which we are outlining, thereby become "more like Christians"). Such ideas give special force to the notion earlier expressed that the church should be a self-forgetful servant of mankind, not a self-aggrandizing institution.

The *Constitution on the Church* makes clear that the role of lay people in this *consecratio mundi* is crucial. They work "for the sanctification of the world from within as a leaven . . . order and throw light upon these [temporal] affairs in such a way that there may come into being and then continually increase according to Christ the praise of the Creator and the Redeemer." They "seek the kingdom of God by engaging in temporal affairs and by ordering them according to the plan of God" (No. 31).

The Christian's work in the temporal realm is thus in some way related to the kingdom of God. The church, so the *Constitution* says, is "the initial budding forth of that kingdom" (No. 5). That kingdom "is to be further extended until it is brought to perfection by Him at the end of time." The church is "a lasting and sure seed of unity, hope, and salvation for the whole human race . . . an instrument for the redemption of all . . . " (No. 9). It "receives the mission to proclaim and to spread among all peoples the kingdom of Christ and of God . . . [and] strains towards the completed kingdom" (No. 5). Apparently one of the ways in which the church "spreads" and "strains towards the completed kingdom" is by helping, through the temporal activities of its members, to build up the earthly city.

This point becomes almost explicit in the "Introduction" to the *Constitution.* The church is there described as a "sacrament" or "sign and instrument," not only of union with God but "of the whole human race . . . so that all men, joined more closely today by various social, technical and cultural ties, might also attain fuller unity in Christ" (No. 1). This seems to say that the progressive unification of mankind which is taking place through modern developments is a preparation, or can become a preparation, for the unity in Christ of which the church is the sacramental sign and instrument. If so, we have here a way of interpreting the vague suggestion, already noted in the first draft of schema 13, to the effect that building up the earthly city is a contributory participation in the redemptive activity of Christ.

Speaking more generally, it is clear that the council documents contain hints of what might be called a "historicized" version of the old principle that grace presupposes and perfects nature. Now that the nature of man is being recognized as historical, as something which develops in and through time, historical developments themselves are being increasingly regarded in Catholic circles as presuppositions for the eschatological triumph of grace in the final manifestation of the kingdom of God. This, then, is the theological answer to the question of why modern developments are to be affirmed, and why the Christian is to throw himself wholeheartedly into the building up of the earthly city: he thereby prepares the conditions for the final coming of the kingdom.

We can advance this interpretation with some confidence because it was clearly and emphatically asserted in a number of council speeches. Cardinal Meyer (Chicago), for example, said that "We must make men realize that their daily work is an essential part of the plan of salvation. . . . The world is not simply a means and a way to salvation, but it is itself an object of redemption. . . . It is

necessary to teach that the improvement of the material order contributes to the improvement of man and to the development of his
superior faculties. . . . Every kind of flight from the world and
enmity to the body which does not take seriously the importance
of the world, including the material world, in the plan of salvation
is unbiblical and unchristian. . . . St. Paul teaches this eloquently
when he speaks of the hope of the world and the redemption of the
body. Both body and soul are to be freed from the slavery of sin.
The material world is to be transformed into the new heaven and
the new earth of which St. John speaks. All things must contribute
to the restoration of the world in Christ."[1] Cardinal Frings (Cologne) made the point "that truly Christian activity in the world
does not consist of making the world into the church, but rather 'it
is truly Christian honestly to deal among men, who often act only
for their own area and their own group, with those things which
are necessary for the welfare of all men without distinction.' Such
activity is a genuine preparation of the kingdom of God."[2] Cardinal
Silva of Chile spoke along the same lines and so did several bishops.

Many readers will by this time have begun to suspect the influence at the council of the French Jesuit paleontologist and philos-
opher-theologian, Teilhard de Chardin, whose works have been repeatedly cautioned against by the Vatican Holy Office. He was, in
fact, favorably cited in a number of speeches in St. Peter's, and
frequently enthusiastically spoken of outside. However, it would be
a mistake to identify the outlook which we are now describing
exclusively with his views. This affirmative attitude towards historical developments, towards human progress, has often been stimulated by Teilhard de Chardin, but sometimes it has arisen independently of him, and even those Catholic theologians who confess to
his influence are generally highly critical of some of his views.[3]

With this preliminary warning, I shall now try to characterize this
new vision of the world in relation to the church which is currently
coming to dominate progressive Roman Catholic thought and which
many bishops and theologians hope will also be evident in the final
versions of schema 13.

It is a vision which seeks to replace the archaic, static, three-story
picture of the universe, developed under Greek rather than biblical
auspices, according to which the world beneath is represented in

sharp distinction from a supernatural realm of created grace and heaven above, with God at some unlocated point beyond. According to this older picture, redemption is basically individualistic. It consists of souls, one by one, escaping—or being catapulted—from here below into heaven above. History is relatively unimportant. To be sure, certain realities within time, such as Christ, the Church, and the Sacraments, provide the means for the ascent of the soul from the lower to the upper levels, but most of what happens on earth, whether the prehistorical evolution of animal species or the material and intellectual progress of humanity, is irrelevant to salvation. In contrast to this, more and more Catholic thinkers are trying to conceive the creative universe as a single whole, a temporal evolutionary development, culminating in a total transformation when all things are reconciled through Christ to the Father (Col. 1:20). In this context, salvation is viewed as the corporate redemption of mankind, indeed of the cosmos, worked out in and through history. Individuals are saved, not atomistically, but through being incorporated into a new and reconciled humanity. Human advancement, even in scientific, technical, and artistic domains, not to mention social and moral ones, is not irrelevant to the Christian's hope, but is in some sense a direct preparation for the final fulfillment, for the ultimate manifestation of the kingdom of God.

This vision supplies the implicit and sometimes the explicit support for the growing engagement of many Catholic circles in promoting so-called "secular" human progress. They believe that Christianity, that the church, has an essential role to play in mankind's journey to final fulfillment. It is at least one of God's means for supplying the religious dynamism and the moral orientation necessary for the opening up of humanity to the coming of the kingdom. The church will do this, not by the dictation and coercive control from above to which it has often been addicted in the past but, as we have seen suggested, by humble and self-effacing service of mankind. It will do this because it recognizes that God is directing the entire world, the entire evolutionary and historical process, toward the consummation. He is working, not simply through the church, but in many ways outside the church, and so he calls the church to the service, not the domination, of advancing humanity.

Sometimes this attitude takes naively enthusiastic forms. While we should not judge this position on the basis of extreme forms, still it is worth noting that the earthly progress of mankind sometimes seems to be considered inseparable from the renewal of the church. If only the churches are reformed along the lines indicated by Pope John, and if only Christians unite, then they will be able to supply the necessary ethical power and guidance which will solve the great problems of war, atomic destruction, poverty, underdeveloped nations, and racial injustice. Further, once the Christian family, which constitutes a third of the world's population, begins acting in this fashion, then, so the enthusiasts say, humanity as a whole will recognize that Christianity is indeed divine.

There are many expressions of this outlook, perhaps particularly among laymen. A good deal of it is to be found in books written by the two most prominent Catholic journalists covering the council.[4]

Theologically trained Catholics, as could be expected, are more restrained, but many of them also share this outlook. Father Houtart, for example, who is the world's leading Catholic organizer of research in the sociology of religion, speaks of the orientation supplied by the church as making an essential contribution to "the social evolution of mankind . . . leading to the spiritualization of mankind and to unity with God."[5]

What should a Protestant make of these views? I am not thinking of the extremes, but of the basic vision. It may not become fully official at this council, but it is exercising an increasingly powerful influence in contemporary Catholicism. It constitutes a logical adaptation to modern historical and evolutionary thought of the traditional principle that grace does not destroy, but presupposes and perfects nature. It may help to make the Roman Church a more dynamic force within human history than it has been for many centuries. It may make its action less triumphalist and authoritarian and therefore more effective in the present situation and less offensive to non-Catholics. The Protestant will surely applaud this, but what should he say of the theological foundation, of the evolutionary vision of cosmic redemption with its implication that building up the earthly city is a direct preparation for the coming of the Kingdom? It is to this question that we must now turn.

IV. A Protestant Evaluation

In this section we shall not deal with the Roman Catholic doctrine of the church, but shall concentrate as much as possible on the new and higher evaluation of earthly realities which we have been describing. It is true that there is much to criticize from the Protestant point of view in the statements about the church which we have had occasion to quote. *The Constitution on the Church,* for example, seems to suggest, even if it does not directly assert, that the growth of the church in history is equivalent to the growth of God's kingdom and that the preparation of the world for the final manifestation of the kingdom is inseparable from the extension of the church's influence. Further, it does not so much as hint that the coming of the kingdom stands over against the church as judgment (e.g., Rev. 2-3), and not only as deliverance, victory, and fulfillment. However, these traditionally exaggerated and triumphalistic claims for the church seem to be both logically and historically independent of the new views. Indeed, they seem to fit in better with the ancient three-story picture of the world within which they arose than with a modern historical-evolutionary outlook.

Further, we must again remind the reader that we are not dealing with a subject on which there is any clear-cut division between Catholics and non-Catholics. Some progressive Catholics,[6] and all real conservatives, repudiate the kind of theology of temporal realities with which we are concerned. Further, some non-Catholics, especially certain Anglicans like Archbishop Temple, L. S. Thornton, and Canon Raven,[7] have long been thinking in terms of an evolutionary vision of cosmic redemption similar to what is now developing in Roman Catholic circles.

However, such thinking is alien and suspect to most contemporary Protestant theologians, whether they belong to the Reformed or the Lutheran traditions. It is both for them and to them that I would like to speak. My approach will be ecumenical. That is, conscious of the fact that we Protestants have much to learn from our Catholic brethren, I shall give as sympathetic an account as I can of the new perspective, and when I present my reservations it will be in full awareness that these have already been expressed, at least in part, by many Catholics, including bishops at the council.

Perhaps the easiest way to proceed will be briefly to list and answer some of the most commonly voiced objections to the new view of earthly realities. I shall try to indicate how such a view can be stated so as to escape these objections. This will clear the way for some final questions directed to all of us, Catholics and Protestants alike.

First, evolutionary-historical versions of cosmic redemption are accused of ignoring the radical discontinuity between all earthly, human history, and the eschatological fulfillment. Closely related to this is the objection that they place their trust, not in God alone, but in the natural, immanent processes of evolution and history and in human effort. A second type of accusation is that they are derived from modern science rather than from revelation and the Bible. Thirdly, it is said that they are far too optimistic, disregarding the continuing evil in human nature. They leave no room for the apocalyptic pictures of the end which are present in the Bible: They do not allow for the possibility that the struggle against wickedness will continue and even intensify until the end of time.

These objections apply to most earlier efforts to Christianize modern evolutionary thought. They certainly apply to the nineteenth century variety which led to the development of Catholic Modernism and the Protestant Social Gospel, whose after-effects are still with us, particularly in the United States.

However, it is doubtful that the first objection, at least, has any validity against a truly cosmic vision of redemption, not even against Teilhard de Chardin's. By definition, this speaks of an infinitely transcendent fulfillment of the entire universe far surpassing anything which natural reason, as long as it knows its limits, could possibly descry. This is utterly different from the rather prosaic, inner-worldly kingdom of God for which the Social Gospel hoped. Further, only those who trust in God have any solid basis for hoping in such a universal fulfillment. They may believe that God is using all the processes of history, including the efforts of both good and wicked men, to further his purposes, but that surely is not to mistrust the *sola gratia*.

My second major point is that it must be admitted in all fairness that there is no need for this view to base itself on the shifting sands of scientific theory. First, the vision of cosmic redemption is present in the Bible, especially in Ephesians and Colossians. Second, it is clear that the biblical authors regard the new heaven and the new earth as much more integrally related to the present heaven and earth than has been recognized during most of Christian history, largely because this has been dominated, as we have mentioned, by a Greek three-story picture of the world. The new heaven and earth, in the biblical view, are not completely discontinuous with our world, but are the restoration, elevation, and transformation of the reality which we experience. This is affirmed, for example, by the doctrine of the resurrection of the body, according to which it is our very physical existence, embedded as this is in the physical cosmos, which will be glorified. Thirdly, because it is this, and not another, world which God will transform, one can argue that the Bible affirms that all the positive aspects of God's progressively unfolding creation including, so to speak, the material, cultural and intellectual values, not simply the narrowly moral or religious ones, are relevant to the eschatological fulfillment. In contributing to human progress, therefore, men are God's instruments in supplying, so to speak, material for the world to come. Lastly, this interpretation of a modern evolutionary world picture in terms of the biblical vision of cosmic redemption can be defended on the grounds that it is not only permitted, but actually commanded by the Bible itself, for instance, by Paul's injunction to bring all thoughts into captivity to Christ. Biological evolution and the historical fact of more and more rapid human development are inescapable parts of our mental equipment, and so we Christians are obligated to try to discern what place they have in God's creative purpose and providential guidance of his world, rather than leaving them like erratic, compartmentalized blocs in our minds unrelated to our Christian faith.

Perhaps, especially for many Protestants, the third major objection is crucial. In part because of past painful experiences with illusory optimism and idealism, we are intensely afraid of any view that minimizes the continuing reality of sin and power of the evil in our lives and in the world. However, it must once again be admitted that, despite what some of its proponents have held, there is nothing in the outlook which we are considering which implies that the world is getting progressively better and better; there is nothing which excludes the apocalyptic vision of an increasing conflict between good and evil culminating in a final cataclysm. Every human advance increases the possibilities of evil as well as of good. The corruption of the best is the worst. Communist ruthlessness is the by-product (as some council fathers pointed out) of a largely Christian-Hebrew view of the good society, of an attempt to bring heaven to earth; Nazi barbarism was worse than any of the barbarisms of the past; the most ghastly of all weapons, the atom bomb, is the result of the most splendid achievements of science, and its sole user up until now is a nation which prides itself on being Christian. However, we must always remember that as the possibilities for evil increase, so also do the possibilities for good. And that, in the cosmic vision of redemption, is precisely why God creatively wills human progress. Through the possibilities of ever greater good which it provides, God is creating the conditions for the coming of his kingdom. Thus Christians can work for the good of the earthly city knowing that they are as directly engaged in their Father's business as when preaching the Gospel *viva voce*, and confidant that, however powerful evil remains, and however dreadful the mutations humanity undergoes, God still wills even man's mundane achievements for his purposes.

Perhaps it would be helpful at this point if the evolutionary-historical outlook were developed in terms of an analogy between the preparation of Israel and the world for the first coming of Christ two thousand years ago in Palestine, and the preparation now taking place for the Second Coming. The New Testament is quite clear that the earlier period is to be viewed as preparation for the Messiah. From the modern perspective this would mean that the billions of years of physical and biological evolution before Christ supplied the physical conditions for his coming. Human evolution and thousands of years of Israelite history created the social and religious preconditions. The early church, you will recall, added to this that the history of other races, Greek philosophy, and Roman peace, also belong to the *praeparatio evangelica*. Until all this physical, intellectual, and political, as well as religious advance had been made, the world was not ready for Christ. He came in the fullness of time and as the fulfillment of all previous times. Yet he also came discontinuously, from above, as an eruption of the kingdom of God into history, not as an ordinary emergent novelty.

It can be argued that an analogous pattern applies to our interim period. Exploration of the atom, the sending of men to the moon, the ever-increasing physical and cultural unification of mankind, are perhaps in a somewhat similar fashion creating the conditions for the final manifestation of the kingdom of God. The world is not getting better in any unambiguous way any more than in the thousands of years before Christ. And yet, perhaps even our ambiguous secular achievements are being used by God to prepare the way for the consummation, just as he used the Greeks and the Romans to prepare for the coming of the kingdom in the person of Jesus. Perhaps he is similarly using our often equally ambiguous religious developments, including the ecumenical movement and the Vatican Council, just as he used and is using his covenant people, the Jews.

We, of course, cannot discern exactly how human and religious progress contribute to God's plan any more than could the people of Israel before Christ, but perhaps it is proper for Christians to believe that in hoping and working for such progress they are hoping and working for the establishment of God's preconditions for the fulfillment, the consummation of all things.

I have cast these suggestions in the hypothetical mood because they do not answer all our problems. We Protestants, when we attempt to state the Gospel in terms of modern thought, have a natural affinity for existentialist rather than evolutionary categories. This is no doubt the result of the overwhelming Reformation emphasis on faith in the sense of total trust in the present forgiving love of God in Jesus Christ. This makes us distrust an eschatology which stresses the horizontal rather than the vertical, which speaks of an objectively future cosmic redemption and not simply of authenticity in human life and in relation to God in the present moment. We are afraid that a futuristic, realistic evolutionary eschatology may, for many people, be simply a modernized version of ancient or contemporary millenniallism or sixteenth century Anabaptist enthusiasm. There is danger that this concentration on the temporal future will distract attention from the one thing necessary. The one thing necessary is our present relation to God. What does the glorious future of the cosmos, or even its present preparation, profit men if they lose their own souls? In other words, this talk of the future eschaton can be used as an excuse for escaping from the eschatological present, from the problem of authentic existence here and now.

I am enough of a Lutheran to believe that the greatest cause for rejoicing both in heaven and earth is the forgiveness of sins, and cannot help reading with dismay the offhand remarks, even by Catholic theologians from whom I have learned much, to the effect that salvation is not merely a matter of the forgiveness of sins, but rather of the divinization of men. Karl Rahner, for example, has said this,[8] and in his case I am sure that what is involved is, not so much a fundamental disagreement as, from my point of view, an extraordinarily limited definition, on his part, of what is involved in the forgiveness of sins. The forgiveness of sins, after all, is the breaking down of the middle wall of partition between man and God, it is the reconciliation of humanity to God, it is the unification of men with God in personal love and communion. As it happens, Karl Rahner makes it quite clear that this is the essence of what he means by divinization. Why then does he use this idea with its misleading connotations? However well-rooted it may be in the Greek fathers, it is, after all, found only once in the New Testament.

Yet, on the other hand, Catholics can justifiably ask us whether we have not so individualized, personalized, and existentialized the forgiveness of sins that we have forgotten its objective, ontological and cosmic dimensions. They can ask us whether we have not so emphasized faith that we have neglected hope. Catholics have also neglected hope, but at least they have left a place for it in their theological systems as one of the three paramount Christian virtues. Does not the fullness of faith and love require hope for an objectively real fulfillment? Does not authenticity in the present often require hope for even the mundane future? How can men fail to be alienated from their work unless they believe in its ultimate significance? How can the Christian fail to be alienated from his participation in the temporal and material progress of mankind unless he is convinced that in some fashion here also, and not simply in his private relations to God and to others, he is playing a part in God's preparations for the eternal kingdom?

These questions, directed to both sides, indicate, it seems to me, that Protestants and Catholics badly need to collaborate in developing a theology of the world, of temporal realities, which is genuinely faithful to biblical eschatology. We need to learn how to hold together a lively hope in the objectively real future coming of Christ (which we shall inevitably visualize in pictures different from those used by first-century Christians) and existential trust in his present forgiveness. If we learn to serve the world together by preaching this Gospel and by working cooperatively in faith, love, and hope to open mankind to the future,[9] we shall do far more for the union of our churches than by all our agonizing, necessary though this is, over our past differences.

Notes

1. Quoted in part from the official council press release, Oct. 20, 1964.

2. *Herder - Korrespondenz*, Jan., 1965, p. 174.

3. For an example of such a sympathetically critical account see Henri de Lubac, S.J., *La pensée religieuse de Père Teilhard de Chardin*, Paris: Aubier, 1962.

4. Robert Blair Kaiser, *Pope, Council and World*, New York: Macmillan, 1963. Henri Fesquet, *Le Catholicisme, Religion de demain?* Paris: Grasset, 1962, and *Trois Questions brulantes à Rome, ibid.*, 1964.

5. F. Houtart, *The Challenge to Change*, New York: Sheed & Ward, 1964, p. 67. For more careful statements of similar points of view applied directly to Schema 13 by theologians who are involved in the preparation of the document, see M.-D. Chenu, "Les signes des temps," *Nouvelle Revue Théologique*, Jan., 1965, pp. 29-39, and E. Schillebeeckx, "The

Church and the World" (a speech delivered in Rome during the third session and appearing in mimeographed form as No. 142 in the "Documentation Hollandaise du Concile," Via S. Maria dell'Anima, 30, Rome).

6. For a description of an earlier phase of the debate among Catholics on these matters, see L. Malavez, "Deux théologies catholique de l'historie," *Bijdragen*, 1949, pp. 224-240.

7. E.g., William Temple, *Nature, Man and God*, London: Macmillan, 1934, L. S. Thornton, *Revelation and the Modern World*, London: Black, n.d. (see also its sequels), C. E. Raven, *Teilhard de Chardin: Scientist and Seer*, New York, Harper, 1962.

8. *Nature and Grace*, London: Sheed & Ward, 1963, p. 24.

9. For an independently Protestant development of somewhat similar ideas, see Jürgen Moltmann, *Theologie der Hoffnung*, Munich: Kaiser, 1964.

Chapter XI

The Council and the Churches
of the Reformation

This book of essays on the most important themes of the council is a contribution by Lutheran observers at Vatican II to the dialogue which is now on the way. Most of the authors have been present at all three sessions. They have been able to follow the developments of the conciliar decrees from first drafts to final versions. They have not been silent observers, but have spoken out with questions and suggestions, not, to be sure, in the council itself, but in countless smaller and larger conferences as well as in private conversations with Roman Catholic prelates and theologians. The fact that the exchange of observers is reciprocal (Catholics, for example, have been present at World Council gatherings as well as at meetings of Anglican, Reformed, and Lutheran international organizations) witnesses to an increasing solidarity among Christians.

In addition, there are still other signs of that increasing closeness among divided Christians in which they approach each other, rediscover each other, learn mutual love, and, it may be, experience mutual disappointments. In many places today, separated churches are experimenting with common services and prayers. Even before the hoped-for improvements in the canon law regulations affecting

253

mixed marriages, an "ecumenical settlement" is being tried out in Holland. In theological work, especially in biblical studies, confessional barriers are falling away. This is not all completely new. There have always been periods of *rapprochement* in the history of divided Christendom. However, an encounter of such depth and breadth as the present one has not been known since the Reformation. The experience of common difficulties in past decades and the growth of explicitly non-Christian and anti-Christian outlooks in modern times have contributed to this. Especially the new conciliar "Decree on Ecumenism" seems to open doors for discussion, cooperation, mutual acquaintance, and also, to be sure, for discovering more clearly our remaining differences.

One can, however, see much that is human, all too human, in the unifying movement in Christendom, in the non-Roman ecumenical movement as well as in the new encounters between Catholic and non-Catholic Christians. However, whoever looks deeper and believes that the history of the church is the workshop of the Holy Spirit will be astonished and amazed to recognize in all this humanness the action of God's Spirit which, according to Martin Luther, "calls, gathers, illumines, sanctifies, and, through Jesus Christ, preserves in the one true faith the whole of Christendom on earth." We do not know whether Christians, the "pilgrim people of God," are being prepared for a new stage on their road. Sometimes one gets the impression that God is bringing the divided parts of Christendom closer together in order, perhaps, to equip them for an arduous journey through the wilderness. It is this which gives seriousness and intensity to the dialogue which is now "on the way." And it is in the light of this that we shall attempt, on the basis of the observers' reports and the council's progress up till now, to present some fundamental considerations and issues for further interconfessional discussion.

1. In the church as the community founded upon Jesus Christ the Savior, the dialogue between the divided confessions ultimately revolves around the question of salvation in Christ. Not all the divisions in Christendom have arisen over this question, but this is the source of Reformation schism, and if there is to be a new unity, it is from this point that it must grow. The existence of Christ's

church is not justified through its cultural importance, nor by its exercise of dominion over men, nor even because it embodies the moral power needed by an aimless and internally weakened world. "You shall receive power when the Holy Spirit has come upon you; and you shall be my witnesses" (Acts 1:8 RSV). This is what Jesus Christ said to his disciples at the moment he bestowed upon them their existence as the church in the world. Jesus Christ, to whom the church bears witness, is God's Anointed, the Savior of the world, of individuals, of generations, and of the whole creation.

In whatever way one judges the Reformation, it must be admitted that what happened then was that the entire life of Christ's church was looked at anew in the light of the question of salvation. Luther puts it this way, "How do I get a gracious God?" This question was answered by the message of the holy God who in Christ justifies sinful men by grace alone through faith—a message which the Reformers found expressed on every page of Scripture. Everything in the life of the church which was irrelevant to the asking or the answering of this question of salvation became peripheral or disappeared in the course of the Reformation. Whatever answered this question of salvation wrongly or obscurely had to be purged or abolished. It was by this norm that distortions of the church's doctrine and practice were corrected. "It must be the chief concern of all the bishops that the people learn the Gospel and Christ's love," Luther wrote to Albert of Mainz on Oct. 31, 1517.[1]

Amidst the welter of themes which are dealt with these days in Christendom, it often seems that clear direction has been lost. Many conversations are taking place between the confessions, but do we know ourselves to be "under God" (Gen. 50:19), or is it rather a matter of hidden human self-assertion which masquerades as love of the church? We say that discussion should be carried on in attentive listening to Holy Scripture—but that is simply another way of insisting on the question of salvation (see John 5:39). It is in insisting on this question that Peter Brunner sees the special task of the Lutheran Reformation also in its dialogue with the churches of the World Council: "The Lutheran Churches must not and cannot permit the ecumenical movement to turn into a kind of Protestant synthesis in which a compromise between the doctrines of the Methodists, Baptists, Calvinists and Lutherans, combined with the adoption of the episcopal polity of the Anglicans, constitutes a uniting principle which enables all to gather together without first reaching clarity and agreement on the truth of the Gospel. It does not matter whether the Lutheran Confessions of the sixteenth century remain completely unchanged in the contemporary ecumenical encounter, but it is crucial that the Gospel given in Scripture be maintained."[2]

It is just as important to say this in reference to the dialogue with Rome. Everyone involved in ecclesiastical matters knows how closely interconnected are questions of doctrine, order, law, history, and tradition. This makes it all the more important to repeat the rule that "Everything in the Christian church is so ordered that we may daily obtain full forgiveness of sins through the Word and through signs appointed to confort and revive our consciences as long as we live."[3] For those members of the churches of the World Council who are familiar with the procedures of ecumenical conferences and discussions, the length and intensity with which Vatican II has dealt with many ecclesiastical and theological problems is truly impressive. However, must not the question of salvation be raised in all the discussions in St. Peter's Basilica? Understandably enough, again and again the view emerges in the conciliar documents that salvation for all men has been entrusted to the church for all time. Further, in many places, those truths and values common to all Christians are expressed with surprising clarity. Even many impulses derived from the Reformation are discernible. Nevertheless, we must seriously ask regarding the relation of Christ's redemptive word and grace to what his church does with them. What is the relation of Christ's church to what appears in the world as the Christian church? We deeply value the breakthrough to a new view of the church understood in terms of poverty, service, and the imitation of Christ. But what bearing does this have on the matter of salvation, on the question of God's Word as the creative and critical force in the church? At the end of the second session, Professor Skydsgaard said in a press conference: "There is no greater mystery in heaven or earth than the forgiveness of sins." He continued, "How much one would have wished— even if it were only once—that the barrier would have burst, that everything else would have faded: the great ecclesiastical institution, the splendidly decorated St. Peter's Cathedral, the bishops, cardinals, and the pope himself—all sanctity and piety—that all this would have become finally irrelevant except one thing, God himself. The Roman Catholic Church, the other churches—we all stand before God alone! That can come to pass through the Word, through the prophetic Word."[4]

The churches of the Reformation, whose vital milieu is the "the living voice of the Gospel," must constantly raise the question of salvation, of the forgiveness of sins, and they must first direct this question to themselves. The Lutheran World Federation Assembly in Helsinki in 1963 grappled anew with the message of justification, with how it can be expressed and lived today. At least as far as appearances go, not much progress was made in these efforts. The Roman Catholic council has finally taken up the draft on "The Church in the Modern World" and will complete this in the fourth session. What, amidst all the ethical themes dealt with there, will be the place of the question of salvation with its essential categories of sin and grace, guilt and forgiveness, faith and works? All the confessions are today brought very close together when they stand before this question. Is Christendom, the whole of Christendom on earth, moving a step forward beyond its internal discussions through the raising, clarification, and answering of these questions of salvation and of its commission to offer salvation to man in the world? Will the "dialogue on the way" on this subject help it to grow in the power of its Lord?

2. The council has attracted world-wide publicity on more than one occasion. Press, radio, and television have done their best to transmit its spectacular moments to the whole earth by both sounds and pictures. Yet it is more important to reflect on those events in the course of the council which affect Christendom as a whole. These were always moments when the question of salvation emerged more clearly than usual. Then arose, not only an inner-Catholic dialogue among the council fathers, but the sparks in some measure shot outwards and kindled a dialogue embracing the whole church.

We do not forget the great witness to Christ given by Pope Paul VI in his address at the beginning of the second session: "Let there be no other light for this gathering but Christ, the light of the world. Let the interest of our minds be turned to no other truth but the words of the Lord, our one master; let us be guided by no other desire but to be unconditionally loyal to him. Let the only trust which sustains us come from those words of his which shore up our pitiful weakness: 'And behold I am with you forever, even to the end of the world' (Matt. 28:30)."[5]

It must be frankly and thankfully said that as soon as these words emphasizing Christ alone were sounded, they re-echoed in other parts of Christendom, and that this was especially true of those phrases which reiterated the theme of the World Council Assembly in New Delhi in 1961. To be sure, one cannot overlook that even these sentences were encased in a strongly Roman Catholic ecclesiology which became dominant in the opening address of the third session. Yet there would, in any case, be a more fruitful dialogue between the churches if we were to set aside all secondary questions and, listening to the Bible, ask ourselves anew the question which Jesus Christ himself asks of us, "What think you of Christ?" (Matt. 22:42). There are countless testimonies to the fact that conversations between members of different confessions proceed best when they are centered, Bibles open before us, around this question.

Much the same can be said of Paul VI's "confession of guilt" in the same speech: "If we are in any way to blame for the separation, we humbly beg God's forgiveness. And we ask pardon too of our brethren who feel themselves to have been injured by us. For our part, we willingly forgive the injuries which the Catholic Church has suffered, and forget the grief endured during the long series of dissensions and separations."[6] It is true that the conditional form in which these sentences are cast is troublesome. The interpretation which the pope gave somewhat later in an audience for the non-Roman Catholic observers did not remove this difficulty. Yet we must say more, because it is precisely where guilt and forgiveness in encounter with Jesus Christ are spoken of that the Churches of the Reformation know themselves to be addressed. They must listen with redoubled attentiveness, and they must answer. Among the many answers which are offered, have we found the answer which is to be given when standing before the Judge and Savior of the church? In its declaration of March 19, 1964, the Evangelical Church of Germany said: "An insight of the Reformation, derived from Scripture, is that the church of Jesus Christ is not in itself pure, but lives only through the justifying grace of its Lord. Self-righteousness and self-justification are the very worst distortions of its nature. So in the conversation between the confessions, let those of us who joyfully call ourselves Protestant Christians take earnest heed of the fifth petition of the Lord's Prayer, 'Forgive us our trespasses even as we forgive those who trespass against us.' Let every individual examine himself in order to see where, in his contacts with his Roman Catholic fellow Christian, he needs to ask or grant pardon. Through God's cleansing forgiveness we become free to testify to his Gospel more clearly." Have we, in such a declaration, found the right answer? The council's "Decree on Ecumenism" repeats the reference to guilt and forgiveness: "in humble prayer we beg pardon of God and of our separated brethren, just as we forgive them that trespass against us." Is it thus that we shall find the right answer? "God be merciful to us sinners!"

Sparks leapt outwards also when discussion centered on the papacy and its importance. Now, however, the sparks kindled fires of controversy. No one can deny the historical greatness of many popes, but it is another matter when the papacy is described as a fundamental presupposition of the true church and as a means of salvation. For instance, Pope John XXIII's encyclical, *Pacem in terris*, contains such words as these: "We, the Vicar on earth of Jesus Christ, Savior of the World and Author of Peace . . . . "

To this day the choice of a new pope is proclaimed with words reminiscent of the annunciation of the Savior (Luke 2:10): "I bring you tidings of great joy, we have a pope!" Even now the decrees of Vatican I—enlarged, to be sure, by the emphasis on episcopal collegiality—are being confirmed even in their fateful formulation of the "irreformabilis." In 1302 Boniface VIII declared "to every human creature that they by necessity for salvation are entirely subject to the Roman Pontiff." The political claims to worldly power involved in this statement are no longer made, but is there not still some resemblance when Pope Paul VI, in his encyclical *Ecclesiam suam* (1964), characterizes the recognition of the exalted place accorded the pope by the dogmas of the First Vatican Council as "a necessary step on the path leading to Christ"? The claims of the papacy relative to salvation are now, as before, one of the most difficult topics in the dialogue regarding salvation and seem once again to divide Christians. One remembers the words spoken by P. Sabatier in 1911: "There are two Catholicisms. One builds bridges and the other destroys them; and one might perhaps say that the papacy stands on the side which destroys."[7]

It is at this point that the third chapter of the "Constitution on the Church" will be an object of critical discussion. Here the importance of the bishops for salvation is placed alongside the importance of the pope for salvation. Each limits the other and is at the same time united with it. It is precisely such affirmations which confirm the need, not of the ecclesiastical structures which grew out of the Reformation nor of the often lamentable church life within these structures, but of the Reformation's understanding of the one church which is "the assembly of saints in which the Gospel is taught purely and the sacraments are administered rightly. For the true unity of the church it is enough to agree concerning the teaching of the Gospel and the administration of the sacraments. It is not necessary that human traditions or rites and ceremonies, instituted by men, should be alike everywhere, as Paul says (Eph. 4:5, 6)."[8] Is there not a wonderful evangelical richness and ecumenical freedom in this "it is enough"?

3. There is one point on which it seems the dialogue acquired special sharpness during the third session. It may be that amidst the tumultuous happenings of the council, only a few at first noted and experienced this sharpness, but that it was there is indirectly confirmed by the later numerous efforts to explain it away. Quite possibly it will be important for us in the later dialogue. It broke to the surface at a place which is of fundamental importance for the understanding of the church as a community of salvation, namely, in reference to the Holy Spirit.

In the Apostles' Creed, the fact that faith in the Holy Spirit is spoken of before the church is mentioned is a sign that the entire life of the church depends on the Holy Spirit. There have often been hesitations on this point in the history of the Lutheran Church. Faith in the Holy Spirit has often receded far into the background behind the "sola scriptura, solus Christus." Defensive reactions resulted from the erroneous appeals to the Holy Spirit made by the sectarian movements. This makes it all the more important to heed E. Brunner's suggestion that the Reformation is to be understood above all as concerned with the work of the Holy Spirit. "It was reserved for the Reformation once again to open the way to the New Testament witness to the Spirit. The whole of the Reformation struggle revolved around the third article, the doctrine of the Holy Spirit, while the first and second articles of the creed were only indirectly involved. Everything which the Reformation restored to us, freedom from priestly mediation, the unity of Word and Sacrament, of faith and communion with Christ, of church and the community of faith, of faith and newness of life—all this can be understood only as a rediscovery of the New Testament consciousness and experience of the Holy Spirit as ever present and active."[9]

There are many indications that the churches of the Reformation must in the immediate future learn to hear and live anew this word regarding the Holy Spirit. One service of the Reformation to the whole of Christendom was its concentration upon Jesus Christ as the only Mediator of salvation. The effects of this emphasis in the realm of the first article changed the entire world: it changed the very course of history as well as the valuation of "secular" callings, of work, of marriage, and of the creation in general. Perhaps an additional step must now be taken in a new comprehension and reception of the Word of the Holy Spirit.

What, in the light of this, is to be made of the apparently trivial change of that section of the Decree on Ecumenism which speaks of the churches of the Reformation? That change was made in the last days of the third session "by higher authority," that is, it was occasioned by the pope himself. We do not need to deal here with the historical details (*v. supra.*, Ch. IV), but it is significant that a sentence already approved by the council was replaced by another, and final, formulation. The statement, "Moved by the Holy Spirit, they find God speaking to them in Christ in the Holy Scriptures" was replaced by "While invoking the Holy Spirit, they seek in these very Scriptures God as [or possibly, "as though"] speaking to them in Christ." In this session, for the first time, Paul VI had addressed other separated communities as "churches." Here, however, precisely in the "Decree on Ecumenism," the very source of the reality of the Reformation churches—or of any church—as churches was contested or, at least, made questionable. To be a church is to live out of the power of the Holy Spirit—if not, there is no church. The seriousness of this change in the decree is in no way altered by its high evaluation of the Christian life of the separated brethren.

Long and wearisome labor in the dialogue will be necessary before there can be some kind of meeting of minds on this fundamental point. We find ourselves remembering Luther's words that the papacy "is nothing but enthusiasm, for the pope boasts that 'all laws are in the shrine of his heart,' and he claims that whatever he decides and commands in his churches is spirit and law, even when it is above and contrary to the Scriptures or spoken Word."[10] The question must be raised whether the concept of infallibility can in any sense be appropriately used in describing that guidance of the church by the Holy Spirit of which the Constitution on the Church often speaks.

Can there be any genuine dialogue when the levels, the presuppositions, of the discussion are so fundamentally different? Yet "for God, nothing is impossible"—that is a certainty which lives through the creative power of the Spirit of God.

4. Closely connected with the Holy Spirit is the question of the renewal of the Church. One must recognize that one of the great effects of the council on the whole of Christendom is that the call, indeed, the drive toward church renewal has been made living in many places. In the Roman Catholic Church itself this includes the reform of the curia, the effort to interpret old dogmas afresh, the criticism of churchly triumphalism and the concern for a new relation to separated brethren, to other religions and to the modern world. Even the concept of "reformation," which for us has become to a large extent worn and lack-luster, is beginning to acquire vitality in the Roman Catholic Church, even if in a different sense. To be sure, no matter how one evaluates the "perennis reformatio" of the Decree on Ecumenism, the great, critical questions of the Reformation refuse to be silenced. If, for example, the papal dogma of 1870, which stands as the great dividing barrier between the confessions, is now being reaffirmed point by point and is simply

being complemented by the emphasis on episcopal collegiality, then one must ask what kind of reformation is taking place. The Marian dogmas, which have, at the very least, deepened the division, remain unshaken, and to them has now been added the title of "Mother of the Church." Is this reformation, or is it perhaps progress in that making of *additamenta,* of additions, against which Luther so fiercely struggled as a perversion of the Gospel?[11]

What is the renewal of the church? "The old church shines anew!" exclaimed Luther as he described the renewal of the church through the Reformation. Renewal is the return to the old, to that which is biblical. It is true that also in the Roman Catholic council many steps of renewal are being taken by means of return to past insights and forms, for instance, in the restoration of the diaconate. On the other hand, however, the church is also subject to the law of becoming and vanishing, of growth and decay, of the change of conditions. We observe with astonishment how the Roman Catholic Church is now trying to take account of this law even while preserving her substance, how she is adapting to the present and seeking to overcome centuries of inertia in the matter of a few years. Renewal of the church means grappling with tradition, with history, with that Roman centralization which is at the same time strength and weakness. Referring to the Decree on Ecumenism, Hans Küng enumerates the new starting-points which have already developed: "Guilt on both sides for the division of the church; the need of the Catholic Church as church of sinners for constant reform in its practical life, and also in its doctrine; the Gospel as the norm of renewal. . . . "[12] What does this signify for a Protestantism which, in adapting to the spirit of the times, all too lightly and all too often oversteps the limits and loses the substance? No one who reads the Constitution on the Church, especially its great first two chapters, can avoid recognizing that every line, every scriptural citation, breathes a concern to maintain the substance of the church as it, the people of God, enters a new epoch. We Protestants, who are tempted too lightly to esteem the bodily form of the church, its visible aspect, must allow ourselves to be reminded that there is a legitimate, biblically-grounded concern for the corporeality of the church, for a corporeality which we can call "pneumatic," spirit-filled.

But how does this renewal of the church through the Holy Spirit take place? Pope John XXIII described one of the goals of the council as that of being "a sublime manifestation of truth, unity and love which will surely also for those separated from this Apostolic See be a friendly invitation to seek out that unity which Jesus Christ prayed for so ardently from his heavenly Father."[13] It has been repeated numberless times since then that the church must renew itself in order to become attractive to those who are outside. One cannot dispute the legitimacy of this way of thinking. A church which does not take itself seriously even in its most external aspects ought not to be surprised if no one listens to it. Why shouldn't there be concern in the church for clarity and right order? No church reforms should be neglected which promise to make the ecclesiastical structures of the time, however imperfect they may be, a little more believable, that is, more transparent to the Gospel.

Yet, to be sure, the Gospel is, not the glad tidings of the church, but of Jesus Christ, of his truth and clarity. The Bible says of the suffering servant of God who is the type of Christ that "He had no form nor comeliness" (Isa. 53:2 f. RSV). Jesus Christ's comeliness is the cross. The beauty of the church, therefore, can be nothing else than the beauty of the cross of the Christ who bears our sins. "The Holy Spirit is he who shows us our sins" is what a mission congregation once answered when asked about the Holy Spirit's work. They spoke rightly of the beauty of the church in which men's sins are uncovered and removed. The Reformation knows no other renewal of the church than that which takes place through constant repentance, and one side of this repentance is an ever-deepening awareness of sin. We in no way deny the signs of this awareness in the course of the council. Yet Luther's bold words show how deeply this awareness penetrates the church's life and being: "There is no man on earth who is such a sinner as Christ; he feels sin more than any other man. So also, there is no greater sinner than the Christian church."[14] Yet she is holy; her holiness consists in the forgiveness of sins which creates life and blessedness. There is nothing more than this that she desires! God says to the people of God in the Old Testament, "When I passed by you, and saw you weltering in your blood, I said to you . . . grow up . . . and clothed your nakedness . . . with embroidered cloth . . . .

And your renown went forth among the nations because of your beauty." But then comes the complaint, "you trusted in your beauty" (Ezek. 16:8-15 RSV). Is this the church's temptation? The Reformation is very sober regarding the renewal of the church. It does not ask sweeping changes provided only that the Gospel is proclaimed ever anew in the power of the Spirit—that makes all things new! The people of God in pilgrimage are soiled with dust and dirt—not only the dust and dirt of the journey, but also of their life, thoughts, and actions. Just as Christ washed the feet of his disciples, so the entirety of church history is the record of how he, through the power of the Holy Spirit, washes the feet of his disciples as they are daily soiled in their journey through this world. Ultimately, what really makes the church new is, not the constantly renewed effort of adaptation to the present, necessary though this is, but the "powers of the age to come" (Heb. 6:5 RSV) communicated through Word and Sacrament, through the living voice of the Gospel. How does the church become appealing to other men? Once again, there seems to me no better answer to this question than one which Luther gave: "The church has always fared best when she has associated herself with those who are most sinful. For it is in bearing their burdens that her love has gained a golden radiance."[15]

5. It is clear enough from what has been said that the dialogue between the churches must be carried on in faith, yet in conclusion, something more may be said of this. Efforts to understand each other's positions, theological examination of problems, comparisons of different forms of piety, cooperation in practical matters—all these levels of conversation must be seen in yet another dimension, that of faith. Faith sees very well the reality of life and the world. Yet within these it reckons, even against all appearances, with the reality of God, with his Word, with the saving work of Jesus Christ and with the power of the Holy Ghost. It recognizes the world as God's creation, and yet knows that this is subject to corruption. Faith lives from the resurrection without denying the cross. It serves God in his creatures and at the same time waits for the new heaven and the new earth in which righteousness dwells.

Perhaps the inter-church dialogue during the remainder of the council will focus even more strongly than before on Christian service and the church's existence in the world. Material for this will be supplied both by the continuation of the consideration of schema 13, with its many urgent ethical themes, and by the declarations of the World Council of Churches on pressing issues in the life of the nations. For the discussion of such questions, it is necessary to be well informed, and so it is precisely here that the church must thankfully accept and allow to become much more effective the help of its members who are not theologically trained but who are experts in these matters. The Constitution on the Church rightly speaks of "laymen" as "participating in the redemptive mission of the church." At the same time, however, it must be considered that the life and action of the church of Jesus Christ in the world is an existence in faith, not in appearance. The great question is whether she has up until now succeeded in speaking consonantly with this attitude to the disturbing problems of today's world. Church pronouncements and programs very often strongly resemble what astute men of the world already know even without Christian faith. This is the question which arises in reference to both the declarations of the World Council of Churches and the encyclicals of the popes. What is the real word of the church of Jesus Christ to war and peace, to the ordering of human life in the world, to love and marriage, to state and society? What is the word which is entrusted to the church unalterably, which it cannot delegate, and in which is expressed both faith in creation and the insight that the world is in turmoil? What is the word which both interprets the commission given to men to bring the world into subjection and which makes resound the eager expectation of the whole creation for the revelation of the sons of God (Rom. 8:19)? What is the word of the church in which God wills that he be proclaimed today? What is this word of the Triune God, of the Creator of the cosmos, which is expanding before our eyes, of the Savior of mankind and of all the world, and of the Holy Spirit which is stronger than all other spirits?

From such a starting point, the dialogue would of itself be drawn into the dimension of faith. There is no certainty of its success in any of the areas we have mentioned. Perhaps it will advance farthest in regard to the question of relations to the world. It will be most difficult in reference to the problem of church unity. What has been divided by human sin and guilt, blindness and passion, but also by good will and piety, will not easily be gathered together again by human efforts, no matter how good and humble the will may be. God will not leave to any reformer, nor to any pope, the honor of a re-united church. It is therefore desirable that in the present moment talk of reunion recede before the consciousness that we are traveling alongside and together with each other. Yet along this common road, faith must reckon with the God who "calls into existence the things that do not exist" (Rom. 4:17 RSV). Our ecumenical discussions proceed "in hope against hope," but perhaps God has already called into existence what we, blind to his deepest initiatives, neither see nor wish to see, viz., the One Holy Christian Church, the communion of saints.

This One Holy Christian Church is present despite all the divisions and amidst all the schisms which we see before us. According to the message of the New Testament, she is present even when she is hidden. She is Jesus Christ's own work of love in the power of the Holy Spirit, in the creative might of the one God and Father (Eph. 4:5 f.). It is in this faith that the dialogue between the churches ought to be pursued. At least from the viewpoint of the Reformation, this is what one should believe, and thus see the work of the Holy Spirit everywhere in Christendom. This faith will very often take the form of suffering because of the visible splintering of Christendom, of suffering because of the impotence of the church and the resulting unbelievableness of its witness. However, faith need not be stifled by this grief, but this rather provides the measure for all human striving for the unity of the church. It purifies passion, gives certainty, and bestows patience for the dialogue, the patience of Christ (Rev. 3:10).

Notes

1. *Briefe,* Weimar Ausgabe (henceforth abbreviated "WA"), 1, 111, 39 ff.

2. *Pro Ecclesia,* Berlin & Hamburg: Lutherisches Verlagshaus, 1962, p. 53.

3. "Large Catechism," *Book of Concord* (tr. & ed. T. G. Tappert), Philadelphia: Fortress Press, 1959, p. 418.

4. "Die zweite Sitzungsperiode des vatikanischen Konzils in den Augen eines Beobachters," in *Ende der Gegenreformation* (ed. J. C. Hampe), Stuttgart: Kreuz-Verlag, 1964, p. 387.

5. *Council Speeches of Vatican II* (ed. H. Küng, Y. Congar, D. O'Hanlon), Glen Rock, N.J.: Paulist Press, 1964, p. 20.

6. *Ibid.,* 146-147.

7. *L'orientation religieuse de la France,* Paris, 1911, p. 188.

8. Augsburg Confession, Art. VII, in *Book of Concord,* op. cit., p. 32.

9. *Vom Werk des Heiligen Geistes,* 1935, p. 7.

10. Smalcald Articles, VIII, in *Book of Concord,* op. cit., p. 312.

11. E. Wolf, *Peregrinatio,* Munich: Kaiser Verlag, 1954, pp. 149 ff.

12. H. Küng, "Bilanz am Ende der 3. Sitzungsperiode," *Frankfurter Allg. Zeitung,* Nov. 18-19, 1964.

13. *Acta et Documenta Concilio Oecumenico Vaticano II Apparando,* Rome, 1960, p. 34.

14. WA 34, I, 276.

15. WA 2, 605, 3 ff.

Bibliographical Appendix

The literature on the Second Vatican Council is already immense and continues to grow month by month. The following bibliographical notes do not aim at completeness, but simply call the reader's attention to some of the more obvious sources in various languages dealing with the preparations and first two sessions of the council. The abbreviations indicated after some of the titles are those used in the footnotes to chapters two and three of this book.

For the background and preparations of the council (including bibliography), see especially *The Papal Council and the Gospel* (ed. K. E. Skydsgaard) Minneapolis: Augsburg, 1961. (In German: *Konzil und Evangelium, Göttingen:* Vandenhoeck & Ruprecht, 1961.) Cited as Skydsgaard, *Council.*

Hans Küng, Yves Congar, and Daniel O'Hanlon have edited a collection of 51 council speeches from the second session which is published in French, German, and English (in English by the Paulist Press, Glen Rock, N.J.)

Especially useful books on the first two sessions are the following:

In English: Xavier Rynne, *Letters From Vatican City: Vatican Council II (First Session),* 1963, and *The Second Session,* 1964, New York, Farrar & Straus (cited as Rynne, I and II); Robert Blair Kaiser, *Pope, Council and World: The Story of Vatican II,* New York: Macmillan, 1963. These two books, by a Roman Catholic priest writing pseudonymously and by the Roman Catholic correspondent of *Time* respectively, are the most informative of those in any language regarding the intrigues and conflicts which surrounded the council. Responsible Roman Catholic reviewers admit that the facts are generally accurate, even though the interpretations are sometimes open to question. The most balanced presentation of the first session is by René Laurentin (translated from the French), "Vatican II: Report on the First Session," *Cross Currents* (XIII) 1963, pp. 401-476. The best interpretation in English of the second session is by Michael Novak, *The Open Church: Vatican II, Act II,* New York: Macmillan, 1964. Two American Protestant observers have published diaries of their stays in Rome: Douglas Horton, *Vatican Diary, 1962,* and *Vatican Diary, 1963,* Philadelphia-Boston: United Church Press; and Robert McAfee Brown, *Observer in Rome,* New York: Doubleday, 1964.

In German, more literature is available than in any other language, but this tends to be specialized, presenting particular aspects of, or particular points of view on, the council; e.g., Bernard Häring, *Das Konzil im Zeichen der Einheit,* and Hans Küng, *Kirche im Konzil.* Both are published by Herder, 1963, and both are also available in English. The public documents of the first two sessions are found in *Zweites Vatikanisches Konzil: 1. Sitzungsperiode,* 1963, and

269

2. *Sitzungsperiode,* 1964, Osnabrück: Fromms Taschenbücher (cited as Z.V.K. I and II). Also useful for its documentation is Johann Christoph Hampe, *Ende der Gegenreformation?* Stuttgart: Kreuz-Verlag and Mainz: Matthias-Grünwald-Verlag, 1964.

In French, the best comprehensive treatments are those of René Laurentin, *L'enjeu du concile,* 1961, *Bilan de la première session,* 1963, and *Bilan de la deuxième session,* 1964; Paris: Editions du Seuil. Indeed, for theologians, these constitute the most useful survey of the council now available in any language. Also to be mentioned are Yves Congar, *Le concile au jour de jour,* Paris: Cerf, 1963, and Antoine Wenger, *Vatican II: Première session,* 1963, and *Chronique de la deuxième session,* 1964, Paris: Centurion. In addition, the French Protestant observer, Hébert Roux, has published *Le Concile et le dialogue oecuménique,* Paris: Editions du Seuil, 1964.

No books on the third session have yet appeared at the time this is written, but as in the case of the previous sessions, full information and documentation can be found by consulting the *Osservatore Romano* (O.R.), *Herder-Korrespondenz* (H.-K.), and *Documentation catholique* (D.C.). Nothing giving equally complete coverage is to be found in English, although, beginning in 1964, this gap has been partially filled by *Herder Correspondence,* an abbreviated version of the German original. Other useful periodicals are *Informations catholiques internationales* (I.C.I.), the lay Catholic *Commonweal* and the Jesuit *America.*

Finally, the new theological developments which have influenced or been stimulated by the council are described in a new international series, *Concilium,* which now has begun to appear in half a dozen languages and is published in the United States by the Paulist Press, Glen Rock, N. J.